# MODEL T

*Ford*

# SERVICE

Detailed Instructions for
Servicing Ford Cars

*by*

*Ford Motor Company*

DETROIT, MICHIGAN, U. S. A.

# *Foreword*

IT IS the purpose of this book to standardize the method of repairing Ford cars, to insure continued and satisfactory performance of our product the world over.

The following pages show in a clear and concise manner the "authorized Ford way" of performing the various repair operations.

The methods recommended have been carefully worked out in the Ford factory for the purpose of giving definite and detailed instructions to skilled as well as unskilled mechanics.

The first section contains a general discussion of the contributing factors in conducting a successful and profitable service organization.

The second section describes the correct method of disassembling and reassembling the Ford car.

The third section outlines the proper method of performing all major repair operations, including the complete overhaul of the various assemblies.

The fourth section deals with the diagnosis of car troubles and explains how these are quickly located and remedied.

By following the methods outlined in this book, dealers and service stations will be able to place their service work on an efficient and profitable basis, with greater satisfaction to their customers.

# Contents

# ESSENTIALS OF GOOD SERVICE

The performance of high grade service work is a vital factor in the development of a successful repair business, in fact it is the only safe foundation on which business of this character can be established.

High grade service advertises the business standards of the dealer. It inspires confidence in customers, and customer satisfaction is the forerunner of business growth.

The elements of high grade service are:

A sincere desire on the part of the automobile dealer or service station to serve car owners so efficiently that they will derive the maximum satisfaction from their investment.

Prompt, courteous and intelligent attention to customers' wants.

Skilled mechanics; men who are specialists in promptly diagnosing and correcting car troubles.

A clean, well laid out repair shop, provided with modern service equipment.

A well arranged parts department carrying a complete stock of parts and supervised by a parts salesman who knows stock and appreciates the value of courtesy and salesmanship.

Too much importance cannot be attached to the employment of competent mechanics, as the quality of their workmanship governs the satisfaction of the customer to a large extent.

A clean, well laid out repair shop provided with modern service equipment is essential to the performance of good service. Modern service equipment not only saves time in performing the various repair operations, but it improves the accuracy of the work. New tools and measuring devices which are now available permit the mechanic to work to limits which practically approach manufacturing standards.

In Fig. 1 is shown an ideal shop layout for the average size dealer. The equipment is conveniently grouped and so arranged that as the work progresses through the shop each repair operation is performed in its regular order.

A feature of this layout is the comparatively small amount of floor space used, the entire layout requiring only 23 x 40', thus making it adaptable for practically any type of building.

The procedure followed when a car is brought in for major repair work is to first assign the car to a section of the shop set aside for repair jobs. The assembly to be overhauled is then removed from the car and by means of chain falls and an overhead track it is delivered to the wash tank for cleaning. After the cleaning operation it is transferred to the stand or repair bench on which the work is to be performed.

When the overhaul work is completed the assembly is returned by means of the overhead track to the car from which it was removed. It is then installed in the car and the job is completed.

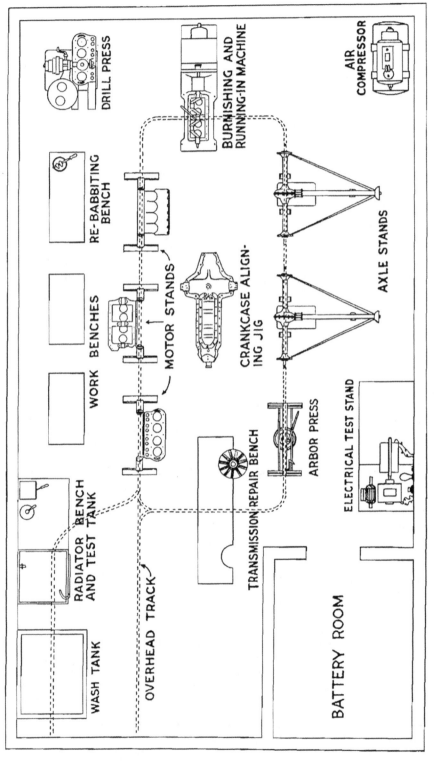

Figure 1

# Essential Shop Equipment

## Engine and Transmission Division

Babbitt furnace
Babbitting fixture
Bending irons . . . . . . .For aligning connecting rods and pedals
Boring machine . . . . . .For main bearings.
Burnishing in machine
Bushing drivers . . . . . .For camshaft, piston pin, and transmission bushings.
Bushing reaming machine . .For transmission bushings.
Camshaft driver
Camshaft puller
Crankcase aligning jig
Crankshaft turning bar
Cylinder gauge
Cylinder hone
Cylinder reboring machine
Drill press . . . . . . . .For use with cylinder reboring machine.
Engine lifting hooks
Engine stand
Gear drivers and pullers . . .For transmission, also large and small time gears.
Piston clamp
Piston and connecting rod alignor
Transmission holding fixture
Transmission band relining machine

## Front and Rear Axle Division

Axle stand
Bearing cup inserter. . . . .For front hub bearing cups.
Bending iron . . . . . . .For aligning front axle.
Bushing drivers. . . . . .For spring, perch, drive shaft, and spindle body bushings.
Front end lifting hooks
Rear end lifting hooks
Pinion gear puller
Sleeve puller and inserter . .For drive shaft and axle roller bearing sleeves.
Wheel alignor

# Carburetor Division

Carburetor repair tools

# Battery Division

Battery recharging outfit including tools

# Electrical Division

Electric test stand including tools
Coil tester
Magnet tester
Magnet gap gauge

# Radiator Division

See pages 189 and 190 for radiator repair tools

# Miscellaneous

Arbor press
Bending iron . . . . . . . .For aligning head lamps.
Car covers
Chain falls
Electric drill
Grinder
Straightening press with dial indicator
Surface plate.

# THE PARTS DEPARTMENT

A clean well arranged stock room gives a lasting impression of good service. In fact the old adage that "Goods well displayed are half sold", is particularly applicable to parts and accessories.

The parts department can be made a splendid advertisement of the dealer's ability to render prompt service, consequently it should be located at the front of the building adjacent to the showroom, where parts can be effectively displayed. If possible the stock room should be located to provide convenient service to the dealer's repair shop, as the despatch with which material is furnished the dealer's mechanics has a relative bearing on the profits earned in the repair department.

With a well kept stock room, it is important that the parts man in charge present a neat appearance. The dealer's customers come in contact with the parts and service department more frequently than with any other branch of the business. Consequently, the dealer should be represented by cleanly attired men, capable of meeting and serving the trade in a manner that will inspire confidence. The courtesy and promptness of the parts man indicates that the entire organization is interested in the customer's welfare.

One of the most important duties of the parts salesman is to know what parts are required to perform each repair job and to diplomatically convey this information to the customer. For example when a customer purchases a front spring, the parts salesman should point out the advisability of installing a new front spring pad as well as new spring perch bushings; new spring hangers may also be required. The purchase of new pistons suggests the purchase of piston rings, piston pins and possibly a new cylinder head gasket or crankcase lower cover gasket are required.

In addition to increasing parts sales, suggestions of this kind are valuable to the customer as it eliminates the necessity of having to make a second trip for the material and insures his receiving the maximum amount of service from the parts installed.

The average quantity of parts sold per car in the dealer's locality should determine the amount of stock to be carried. As all parts do not move with the same regularity each month, it is usually necessary for the dealer to maintain an inventory representing approximately a 90 day turnover. Care must be taken not to allow the parts stock to become depleted. This condition means not only a loss of revenue from parts sales, but also a loss of goodwill on the part of customers who are obliged to wait until replacement parts are obtained from the factory. It means the additional and unnecessary expense of a rush shipment from the factory.

A thorough check should be made monthly of every part regularly sold for service and replenishment made accordingly, consideration being given to seasonal demands.

Steel storage bins can be used advantageously, particularly where space is limited. In addition to presenting a more attractive appearance, the stock can be more readily checked and maintained than is ordinarily possible with wooden box systems. The parts bins should be placed back to back in double rows and arranged at a right angle to the customer's counter. The height of the bins should not be over 7 feet. All aisles should be at least 3 feet in width if space will permit.

AN ATTRACTIVE PARTS DEPARTMENT

Figure 2

# SERVICE FOLLOW-UP SYSTEM

That the advantages derived from the proper use of service follow-up systems are being recognized, is evidenced by the increasing number of dealers who have installed systems of this kind, with profitable results.

There are several satisfactory systems which may be employed, from the simple card record in a box to the elaborate visible record housed in metal cabinets.

While the highly developed costly system can be profitably used by the dealer who has a sufficient volume of business, good judgment must always be exercised to prevent an over-investment in system by smaller dealers.

No follow-up system, however, is self-actuating; each requires a certain definite amount of WORK to become effectual.

The purpose of the service follow-up system is to enroll the names of the dealer's customers, as well as all Ford owners living within a reasonable distance, or within the dealer's natural trade area, so that contact can be maintained with them through personal visits, telephone calls and frequent letters of solicitation. The service follow-up is the key to the dealer's service market as it constitutes a record of prospects for the future sale of Ford parts, repair labor, accessories, gas, oil and other commodities and eventually another Ford car, truck or Fordson tractor.

When completed all repair orders should be computed, showing the total amount of the bill for labor and parts. Before filing the orders they should be routed to some definite person in the office designated to make entries on the service card record. This is particularly important, for unless some employee is held to strict accountability for the maintenance of the follow-up system, it is likely to be slighted, with the result that it will eventually become useless.

All entries on the service card should show date, repair order number and the amount of repair work performed, in dollars and cents.

There are some small service jobs performed on cars where no repair order is issued due to the small amount involved; in such cases job tickets should be issued and postings made on the service cards from them.

Dealers will find a service record of great value in keeping the shop working to capacity during dull periods. Service follow-up cards assist the service floor man to sell a repair job to the customer on the basis of past experience.

A service follow-up properly used keeps the dealer in contact with his customers. It shows him how many service customers are lost and the reason for each case of customer dissatisfaction. It shows whether or not his service is satisfactory and suggests the changes which are necessary to improve it.

## Operation of Service Follow-up System

When a new car is sold, the following data should be noted on the service follow-up card (Figs. 3 and 4 show a front and back view of this card).

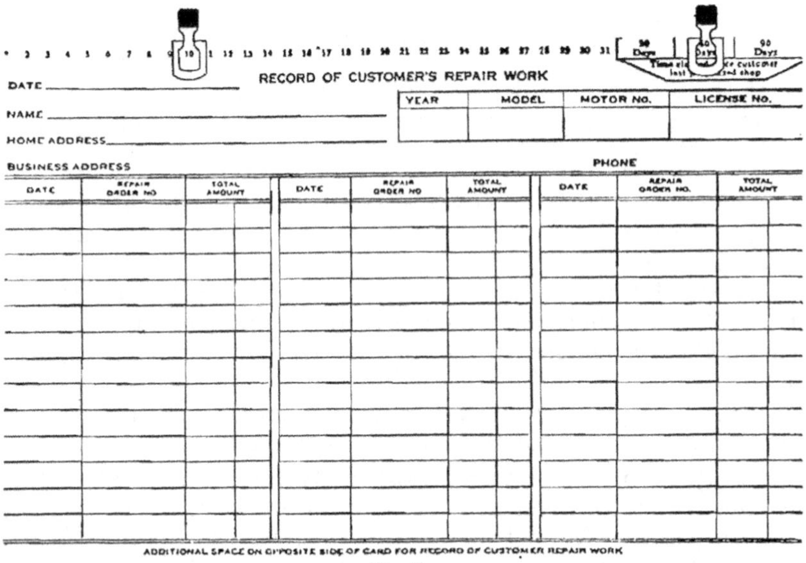
RECORD OF CUSTOMER'S REPAIR WORK

DATE

NAME

HOME ADDRESS

BUSINESS ADDRESS

| YEAR | MODEL | MOTOR NO. | LICENSE NO. |
|---|---|---|---|

PHONE

| DATE | REPAIR ORDER NO | TOTAL AMOUNT | DATE | REPAIR ORDER NO | TOTAL AMOUNT | DATE | REPAIR ORDER NO. | TOTAL AMOUNT |
|---|---|---|---|---|---|---|---|---|

ADDITIONAL SPACE ON OPPOSITE SIDE OF CARD FOR RECORD OF CUSTOMER REPAIR WORK

Fig. 3

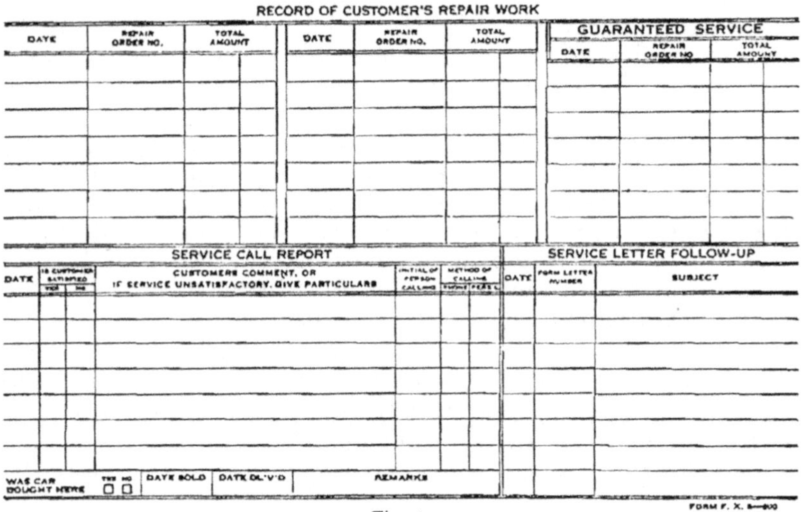
RECORD OF CUSTOMER'S REPAIR WORK

| DATE | REPAIR ORDER NO. | TOTAL AMOUNT | DATE | REPAIR ORDER NO. | TOTAL AMOUNT | GUARANTEED SERVICE DATE | REPAIR ORDER NO | TOTAL AMOUNT |
|---|---|---|---|---|---|---|---|---|

SERVICE CALL REPORT

| DATE | IS CUSTOMER SATISFIED | CUSTOMERS COMMENT, OR IF SERVICE UNSATISFACTORY, GIVE PARTICULARS | INITIAL OF PERSON CALLING | METHOD OF CALLING |
|---|---|---|---|---|

SERVICE LETTER FOLLOW-UP

| DATE | FORM LETTER NUMBER | SUBJECT |
|---|---|---|

WAS CAR BOUGHT HERE — DATE SOLD — DATE DL'V'D — REMARKS

FORM F. X.

Fig. 4

Name and address of customer
Telephone number
Type of car
Motor number
Delivery date
Name of salesman who sold car.

Within three days after delivery it is a good plan to send out a letter similar to the one which follows:

"My dear Mr. (Mrs. or Miss):

With the delivery of your new Ford car, we extend to you our best wishes for many years of motoring satisfaction. Ford cars are built to give years of economical service. We aim to help you get the most out of your investment. You, of course, realize that every piece of high grade machinery requires a certain amount of attention, if it is to continue to operate satisfactorily for an indefinite period. Accordingly, it will be to your interest to carefully study the Ford manual containing instructions on the care and operation of Ford cars, in order that you may be generally familiar with the mechanism of the car.

In driving a new car the following points of care are of particular importance: Do not drive over 20 miles per hour for the first 500 miles. Change the oil in the crankcase at the end of the first 400 miles and every 750 miles thereafter, except during cold weather, when it is advisable to change oil every 500 miles.

Keep car well oiled and greased throughout.

Have adjustments made as soon as possible after need for them is noticed.

Drain and refill radiator frequently, especially while your car is new. Have the battery inspected every two weeks and fresh distilled water added. Keep all bolts and nuts properly tightened.

We invite you to take advantage of our thirty-day free inspection and adjustment service, and suggest that you drive your car into our service station every ten days during this period. This will insure your receiving maximum service from your car at the minimum of expense.

The knowledge and skill of our mechanics is at your service at all times, and we want you to always consider our service department the proper home for your Ford car.

May we have an opportunity to show our appreciation of your patronage?

READY MOTOR COMPANY

By.............................''

A signal is placed on service card for follow-up ten days following date of sale.

When service card comes up for attention 10 days after delivery, the salesman who sold the car is advised on his daily report sheet to make a personal call on the purchaser to see how he or she is getting along, and incidentally to pick up any possible prospects. Result of call as reported by salesman is noted on service card, and a signal is placed on card for follow-up 30 days after date of salesman's call. (If the customer calls before the expiration of the 30 days, move the signal ahead for follow-up 30 days from date of his visit.)

Thirty days after salesman's call, or customer's visit, the service card will turn up and a letter carrying signature of the service manager should be written along the following lines:

"My dear Mr. (Miss or Mrs.):

You have been using your car for about ... days and we are interested in knowing if it meets with your expectations. If there is any way in which we can be of service to you, we want you to know that we are always ready and willing to assist you.

We would suggest that you bring your car into our service station and allow our battery man to examine the water level in your battery. There will be no charge for this service.

READY MOTOR COMPANY

By.............................''

Signal is then placed on service card for follow-up 30 days from date of letter. Should the customer call before the expiration of the 30 days, simply move the signal ahead for follow-up 30 days from date of his visit.

Thirty days after date of letter, or customer's visit, service card will again turn up and a letter or post card, signed by the service manager, should be mailed to the following effect.

"My dear Mr. (Mrs. or Miss):

If there is anything we can do to make your car a source of more pleasure or more comfort to you, please remember we are always ready to cheerfully serve you.

Have you had the water level in your battery examined recently? If not, we suggest that you drive your car into our service station and let us attend to it for you.

Yours for better service.

READY MOTOR COMPANY

By............................"

Signal is placed on service card for follow-up seven days before the expiration of three months from date of purchase of car.

On this day service card will turn up. If the purchaser has not been in recently, a letter, signed by the service manager, should be written similar to the following:

"My dear Mr. (Miss or Mrs.):

"As you have had your car in operation about three months we would suggest that you bring it to our service station and allow our mechanics to inspect it and make any necessary adjustments.

"There will be no charge to you for this work, which is a part of our service to customers.

"Assuring you that we desire to accord real Ford service at all times, we remain, Very truly yours,

READY MOTOR COMPANY

By............................"

The owner should now be considered a prospect for service work, and the service card carried under a separate index, operated by months and days—12 dividers being used to designate months. The file is now used as a mailing list, record of service work and to see which customers it is necessary to follow by reason of their not coming in for service—the latter the most important function of the file.

All repair orders are entered on service cards each day by clerk who notes R. O. number, date, and dollars and cents amount in space provided. After entry is made, a signal is placed on service card on date of repair order entry, and filed under the month designated for follow-up, (either 60 or 90 days hence, as desired).

As stated in the foregoing, it is essential that the service follow-up be conducted in a regular and systematic manner. Good results cannot be obtained from a system which is handled haphazardly. The usual practice in larger dealerships is to have the service file clerk examine and pull all service cards from file on the date they are scheduled for follow-up and place them on service manager's desk who will dictate the type of follow-up to be employed. Smaller dealers usually make a practice of dividing the alphabet into four sections, and pulling each section once a week. A letter should be written by the service manager to the customer, along the following lines:

"My dear Mr. (Miss or Mrs.):

It has been two months since your car was in our shop. No doubt the reason we have not seen you is because your car is giving good service.

Possibly you would like to have one of our mechanics check your car for you to insure satisfactory future operation. A call on (Glendale 1000) will put us into immediate action for you.

READY MOTOR COMPANY

By............................."

If no response is received, the owner should be called on the phone or a personal call made. The latter is preferable.

Service card is held on service manager's desk and follow-ups made until the owner comes in for service, when card is placed back in file.

# SERVICE

## CHAPTER I

1   So that the mechanic will have complete information on how each part of the car is removed and installed, we will first describe, step by step, the correct procedure in disassembling, and reassembling the car.

2   Before commencing a service job, it is important that car covers be placed over the running boards, fenders, steering wheel and upholstery. This prevents the parts becoming scratched or marred and protects the upholstery from grease spots and stains.

3   When disassembling, it is a good plan to provide a clean box for holding small parts, such as bolts, nuts, washers, etc. This will keep the parts conveniently grouped and eliminate the possibility of misplacement.

4   When performing major repair work, it is advisable to first disconnect the starting motor to switch cable (See "C" Fig. 35). Disconnecting this cable prevents injury to the mechanic in the event the starting switch is accidentally depressed while working on or underneath the car.

## Disassembling the Car

5   *Remove rear fenders—*

   (a) Run out the two running board to rear fender bolts and nuts (See "A" Fig. 5).

   (b) Run out the two shield to fender bracket bolts and nuts "B".

   (c) Loosen fender eye bolt nut "C". Fenders can now be lifted from fender irons.

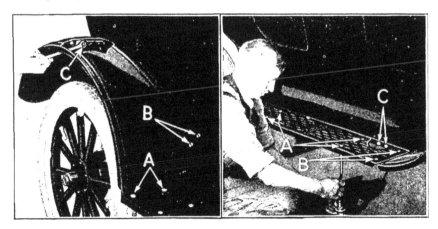

Fig. 5                                       Fig. 6

**6** *Remove running board—*

    (a) Run out the four running board bolts and nuts (See "A" Fig. 6).

    (b) Run out the two running board to front fender bolts and nuts "B".

    (c) Run out the two running board to shield bolts and nuts "C". Running boards can now be lifted from brackets.

**7** *Remove headlamps—*

    (a) Disconnect headlamp plugs; this is done by pressing in on the plug and turning it counter-clockwise.

    (b) Run off headlamp nut (See "A" Fig. 7).

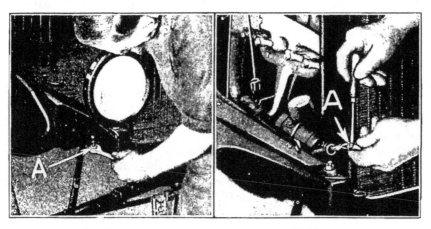

Fig. 7        Fig. 8

**8** Release the four hood clips and lift off hood.

**9** *Disconnect headlamp wires* by unscrewing thimble from plug and loosening headlamp wire screws (See "A" Fig. 8).

**10** *Remove hood blocks from frame* by running off the nuts on the ends of the engine pan bolts (See "A" Fig. 9), and lifting off blocks.

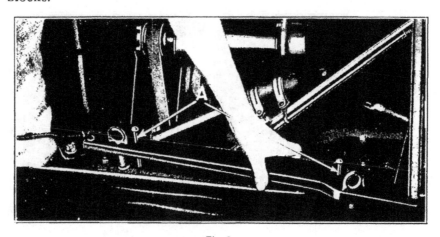

Fig. 9

Fig. 10               Fig. 11

**11   *Remove front fenders*—**
  (a) Run off the two fender apron to frame bolt nuts and withdraw bolts and loom supports (See "A" Fig. 10).
  (b) Loosen nut on fender eye bolt (See "A" Fig. 11).
  (c) Run out fender apron to frame bracket bolt "B" and lift off fender.

**12   *Remove body from chassis*—**
  (a) Run off nuts on the six body bolts, (three on each side of car, See "A" Fig. 12). Run out the two wood screws "B", which hold each running board shield to body.

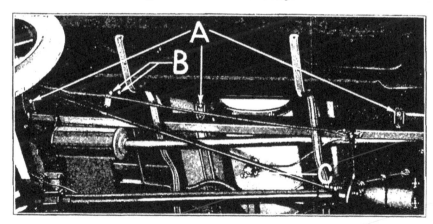

Fig. 12

  (b) Run off nuts on the four dash to body bolts, (See "A" Fig. 13), and withdraw bolts.
  (c) Loosen the six terminal block wire screws "B" and withdraw switch loom wires from terminal block. Run off coil wire terminal nut "C" and pull switch loom wires into body through opening in dash.
  (d) Disconnect priming rod from bell crank by withdrawing cotter pin "D". Priming rod is then withdrawn through dash.

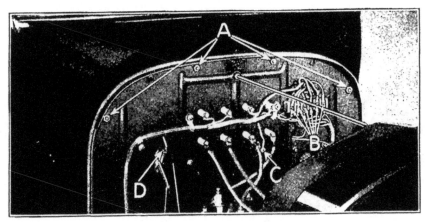

Fig. 13

(e) Remove steering wheel by running off steering wheel nut and withdrawing wheel from drive pinion with a puller (See Fig. 14).

(f) Swing steering gear bracket cap to one side by removing one of the two steering gear bracket bolts and loosening the other bolt (See "A" Fig. 15).

(g) Lift out front mat and floor boards. Remove spare rim by running off nut on spare rim carrier clamp bolt.

(h) Remove body—If no equipment is available for lifting off the body with chain falls, it can be removed by tipping up the ends and inserting a hardwood lifting bar under each end of body. Four men (two to a side) can then lift body from chassis (See Fig. 16). When body is removed it should be placed on a flat truck and wheeled to a section of the shop where it will be out of the way, and there will be no possibility of it being damaged.

13    *Remove running board shields.* Run off running board shield to frame bolt nut (See "A" Fig. 17) and withdraw bolt.

Fig. 14                                    Fig. 15

Fig. 16

Fig. 17

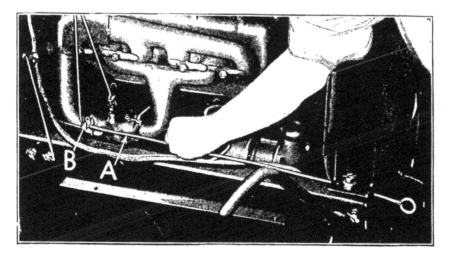

Fig. 18

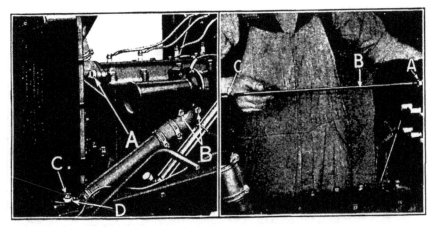

Fig. 19              Fig. 20

**14**   *Remove radiator—*

(a) Open pet cock underneath radiator, while water is draining, disconnect priming wire (See "A" Fig. 18), by unhooking it from carburetor butterfly "B" and withdrawing it through radiator apron.

(b) Withdraw the two cylinder head outlet connection screws (See "A" Fig. 19) and the two cylinder water inlet connection screws "B".

(c) Run off radiator stud nut "C" and lift off upper thimble "D" from each side of radiator.

(d) Loosen radiator rod nut (See "A" Fig. 20) and unscrew radiator rod "B" from radiator rod bracket "C".

(e) Lift off radiator, lower thimbles and springs (See Fig. 21).

(f) Withdraw radiator rod through dash by running off radiator rod nut (See "A" Fig. 22).

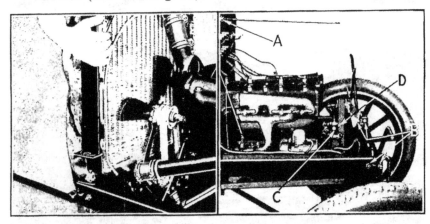

Fig. 21              Fig. 22

**15**   *Remove radiator apron—*

(a) Run off the four front fender iron bolt-side nuts "B" and with draw bolts. Apron can then be slipped off over end of starting crank handle.

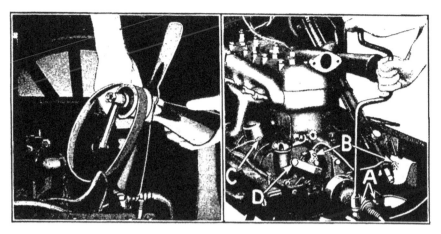

Fig. 23                                Fig. 24

**16  *Remove fan*—**
  (a) Loosen fan adjusting screw "C". (Fig. 22.)
  (b) Withdraw cotter pin from end of bolt and run out fan bracket bolt "D".
  (c) Fan together with fan belt can now be removed (See Fig. 23).

**17  *Remove crankcase front bearing cap*** by running out the two cap screws (See "A" Fig. 24), which hold bearing cap to front bearing.

**18  *Remove commutator pull rod*** by withdrawing the two cotter pins "B", which hold pull rod to commutator case and lead rod lever.

**19  *Disconnect ammeter to cutout wire at cutout*** by running out ammeter to cutout wire screw "C".

**20  *Remove commutator case*** by loosening commutator case spring bolt "D" and lifting case out of recess in cylinder front cover.

Fig. 25                                Fig 26

21  *Remove horn* by disconnecting horn wire at horn (See "A" Fig. 25) and running out cylinder head bolt "B" which holds horn to cylinder head.

22  *Disconnect spark plug wires* "C" at plugs.

23  *Remove engine pan-left* by loosening the three crankcase bolts which hold pan to crankcase (See "A" Fig. 26) and withdrawing pan.

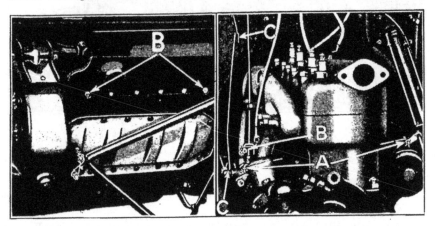

Fig. 27                              Fig. 28

24  *Remove engine pan-right* by loosening crankcase bolt and cap screw which holds pan to crankcase (See "B" Fig. 27) and withdrawing pan.

25  *Remove carburetor pull rod* by withdrawing the two cotter pins which hold pull rod to carburetor throttle and throttle rod lever (See "A" Fig. 28).

Fig. 29                              Fig. 30

26  *Remove carburetor adjusting rod* by withdrawing cotter pin "B". Forked end of rod can then be lifted from carburetor needle valve and head of rod withdrawn through dash.

27  *Remove priming wire* by unhooking priming wire "C" at carburetor butterfly and bell crank.

28 *Shut off gasoline* by closing the cock on sediment bulb underneath gasoline tank (See "C" Fig. 12).

29 *Disconnect feed pipe from carburetor* by running off gasoline feed pipe pack nut from carburetor inlet elbow (See "A" Fig. 29). (To prevent any possibility of the motor lifting hooks slipping when lifting engine out of frame it is advisable to remove the carburetor hot air pipe. This is done by running off manifold stud nut "B" and lifting off clamp and pipe.)

30 *Disconnect exhaust pipe from manifold* by running off exhaust pipe pack nut (See "A" Fig. 30).

31 *Disconnect magneto terminal wire* by running off magneto terminal nut "B" and lifting wire off terminal post.

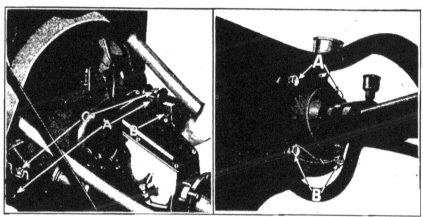

Fig. 31          Fig. 32

32 *Remove crankcase arm blocks* by running off nuts from ends of the two crankcase arm bolts—side (See "A" Fig. 31). Crankcase side arm blocks "B" can then be slipped from behind crankcase arms and lifted out of channel of frame.

33 *Remove crankcase arm bolts—top* by withdrawing cotter key and running off nuts on the ends of the two crankcase arm bolts "C".

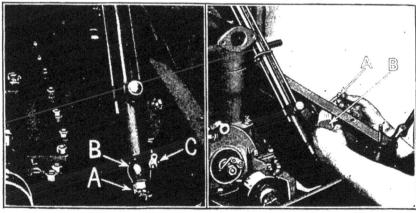

Fig. 33          Fig. 34

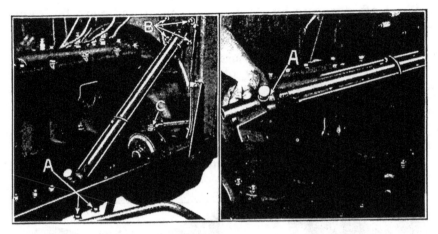

Fig. 35                    Fig. 36

34 *Disconnect axle from transmission* by running out the two universal ball cap bolts and nuts (See "A" Fig. 32). Break wire and run out the two cap screws "B".

35 *Remove steering gear assembly—*

(a) Run off nut on end of steering post (See "A" Fig. 33) and remove ball arm "B" from end of post by tapping it with a brass or lead hammer. The steering gear ball arm key can then be removed by tapping it out of keyway with a hammer and drift.

(b) Run off nut on end of steering gear bracket bolt—side and withdraw bolt (See "A" Fig. 34). Steering gear bracket block "B" can now be lifted from channel of frame.

(c) Run off nuts on the ends of the two steering gear bracket bolts —lower (See "A" Fig. 35) and withdraw bolts.

(d) Run off nuts and withdraw the four steering gear tube flange bolts "B".

(e) Drive out the lead rod lever pin (See "C" Fig. 33), and slip lever and bracket off end of steering gear shaft (See "A" Fig. 36).

(f) Steering gear assembly can now be withdrawn through dash.

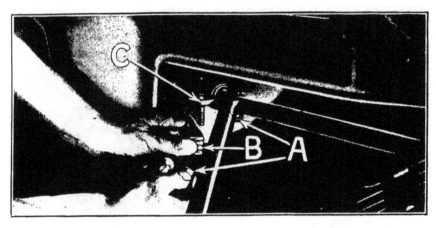

Fig. 37

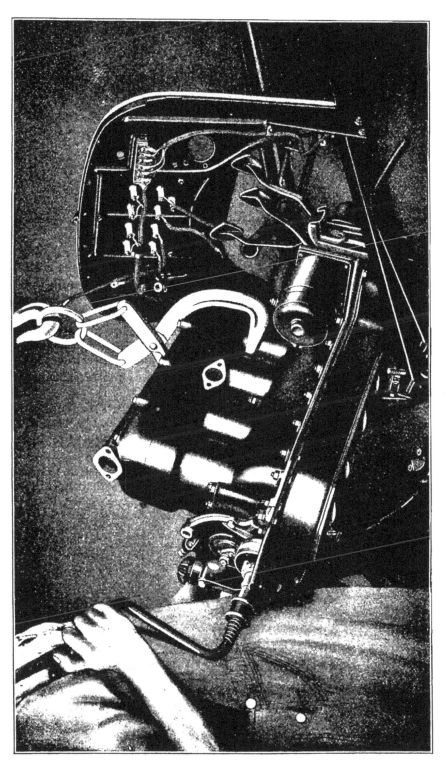

Fig. 38

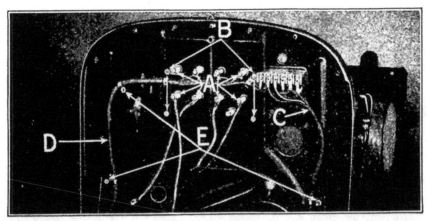

Fig. 39

36  *Disconnect starting motor to switch cable* by running off terminal nut (See "C" Fig. 35) on starting motor, and lifting off cable.

37  *Remove radius rod ball cap and springs* by running off the two radius rod ball cap stud nuts (See "A" Fig. 37), and lifting off ball cap springs "B" and ball cap "C".

38  *Remove spark plugs,* replacing them with pipe plugs. This prevents any possibility of damaging the spark plugs when removing engine. The pipe plugs prevent any foreign matter entering cylinders.

39  *Remove engine from chassis* by means of motor lifting hooks and chain falls (See Fig. 38).

40  *Remove coil box* by running off the eight nuts on ends of coil box terminals (See "A" Fig. 39) and the four coil box bolt nuts "B".

41  *Remove lighting wire loom terminals.* Withdraw lighting wire loom terminals "C" from terminal block.

42  *Remove commutator loom and case.* Commutator loom "D" together with commutator case can be removed from car and lighting wire "C" disconnected at dash by loosening the three loom clip nuts "E" on dash and lifting out loom wire from underneath loom clips.

Fig. 40

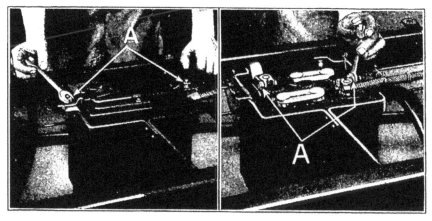

Fig. 41                    Fig. 42

**43  *Disconnect tail lamp wire—***

(a) Disconnect tail lamp wire at tail lamp (See "A" Fig. 40) and withdraw wire through the five tail lamp wire bushings "B".

**44  *Remove battery, battery cable, battery box, battery box support, ground connector and battery to switch cable support.***

(a) Run off the two battery clamp bolt nuts (See "A" Fig. 41) and lift off battery box cover.

(b) Disconnect ground connector and battery to switch cable from battery by loosening the nuts on the two battery terminal bolts (See "A" Fig. 42) and lifting cable and ground connector off of positive and negative terminal posts. Battery and battery box can now be lifted out of battery box support.

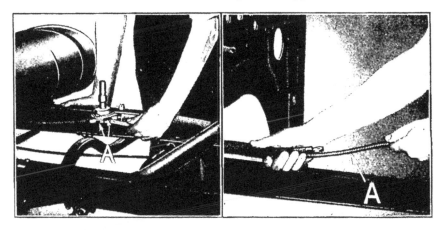

Fig. 43                    Fig. 44

(c) Disconnect battery to switch and motor to switch cables at starting switch by running off the two starting switch terminal nuts (See "A" Fig. 43), and lifting cables off ends of terminals.

(d) Lighting switch loom can then be removed by withdrawing wires through cable sleeve (See "A" Fig. 44).

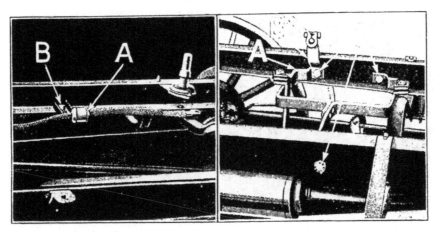

Fig. 45                              Fig. 46

(e) Withdraw battery to switch cable through cable support bushing (See "A" Fig. 45), remove battery to switch cable support
by running out cable support bolt and nut "B". Remove battery box support (See "A" Fig. 46) and ground connector "B"
by running out the three battery box support bolts and nuts
"C", which hold connector and support to frame.

Fig. 47

**45** *Remove feed pipe* by running out feed pipe pack nut (See "A"
Fig. 47) at sediment bulb and withdrawing pipe from feed pipe
clamp.

**46** *Remove gasoline tank* by running out the three gasoline tank
support bolts and nuts "B" which hold tank to frame.

**47** *Remove terminal block* by running out the two terminal block
wood screws (See "A" Fig. 48).

**48** *Remove dash* by running off nuts on ends of four dash to bracket
bolts "B".

Fig. 48

49  *Remove the two dash brackets* by running off the four dash bracket to frame bolt nuts "C" and withdrawing bolts.

50  *Remove radiator studs, nuts and springs.* The two radiator studs, washer nuts and springs "D" are removed by withdrawing cotter pins and unscrewing studs from washer nuts.

51  *Remove front fender irons* by running off the two nuts "E" from ends of the two fender iron bolts—bottom and withdrawing bolts.

52  *Remove starting switch* by running out the two starting switch bolts and nuts (See "A" Fig. 49).

53  *Remove tail lamp and license bracket* by running out the two bolts and nuts which hold bracket to spare rim carrier (See "A" Fig. 50).

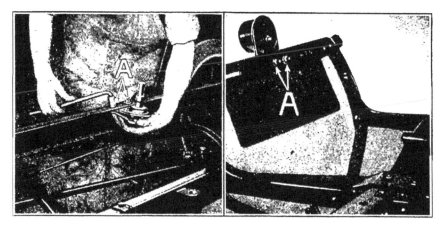

Fig. 49                              Fig. 50

54  *Remove exhaust pipe and muffler* by running off muffler head to frame bolt nut and withdrawing bolt (See "A" Fig. 51).

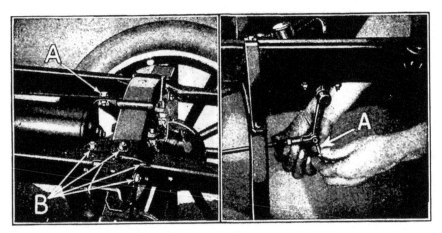

Fig. 51                    Fig. 52

**55    Remove spare rim carrier** by running out the four spare rim carrier bolts and nuts "B" which hold each side of carrier to rear cross member and corner bracket.

**56    Remove brake rods from control shaft** by removing cotter key and withdrawing clevis pin (See "A" Fig. 52).

**57    Remove rear axle—**
(a)  Remove hub caps and run off axle shaft nuts (See "A" Fig. 53).
(b)  Lift up rear end of chassis with chain falls and lifting hooks "B".

Fig. 53

(c)  Withdraw rear wheel from axle shaft with a wheel puller; the puller is screwed onto hub and drawn down tightly by means of a clamp screw. The screw in the end of the puller is then drawn down against end of shaft until wheel is forced off (See "A" Fig. 54).

Fig. 54      Fig. 55

(d) Remove brake shoe by running off brake shoe bolt nut (See "A" Fig. 55) and running out brake shoe bolt. This operation is performed by loosening the nut, the nut is then held stationary while the bolt is run out as shown above.

(e) Run off spring perch nut "B" from ends of both spring perches. Axle is now disconnected and can be removed from chassis.

**58** *Remove rear spring, hangers, and perches—*

(a) Run off spring hanger nuts (See "A" Fig. 56) and withdraw hanger bars "B", perches and hangers can then be withdrawn as shown at "C".

(b) Run off the four spring clip nuts "D" and lift off spring clip bars "E". Spring can now be removed from cross member by tapping the spring with a brass or lead hammer. If spring fits tightly in cross member it can be pried out with a pinch bar which is inserted between the spring and cross member.

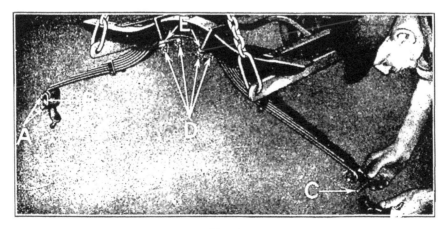

Fig. 56

Fig. 57                    Fig. 58

**59**  *Remove control shaft* by running out the four control shaft bracket bolts and nuts (See "A" Fig. 57).

**60**  *Remove front axle assembly—*

(a) Jack up front end of chassis.

(b) Unscrew hub caps (See "A" Fig. 58).

(c) Withdraw cotter pin "B", run off spindle nut "C" and lift off washer "D".

(d) Run off adjusting cone "E" from spindle, and lift off wheel.

(e) Remove crankcase front ˙bearing and spring clip by running off the two crankcase front bearing and spring clip nuts and lifting off license bracket (See "A" Fig. 59) and spring clip bar "B". Spring clip is then lifted off of cross member.

**61**  Front axle assembly can now be removed from frame which completes the disassembly of the car.

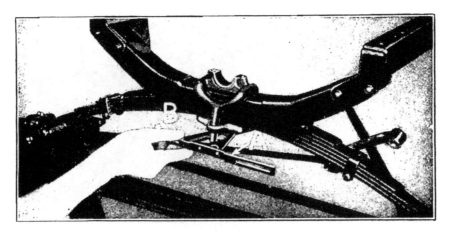

Fig. 59

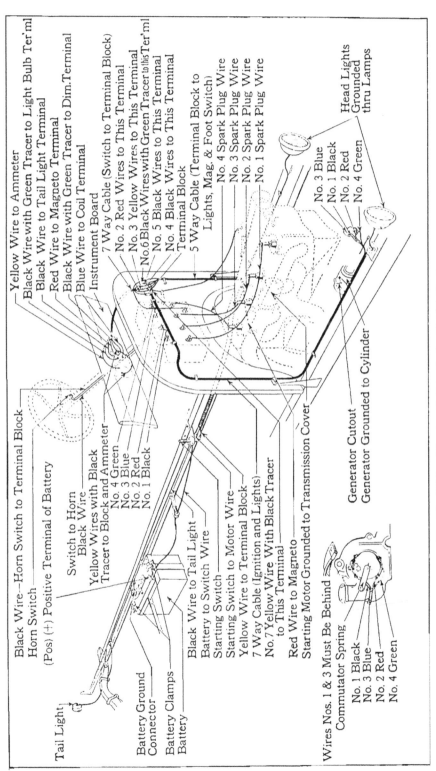

Yellow Wire to Ammeter
Black Wire with Green Tracer to Light Bulb Ter'ml
Horn Switch
Black Wire to Tail Light Terminal
Red Wire to Magneto Terminal
Black Wire with Green Tracer to Dim.Terminal
Blue Wire to Coil Terminal
Instrument Board
7 Way Cable (Switch to Terminal Block)
No. 2 Red Wires to This Terminal
No. 3 Yellow Wires to This Terminal
No.6 Black Wires with Green Tracer to this Ter'ml
No. 5 Black Wires to This Terminal
No. 4 Black Wires to This Terminal
Terminal Block
5 Way Cable (Terminal Block to
Lights, Mag. & Foot Switch)
No. 4 Spark Plug Wire
No. 3 Spark Plug Wire
No. 2 Spark Plug Wire
No. 1 Spark Plug Wire

No. 3 Blue
No. 1 Black
No. 2 Red
No. 4 Green

Head Lights
Grounded
thru Lamps

Black Wire—Horn Switch to Terminal Block
(Pos) (±) Positive Terminal of Battery

Tail Light

Switch to Horn
Black Wire
Yellow Wires with Black
Tracer to Block and Ammeter
No. 4 Green
No. 3 Blue
No. 2 Red
No. 1 Black

Battery Ground
Connector
Battery Clamps
Battery

Black Wire to Tail Light
Battery to Switch Wire
Starting Switch
Starting Switch to Motor Wire
Yellow Wire to Terminal Block
7 Way Cable (Ignition and Lights)
No. 7 Yellow Wire With Black Tracer
to This Terminal
Red Wire to Magneto
Starting Motor Grounded to Transmission Cover

Generator Cutout
Generator Grounded to Cylinder

Wires Nos. 1 & 3 Must Be Behind
Commutator Spring
No. 1 Black
No. 3 Blue
No. 2 Red
No. 4 Green

Fig. 60. Wiring Diagram of Cars Equipped with Starter.

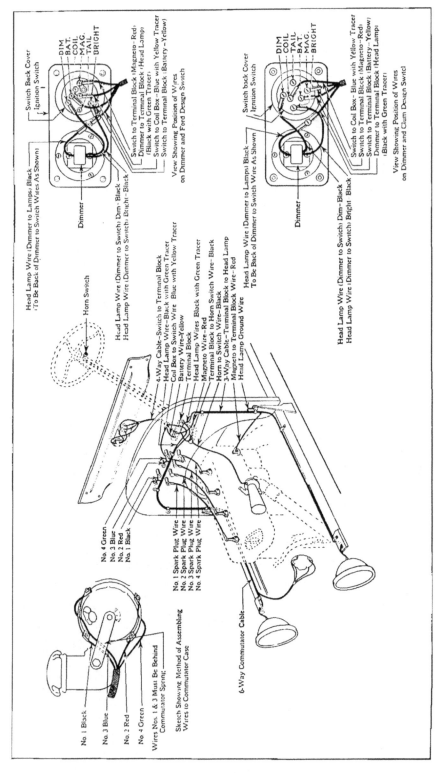

Fig. 61.  Wiring Diagram of Cars Not Equipped with Starter.

# CHAPTER II
# Assembling the Car

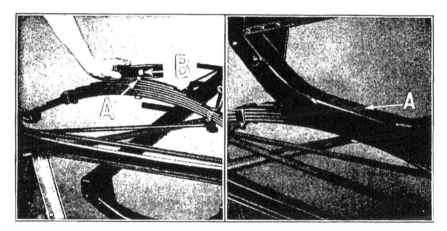

Fig. 62                    Fig. 63

**62** *Install spring pad*—Place front axle assembly on jacks. Position spring pad on top of front spring, making sure that head of tie bolt (See "A" Fig. 62), enters hole "B" in spring pad.

**63** *Connect frame to front axle assembly*—Position frame on front axle assembly, making sure that head of tie bolt (See "A" Fig. 63) enters hole in cross member.

Fig. 64

**64** *Install crankcase front bearing and spring clip assembly*—Position crankcase front bearing (See "A" Fig. 64) on cross member, inserting spring clip bar "B" over ends of spring clip.

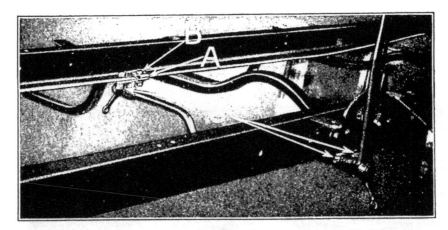

Fig. 65

**65** *Insert license bracket over ends of spring clip* (See "A" Fig. 59). Run down the two spring clip nuts on ends of spring clips; draw nuts down tightly and lock with cotter keys.

**66** *Install front wheel—*
- (a) Fill hub with grease.
- (b) Slip wheel over end of spindle.
- (c) Screw on adjusting cone (See "E" Fig. 58). Run down cone sufficiently far to permit wheel turning freely yet have no play between bearing cup and cone bearing.
- (d) Insert spindle washer "D" over end of spindle, positioning it against adjusting cone.
- (e) Run down spindle nut "C" locking nut with cotter key "B".
- (f) Fill hub cap "A" with grease and screw cap on hub.

**67** *Install control shaft and feed pipe clamp—*
- (a) Insert the four control shaft bracket bolts and nuts which hold shaft to frame, positioning feed pipe clamp (See "A" Fig. 65) under head of bolt "B".
- (b) Run down nuts "C" on ends of control shaft bracket bolts, drawing down three of the nuts tightly and locking with cotter keys. The fourth nut is not tightened until feed pipe is inserted through clamp.

**68** *Install rear spring* by entering spring into cross member, making sure that head of tie bolt (See "A" Fig. 66), enters hole in cross member.

**69** *Install rear spring clips*—Position spring clips on cross member, making sure that locking pin "B" on spring clip enters hole "C" in cross member.

**70** *Install spring clip bars* (See "A" Fig. 67) over ends of spring clips. Run down and securely tighten the four spring clip nuts, locking three of the nuts with cotter keys and using the wire on the tail lamp wire bushing "B" to lock the fourth nut.

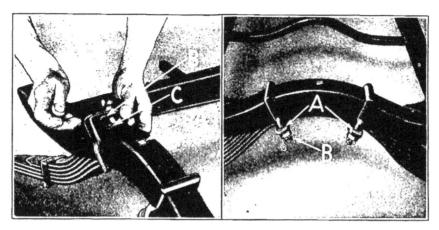

Fig. 66          Fig. 67

**71  Install rear spring hangers and perches—**

(a) Insert hangers through ends of spring and perches (See "C" Fig. 56).

(b) Position spring hanger bars "B" over ends of hangers.

(c) Run down and tighten the two spring hanger nuts "A" on each hanger, locking the nuts with cotter keys.

**72  Install rear axle assembly—**

(a) Lift up rear end of frame with chain falls and lifting hooks and position axle on horses (See Fig. 68).

(b) Insert end of perch "A" through hole "B" in flange on both axle housings. A spring spreader can be used to facilitate entering perches through holes in flanges or two blocks of wood can be used as shown in Fig. 366.

(c) Run down nuts on ends of perches and lock with cotter keys.

Fig. 68

Fig. 69                                    Fig. 70

**73   *Install brake shoes—***

(a) Position brake shoe on housing flange with flat side of shoe against flange making sure that hub cam enters slot in brake shoe (See "A" Fig. 69).

(b) Insert brake shoe bolt "B" through brake shoe, running bolt down into housing flange; run down nut tightly on end of bolt, and lock the nut with a cotter key.

(c) Place a little grease around cam and bolt.

**74   *Install rear wheel—***

(a) Before installing wheel, examine hub key (See "A" Fig. 70) in axle shaft, and hub felt "B" in wheel to make sure they are in good condition.

(b) Slip wheel over end of axle shaft, making sure that key "A" in shaft enters keyway "C" in hub of wheel.

(c) Run down and securely tighten axle shaft nut, locking the nut with a cotter key.

(d) Tightening rear wheels on axle shafts is an operation requiring special attention. If the axle shaft nut is not draw down tightly, the wheel hub will clash against the key on the shaft, ultimately resulting in breakage of the shaft either from crystallization or because of the chipping off of small pieces of steel, which work around the shaft, eventually cutting both shaft and hub. Owing to the importance of this operation, hexigon head box shaped wrenches, having handles 20″ and 25″ long, should be used in tightening axle shaft nuts on both car and truck (See "A" Fig. 71). Wrenches of this description can be obtained from nearest Ford Branch. The wrench used on the car is listed under symbol No. 5-Z-248, while the one used on the truck is listed under symbol No. 5-Z-591. When wheels are installed while car is on assembly line, a bar, details of which are shown in Fig. 72, can be used to prevent the wheels from turning. The forked end of bar is placed over drive shaft tube as shown at "B" Fig. 71 with the flat end of bar resting on spoke of wheel.

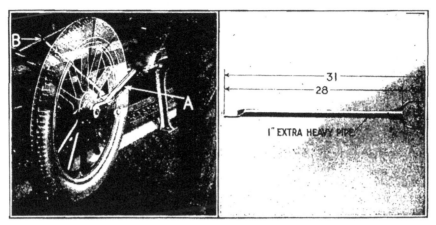

Fig. 71            Fig. 72

**75** *Connect brake rods to control shaft and adjust brakes—*

(a) Insert levers on control shaft into clevises on brake rods.

(b) Line up holes in shaft and clevis and insert clevis pin (See "A" Fig. 73).

(c) The brake pull rods are adjusted so they will pull evenly on both wheels, and the brakes will set tightly when the hand brake lever is in a vertical position. The adjustment is made by turning the threaded clevises "B" on the ends of the pull rods. Ordinarily the pins will slip into the clevises readily. However, if trouble is experienced, place the hand brake lever forward and draw the pull rod forward until the lever enters the clevis. Insert a drift through the clevis and lever holes to draw them into line. The drift can be made from a piece of $\frac{1}{4}''$ round steel tapered at the ends. When the clevis and lever holes line up properly withdraw drift and insert clevis pin. Then try the brakes to see that they are set evenly, proceeding as follows: With the rear axle jacked up pull the hand brake lever back as

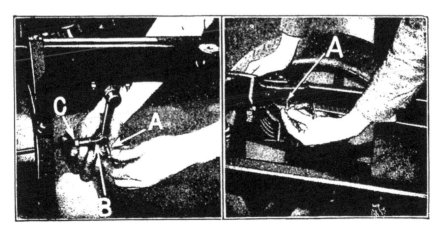

Fig. 73            Fig. 74

far as it will go.  Next examine wheels to see whether they are both tightly locked, if not readjust until both wheels are locked, then release hand brake and examine wheels to make sure the brakes are not dragging.

(d) When correct adjustment is obtained lock clevis pin with cotter key and run down clevis lock nut "C" tightly against clevis.

76  *Install rear hub caps.*  Screw hub caps onto hubs of rear wheels.

77  *Install spare rim carrier* by running down the four spare rim carrier bolts, lockwashers and nuts which hold each side of carrier to rear cross member and corner brackets (See "B" Fig. 51).  Before installing bolt in front end of left side of carrier, place tail light wire spring with fibre clamp attached over end of bolt (See "A" Fig. 74).

78  *Install tail light wire bushing* (See "A" Fig. 75) by slipping ends of wires through hole in spare rim carrier and bending ends of wires to hold bushing in place.

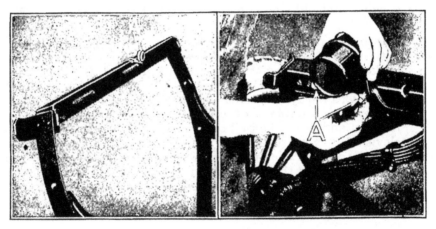

Fig. 75                    Fig. 76

79  *Install tail lamp and license bracket* by inserting the two tail lamp and license bracket bolts, through bracket and carrier.  Place lockwashers over ends of bolts and run down nuts tightly (See "A" Fig. 76).

80  *Install starting switch.*  Position starting switch under upper edge of channel of frame and run in the two starting switch to frame bolts and nuts which hold switch to frame.  Draw nuts down tightly and lock with cotter keys (See Fig. 49).

81  *Install battery bracket assembly and ground connector—*
(a) Position battery bracket (See "A" Fig. 46), on frame and run in the three battery bracket bolts "C" placing ground connector "B" over end of bolt before inserting bolt through bracket and frame.

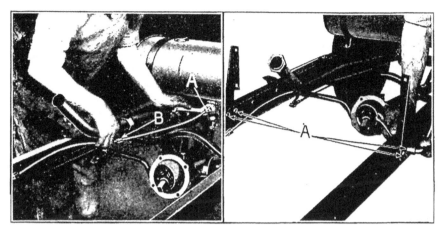

Fig. 77      Fig. 78

(b) Before running in the bolt which holds ground connector to battery bracket, make sure that the point where connector is bolted to bracket, is thoroughly clean, and all paint removed, this insures a good connection.

(c) Run down nuts on ends of battery bracket bolts and lock with cotter keys.

**82** *Install muffler and exhaust pipe assembly—*

(a) Position muffler head to frame bracket on frame lining up bolt hole in bracket with hole in frame.

(b) Insert muffler head to frame bolt (See "A" Fig. 51) through frame and muffler.

(c) Run down nut on end of bolt and lock the nut with a cotter key.

**83** *Install gasoline tank* by positioning it on frame, lining up the bolt holes in support with holes in frame. Insert the three gasoline tank support bolts through frame and support. Run down nuts on ends of bolts and lock with cotter keys (See "B" Fig. 47).

**84** *Install feed pipe—*

(a) Clean out feed pipe with compressed air.

(b) Examine feed pipe gasket inside of pack nut on both ends of feed pipe (See "A" Fig. 442).

(c) Connect feed pipe to sediment bulb by running down pack nut (See "A" Fig. 77).

(d) Insert feed pipe through feed pipe support "B", tightening the nut on end of bolt and locking it with a cotter key.

**85** *Install dash brackets* by running in the four dash bracket to frame bolts and nuts which hold brackets to frame (See "A" Fig. 78). Tighten nuts and lock with cotter keys. (Due to an Engineering change, only one bolt is now being used in each dash bracket, when assembling brackets to frame).

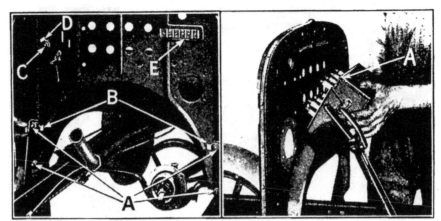

Fig. 79                                Fig. 80

**86  *Install dash*—**
   (a) Position dash against dash brackets.
   (b) Insert the four dash to bracket bolts (See "A" Fig. 79) through dash and brackets.
   (c) Position loom supports "B" over ends of two upper bolts.
   (d) Run down lockwashers and nuts on ends of the dash to bracket bolts, drawing nuts down tightly.

**87  *Install loom support bolt and support*—**Insert loom support bolt "C" through dash. Place loom support "D" over end of bolt and run down lockwasher and nut.

**88  *Install terminal block "E" on dash*** by running in the two terminal block screws through back of dash and into terminal block (See "A" Fig. 48).

**89  *Install coil box*—**
   (a) Position coil box on dash (See "A" Fig. 80).
   (b) Insert the four coil box bolts through coil box and dash (See "A" Fig. 81).
   (c) Place loom clips "B" over ends of the two top bolts.
   (d) Run down lockwashers and nuts on ends of bolts.

**90  *Install lighting wire loom on dash*** by inserting it through loom support (See "A" Fig. 82). Insert tail lamp wire "B" (black) together with battery wire "C" (yellow), and switch to motor cable "D" through cable sleeve, leaving headlamp wire "E" (black with green tracer) and magneto terminal wire "F" (red) outside of sleeve·

**91  *Install battery box and battery.*** Place battery box into battery bracket assembly and insert battery into battery box with negative post (See "A" Fig. 83) nearest frame.

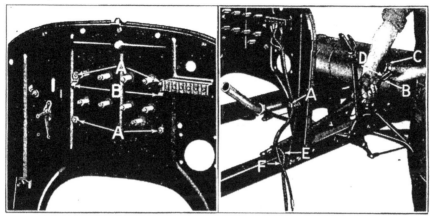

Fig. 81                    Fig. 82

**92** *Install battery to switch cable support* by positioning support on frame and inserting the cable support bolt "B" through support and frame.   Run down nut on end of bolt and lock the nut with a cotter key.   (See "A" Fig. 45).

(a) Insert battery to switch cable through cable support "A" Fig. 45.

(b) Clean positive and negative battery terminal posts thoroughly after which they should be given a coating of vaseline.

(c) Position battery to switch cable terminal over positive terminal post, and ground connector terminal over negative terminal post.

(d) Draw down terminal bolt nuts tightly (See "A" Fig. 42).

**93** *Connect motor cable, battery wire and switch cable.* Connect switch to motor cable at starting switch terminal point "A" Fig. 84; and battery wire and battery to switch cable at point "B" by running down the two lockwashers, and nuts on starting switch terminals.

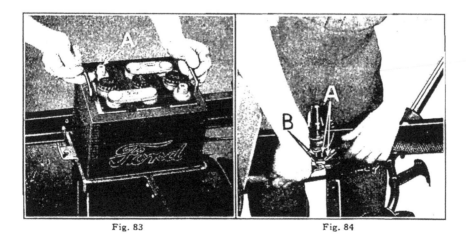

Fig. 83                    Fig. 84

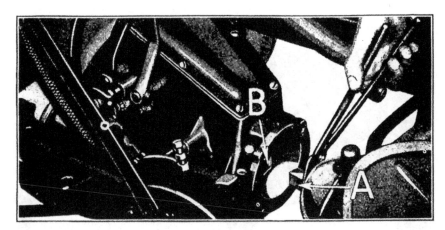

Fig. 85

**94** *Install battery box cover*—Place cover on battery box. Position battery clamps on battery cover and run down the two battery clamp bolt nuts tightly (See "A" Fig. 41).

**95** *Connect tail lamp wire to tail lamp*—Insert tail lamp wire through tail lamp wire bushings "B" and connect terminal of wire "A" to tail lamp (See Fig. 40).

**96** *Mount engine in frame* using motor lifting hooks and chain falls, exercising care when sliding engine back in frame to prevent pedals striking coil box (See Fig. 38).

**97** *Enter universal joint into drive plate assembly*—Fill universal joint housing with grease and enter joint (See "A" Fig. 85) into drive plate assembly "B" with an entering tool. When performing this operation one man stands in front of car and slides engine back in frame while joint is being entered into drive plate. In order that universal joint may be turned freely when entering it into drive plate, one of the rear wheels should be jacked up. After the joint has been entered, the two ball cap, cap screws are run down through ball cap into crankcase, but not tightened until the two ball cap bolts are entered.

**98** *Install crankcase arm bolts—top*—Insert the two crankcase arm bolts—top through frame and crankcase arms, running down nuts on ends of bolts and locking nuts with cotter keys (See "A" Fig. 86).

**99** *Install crankcase arm blocks*—Insert the two crankcase arm blocks into channel of frame and position them behind crankcase arms, lining up the holes in the blocks with bolt holes in frame and crankcase arms (See "B" Fig. 86).

**100** *Install crankcase arm bolts—side*—Insert crankcase arm bolts —side (See "C" Fig. 86), through frame block, and arm. Run down nuts on ends of bolts and lock with cotter keys (See "A" Fig. 87).

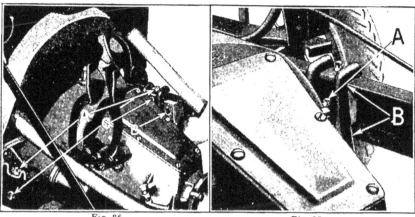

Fig. 86          Fig. 87

The nuts should be run down as far as they will go, but absolutely no force applied in tightening them, as there is a possibility of drawing the crankcase arms so tightly against frame that they become imbedded in that part, eventually resulting in crystallization of the frame at points "B".

**101** *Connect axle to transmission* by entering the two ball cap bolts (See "A" Fig. 32), running down the nuts and locking with cotter keys. Tighten the two universal ball cap, cap screws "B". Screws are then wired together.

**102** *Connect magneto terminal wire to terminal post*—Position magneto terminal wire on terminal post (See "B" Fig. 30), and run down lockwasher and nut on end of post.

**103** *Connect exhaust pipe to manifold* by running down exhaust pipe pack nut (See "A" Fig. 30).

**104** *Connect front radius rod to crankcase*—
(a) Place cup grease in ball socket in crankcase.
(b) Insert ball on radius rod into socket in crankcase (See "A" Fig. 88).

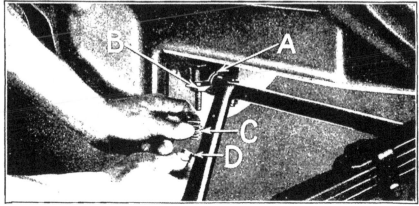

Fig. 88

(c) Position ball socket cap "B" over ends of radius rod ball cap studs.

(d) Place ball cap springs "C" over ends of studs and run down the two radius rod ball cap stud nuts "D" and wire the nuts together.

105  *Install crankcase front bearing*—Position crankcase front bearing cap on front bearing; place lockwashers over ends of bearing cap cap screws, and run down screws through bearing cap and into bearing, drawing screws down tightly (See "A" Fig. 24). After cap has been installed it should be carefully inspected to make sure that crankcase front end support is held firmly in bearing. If there is any play at this point it is necessary to remove and lightly file face of cap in the same manner as a connecting rod cap is filed (See Fig. 232).

106  *Assemble engine pan—right to engine* by slipping the pan under the heads of the two crankcase bolts shown at "B" Fig. 27, which have been previously loosened.

107  *Assemble engine pan—left to engine* in the same manner with the exception that the pan is inserted under the heads of three of the crankcase bolts (See "A" Fig. 26).

108  *Install front fender iron bolts, radiator springs, studs, and washer nuts* by inserting the two front fender iron bolts—bottom through bolt holes in bottom of frame (See "A" Fig. 89). Insert radiator studs "B" through stud holes in upper part of frame. Place radiator spring "C" over lower end of each stud. Position washer nut "D" under stud and run stud down through washer nut until a cotter pin can be inserted through hole "E" in stud.

109  *Install radiator apron* by slipping apron over starting crank handle (See "A" Fig. 90).

Fig. 89

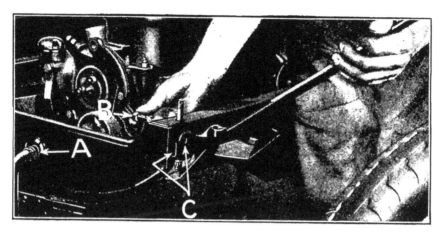

Fig. 90

**110** *Install front fender irons*—right and left.
- (a) Position front fender irons over ends of the two fender iron bolts—lower and run down nuts on ends of bolts with fingers.
- (b) Insert front fender iron bolts—side "B" through frame, apron, and fender irons as shown at "C". After entering bolts run down nuts tightly on ends of fender iron bolts—side and tighten nuts on fender iron bolts—lower, locking all nuts with cotter keys.

**111** *Connect feed pipe to carburetor* by running down pack nut on end of feed pipe onto carburetor inlet elbow (See "A" Fig. 29). making sure that gasket in pack nut is in good condition.

**112** *Turn on gasoline* by opening cock on sediment bulb underneath gasoline tank.

**113** *Install carburetor hot air pipe*—
- (a) Insert end of manifold clamp into hole in hot air pipe (See "A" Fig. 91).
- (b) Clamp and pipe are then installed over manifold stud "B".
- (c) Place lower end of hot air pipe "C" into carburetor mixing chamber "D". Run down nut on end of manifold stud "B", drawing nut down tightly against manifold clamp.

**114** *Connect carburetor pull rod to throttle lever* by inserting carburetor pull rod through hole in valve door (See "A" Fig. 92). Insert end of rod through throttle lever "B" and lock the rod in position by inserting a cotter pin through end of rod.

**115** *Install carburetor adjusting rod* by inserting head of rod through slot in dash. Place forked end of rod "C" through head of carburetor needle valve, locking the rod in position by inserting a cotter key through end of rod.

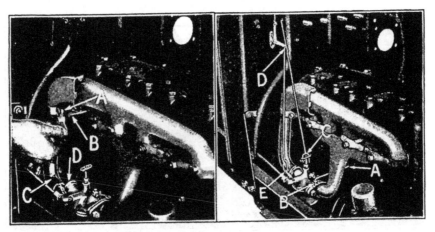

Fig. 91                    Fig. 92

**116**  *Install priming wire* by slipping end of wire through bell crank
"D" the other end of wire is inserted through butterfly valve "E"
on carburetor, and is locked in position by bending ends of wire
with a pair of pliers.

**117**  *Install commutator loom—*
  (a)  Insert loom under the four loom clips on dash ( See "A" Fig. 93).
  (b)  Position commutator wire terminals over ends of the four coil
       box terminals "B".
  (c)  Run down nuts on ends of coil box terminals.

**118**  *Connect headlamp and cutout to ammeter wires* at terminal
block by inserting terminals of headlamp wires (See "C" Fig. 94
black with green tracer) under heads of terminal block wire screws
"A", and cutout to ammeter wire "D" (yellow with black tracer)
under head of screw "B".

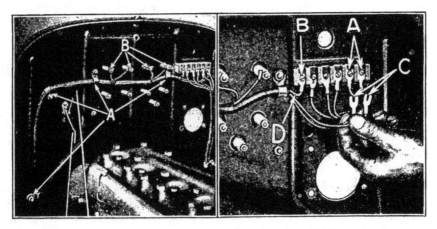

Fig. 93                    Fig. 94

Fig. 95                    Fig. 96

**119** *Install commutator case—*

(a) Position commutator case (See "A" Fig. 95) into recess in cylinder front cover.

(b) Insert commutator case spring bolt "B" through commutator case spring. Position spring in center of case and run down commutator case bolt through cylinder front cover.

(c) Connect ammeter to cutout wire to cutout by placing a lock-washer over end of ammeter wire to plate screw "C". Insert the screw through terminal on wire and run down screw into plate.

**120** *Install steering gear assembly—*

(a) Insert steering gear post through hole in dash, positioning steering gear bracket over end of steering gear post (See Fig. 36).

(b) Install lead rod lever (See "A" Fig. 96) on lead rod by slipping lever over end of rod and locking it in position by driving lead rod lever pin "B" through lever and lead rod; the ends of the pin are then riveted.

(c) Position steering gear bracket on frame. Insert the two steering gear bracket bolts—short through frame and bracket. Run down nuts tightly on ends of bolts and lock with cotter keys (See "A" Fig. 97).

**121** *Install steering gear bracket block* by placing steering gear bracket block "B" between bracket and frame. Insert steering gear bracket bolt—long "C" through frame, block and bracket. Run down nut on end of bolt and lock with cotter key.

Fig. 97

**122**   *Connect carburetor pull rod to throttle rod lever* by inserting end of carburetor pull rod through throttle rod lever (See "A" Fig. 98) and locking pull rod in position by inserting a cotter key through hole in end of rod.

**123**   *Install steering gear ball arm key* by inserting steering gear ball arm key "B" into keyway in end of steering gear post. Tap key into position with a small hammer. It is very important that key fits tightly into keyway in steering gear post.

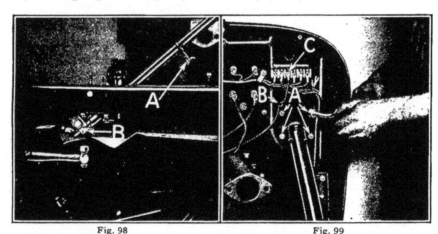

Fig. 98                          Fig. 99

**124**   *Install ball arm,* by placing ball arm (See "B" Fig. 33) over end of steering gear post, making sure that key in post enters keyway in arm. Drive ball arm tightly onto shaft with a lead or copper hammer. Run down nut on end of steering gear post, locking the nut with a cotter key (See "A" Fig. 33).

**125**   *Connect steering gear tube flange to dash—*

(a) Insert the four steering gear tube flange screws through flange and dash and run down lockwashers and nuts on ends of screws (See "A" Fig. 99).

(b) Insert horn wires "B" through hole in dash, slipping terminal on the shortest of the two horn wires under head of screw "C" on terminal block.

**126** *Install commutator pull rod* by inserting ends of rod through lead rod lever and commutator case; the rod is locked in position by means of two cotter pins, which are inserted through ends of rod (See "B" Fig. 24). When installing the commutator it is important that it is accurately set, as an incorrectly timed spark results in burned valves, knocking and broken parts. The method of setting the Ford commutator is to set it $2\frac{1}{2}''$ from the center of the commutator case pull rod to center of commutator case spring bolt, with the spark lever fully retarded. The adjustment is made by bending the pull rod (See "A" Fig. 100). The use of a gauge "B" facilitates making the adjustment.

**127** *Install fan and fan belt—*

(a) Run out fan adjusting screw (See "A" Fig. 101) sufficiently far to prevent lug "B" on fan bracket coming in contact with adjusting screw.

(b) Slip fan belt over drive pulley on crankshaft.

(c) Insert fan bracket bolt "C" through fan bracket and position fan belt over fan pulley.

(d) Run down fan bracket bolt into cylinder block and insert cotter pin through end of bolt.

(e) Adjust fan belt, by running in fan adjusting screw and tightening the lock nut. The correct adjustment is obtained by attaching a spring balance on a blade of the fan and adjusting the belt so that a pull of five pounds on the spring balance will just be sufficient to cause the belt to slip on the pulley.

(f) Belt dressings or oils should not be used on the fan belt adopted as standard equipment on Ford cars.

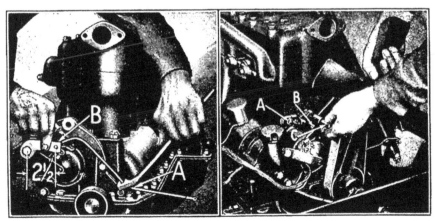

Fig. 100          Fig. 101

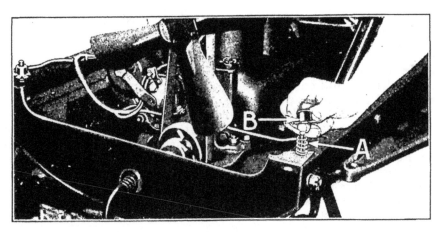

Fig. 102

**128** *Install radiator and horn—*

(a) Insert radiator stud spring (See "A" Fig. 102), and lower thimble "B" over radiator studs.

(b) Insert radiator support (See "A" Fig. 103) over studs and thimbles "B".

(c) Place upper thimble (See "A" Fig. 104) over the two radiator studs and run down castle nuts "B" sufficiently far to permit locking the nuts by inserting cotter pins through radiator studs.

(d) Connect cylinder head outlet connection to radiator and cylinder head by placing gasket "C" between connection and cylinder head and running down the two cap screws "D" which hold connection to head.

(e) Connect cylinder water inlet connection to cylinder block by placing cylinder water inlet gasket "E" between connection and block and running down cylinder inlet connection screw "F".

(f) Position horn on cylinder block and run down cylinder head bolt "G" and remaining cylinder inlet connection screw "H".

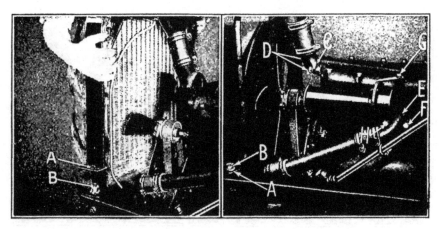

Fig. 103                         Fig. 104

Fig. 105

(g) Install radiator rod (See "A" Fig. 105), by inserting it through dash and placing lockwasher and nut "B" over end of rod.

(h) Threaded end of radiator rod "C" is then screwed into radiator rod support "D" and radiator rod nut "B" run down but not tightened until hood is installed.

129  *Install carburetor priming rod* by inserting end of carburetor priming rod (See "A" Fig. 18), through radiator shell and connect it to carburetor butterfly "B" by bending end of wire.

130  *Install spark plugs* by removing the pipe plugs which had previously been installed (See Par. 38) and screw in spark plugs, connecting the wires to coil box posts (See "A" Fig. 106) and spark plugs "B".

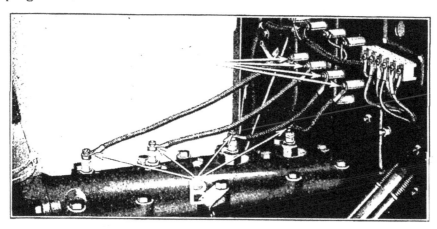

Fig. 106

131  *Install running boards and shields—*

(a) Position shield on frame; insert running board shield to frame; bolt through frame and shield, and run down lockwasher and nut (See "A" Fig. 17).

(b) Place running board blocks (See "A" Fig. 107) on running board brackets.

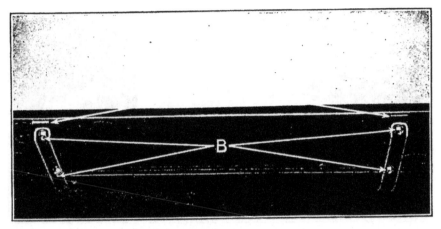

Fig. 107

(c) Position running board on blocks and insert the four running board to bracket bolts "B" through running board, blocks and brackets. Place lockwashers over ends of bolts and run down nuts.

(d) Insert the two running board to shield bolts through running board and shield (See "C" Fig. 6). Position running board to shield clamp over ends of the two bolts and run down lock-washers and nuts.

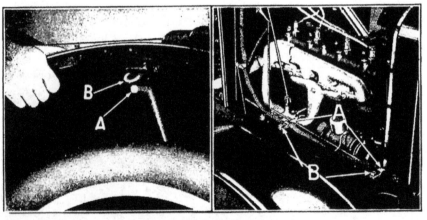

Fig. 108                          Fig. 109

**132  Install front fenders—**

(a) Insert fender iron (See "A" Fig. 108) through fender eye bolt "B".

(b) Insert fender apron to frame bracket bolt (See "B" Fig. 11) through frame and bracket starting nut on end of bolt, but not tightening nut until all bolts have been entered.

(c) Insert the two fender apron to frame bolts through frame and fender, slipping loom supports over ends of bolts (See "A" Fig. 109) and running down fender apron to frame bolt nuts "B" on ends of bolts.

Fig. 110

(d) Place two spacer washers between fender and running board (See "A" Fig. 110). A slight change was made in the fenders which eliminates the necessity of installing spacer washers between fenders and running boards on cars manufactured subsequent to August 1924.

(e) Line up spacer washers and insert the two fender to running board bolts through running board, spacer washers and front fenders. Place lockwashers over ends of bolts and run down nuts.

(f) Tighten the nut on fender apron to frame bracket bolt and lock the nut with a cotter key.

(g) Tighten fender iron eye bolt nut.

**133** *Install hood blocks—*

(a) Insert headlamp wire bushing (See "A" Fig. 111) over ends of headlamp wires "B" slipping bushing down on loom.

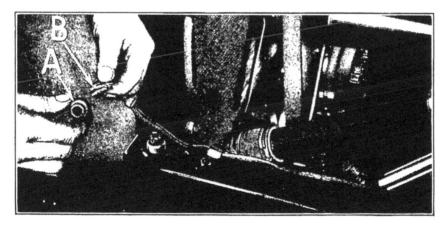

Fig. 111

Fig. 112

(b) Position hood block on frame and insert headlamp wire through headlamp wire hole in hood blocks. Place headlamp wire bushing into hole in hood block (See "A" Fig. 112). This prevents headlamp wires from becoming chafed.

(c) Insert the two engine pan bolts "B" through hood block, frame and engine pan. Place lockwashers over ends of bolts and run down nuts.

**134** *Install headlamps—*

(a) Insert headlamp spindle through fender iron. Run down headlamp nut (See "A" Fig. 7), on end of spindle, locking the nut with cotter key.

(b) Slip head lamp plug thimble (See "A" Fig. 113) over ends of headlamp wires. Insert headlamp wires "B" into headlamp plug "C". The wires are held in place by running down the two headlamp wire plug screws "D".

(c) Run down headlamp plug thimble on threaded end of plug.

(d) Install plug in headlamp by pressing plug into headlamp and turning plug clockwise.

Fig. 113                    Fig. 114

**135** *Assemble body to chassis—*
- (a) Lift body onto chassis either with chain falls or as shown in Fig. 16.
- (b) Install dash felt between body and dash (See "A" Fig. 114).
- (c) Insert the six body bolts through body and body brackets (See "A" Fig. 12), running down lockwashers and nuts on ends of bolts.
- (d) Run in the two running board shield screws which hold running board shields to body (See "B" Fig. 12).
- (e) Insert the four dash to body bolts through body and dash, place lockwashers over ends of bolts and run down nuts (See "A" Fig. 13).
- (f) Install floor boards and mat.

**136** *Install priming rod* by inserting priming rod through dash and connect it to bell crank with a cotter pin (See "D" Fig. 13).

**137** *Connect switch loom wires* by inserting switch loom through hole in dash (See "A" Fig. 115). Slip terminals of the two head lamp wires "B", tail lamp wire "C", battery wire "D" magneto wire "E", ammeter wire "F" under heads of screws on terminal block and tighten the screws. Connect ignition wire to coil box terminal "G" by placing wire over end of terminal and running down nut.

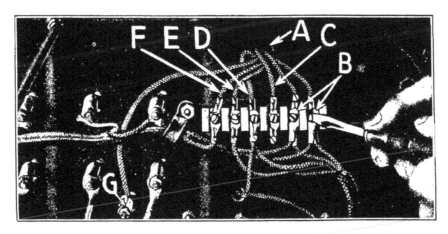

Fig. 115

**138** *Connect horn wire to horn* by positioning terminal of wire on horn and running down nut (See "A" Fig. 25).

**139** *Connect starting switch to motor cable* by positioning cable on starting motor terminal and running down lockwasher and nut (See "C" Fig. 35).

**140** *Install steering post bracket cap* (See "A" Fig. 15) by running down the two screws which hold cap to steering post bracket.

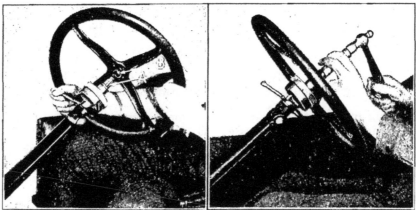

Fig. 116                    Fig. 117

### 141  *Install steering wheel—*

(a) Insert steering gear drive pinion key into keyway in steering gear drive pinion (See "A" Fig. 116), making sure that key fits tightly in keyway.

(b) Position steering wheel on end of steering gear drive pinion, inserting key in pinion into keyway "B" in steering wheel.

(c) Force wheel onto pinion with a driver as shown in Fig. 117.

(d) Run down and tighten steering wheel nut on end of drive pinion.

### 142  *Install rear fenders—*

(a) Insert fender iron (See "A" Fig. 118) through fender eye bolt "B".

(b) Insert the two fender to shield bolts through shields and fenders (See "B" Fig. 5). Place lockwashers over ends of bolts and run down nuts.

(c) Insert the two fender to running board bolts (See "A" Fig. 5), through running board and fender. Place lockwashers over ends of bolts and run down nuts.

(d) Draw down fender eye bolt nut (See "C" Fig. 5) tightly.

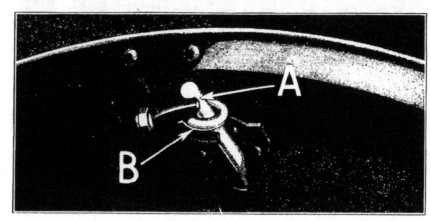

Fig. 118

**143** *Install spare rim on carrier* by running down clamp and nut on carrier.

**144** Check oil level in crankcase and see that there is fuel in the gasoline tank.

**145** *Install hood on car,* making sure that hood fits properly on dash and radiator shell; the adjustment is obtained by screwing in or running out the radiator rod, after which the rod nut is tightened against dash. Close drain cock in bottom of radiator and fill radiator with clean water. Car is now completely assembled.

## Alignment of Front Axle and Wheels

Fig. 119

**146** The front axle should now be checked for pitch and the front wheels checked for alignment.

**147** The front axle should have a $5\frac{1}{2}°$ pitch toward rear of car. To check the pitch, place the car on a floor having a level surface. A square is then positioned with one edge on the floor and the other edge resting against lower spindle body bushing in front axle (See "A" Fig. 119).

**148** The distance between the square "B" and the upper spindle body bushing "C", should now be measured. The distance between these points should measure not less than $\frac{1}{4}''$ or more than $\frac{5}{16}''$. If the distance is greater or less than these limits, it can be adjusted by slightly tilting the front axle with straightening bar until the correct adjustment is obtained. The bar is placed on the lower side of the axle over the ends of the spring perches.

# Alignment of Front Wheels

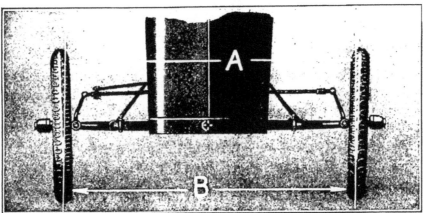

Fig. 120

**149**    The front wheels are checked for camber and gather. Gather is the toe in at the front of the wheels measured on a horizontal plane through the center of the hub. Camber is the outward pitch at the top of the wheels.

**150**    The gather of the front wheels should measure $\frac{3}{16}''$ to $\frac{1}{4}''$ while the camber should measure approximately $3''$.

**151**    The gather is checked by drawing a horizontal line from center of hub to the front and rear of the wheel felloe on both front wheels (See "A" and "B" Fig. 120), and measuring the distance between the wheel felloes at these points. There should be a difference of $\frac{3}{16}''$ to $\frac{1}{4}''$ between the two measurements. If the gather is greater or less than these limits it can be adjusted by running off the spindle connecting rod yoke ball nut (See "A" Fig. 121) and withdrawing ball from yoke. Run off spindle connecting rod bolt nut "B" and spindle connecting rod bolt "C". The spindle connecting rod yoke "D" is then turned until the correct adjustment is obtained. The connecting rod bolt is then replaced and the nut run down and cottered. The yoke ball is inserted through yoke and nut run down and cottered.

Fig. 121

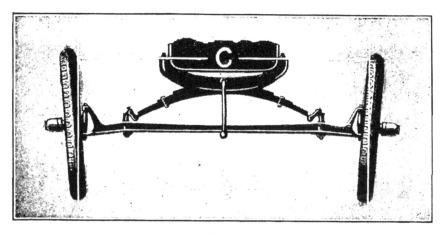

Fig. 122

**152** The camber is not adjustable as it is provided for in the forging of the spindle. The only possibility of the camber being changed would be due to a bent axle or spindle, or badly worn spindle body bushings.

**153** The camber is checked by drawing a vertical line through center of hubs to the top and bottom of the wheel felloes (See "C" and "D" Fig. 122) and measuring the distance between the wheel felloes at these points. The difference between the measurements at "C" and "D" should be approximately 3″; in other words there should be a 1½″ pitch on each front wheel.

**154** The use of an automatic wheel alignor (See Fig. 123), will facilitate checking the camber and gather of the front wheels, as it is not only a time-saver but furnishes a more accurate check on the alignment of the wheels than it is possible to obtain with ordinary devices.

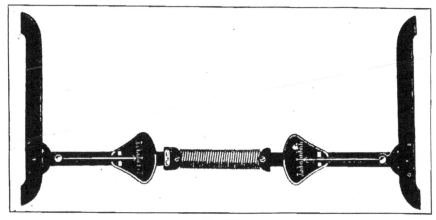

Fig. 123

## Alignment and Focus of Headlamps

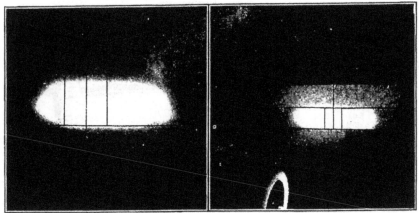

Fig. 124                    Fig. 125

**155**   The headlamps should be checked for alignment and focus. This
is done with the empty car standing on a level surface and facing a
white wall or screen 25 feet in front of the headlamps. The wall
must be marked off with black lines as shown in Fig. 124 and 125,
and must be shielded from direct light, so that the light spots from
the headlamps can be clearly seen.

## Focusing Headlamps

**156**   First turn on bright lights, then focus first one lamp and then
the other, by means of the adjusting screw at back of lamps (See
Fig. 126). Adjust the bulb filaments until an elongated elliptical
spot of light appears on the wall with its long axis horizontal (See
Fig. 124). When focusing, adjust the bulb to obtain as great a
contrast and as well defined cutoff across the top of the spot of
light as possible. With lamps thus focused for the "bright" filament,
the "dim" will be in correct position.

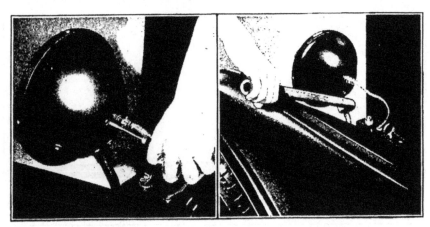

Fig. 126                    Fig. 127

# Alignment of Headlamps

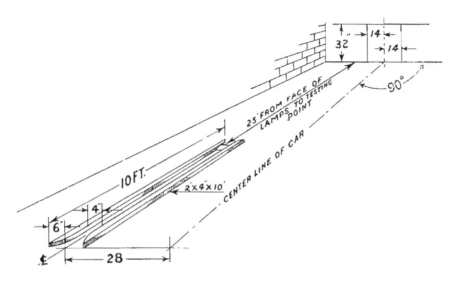

Fig. 128

**157** Headlamps are aligned by bending the headlamp brackets (See Fig. 127), as follows:

(a) The tops of the bright spot on the 25-foot wall are set at a line 32″ above level of surface on which car stands (See Fig. 128). With top lines thus set for empty car, the headlamps will also have the proper tilt under full loads.

(b) The beam of light from each headlamp is to extend straight forward, i. e., the centers of the elliptical spots of light must be 28″ apart.

**158** With the car facing a white wall 25 feet in front of headlamps, proper alignment can readily be checked by means of a horizontal line drawn on the wall 32″ above the level surface of car, and two vertical lines 28″ apart, each one 14″ from center line of car. Proper alignment of car relative to marks on the wall can be provided by the use of wheel guide blocks for one side of the car, as shown in Fig. 128. If it is impractical to tie up the floor space required by these blocks, marks painted on the floor can be used to show where one set of wheels should track and where the car should be stopped.

# CHAPTER III
# Major Repair Operations

159 In this section of the book is described the correct procedure for overhauling the various assemblies and performing the principal repair operations.

160 When removing a part do not use unnecessary force; the use of a puller, soft hammer or drift will facilitate the work and prevent damaging the part.

161 New gaskets will usually prove more satisfactory when reassembling, although an old gasket, if in good condition, will render satisfactory service. Inspect each gasket before installing; see that the surface against which it fits is clean and in good condition.

162 Before assembling, clean all parts thoroughly, also lubricate all moving parts and the surfaces upon which they move, such as bearings, bushings, pistons, cylinders, etc. Draw all bolts, nuts and cap screws down tightly, making sure to replace lock washers and cotter pins as required.

## Complete Engine and Transmission Overhaul

### (Removing Engine from Car)

163 Drain water from radiator.

164 Shut off gasoline at sediment bulb underneath gas tank (See "C" Fig. 12.

165 Break wire and run out the two universal ball cap cap screws (See "B" Fig. 32).

166 Break wire and run off radius rod ball cap stud nuts and lift off ball cap springs, and ball cap (See "A" Fig. 37).

167 Run off nuts on ends of the four engine pan bolts (See "A" Fig. 9).

168 Lift off hood.

169 Disconnect carburetor priming rod at carburetor and withdraw rod through radiator apron (See "A" Fig. 18).

170 Disconnect bell crank priming wire at carburetor (See "C" Fig. 28).

171 Disconnect carburetor adjusting rod at carburetor (See "B" Fig. 28).

172 Remove carburetor pull rod from carburetor and throttle rod lever (See "A" Fig. 28).

173 Disconnect feed pipe at carburetor by running off the feed pipe pack nut from carburetor elbow (See "A" Fig. 29).

174 Run out the two cylinder head outlet connection screws and two cylinder head inlet connection screws (See "A" and "B" Fig. 19)

175   Loosen radiator rod nut and run out rod from radiator top tank. Run off radiator stud nuts and lift off upper thimble from radiator stud.   Radiator can now be lifted from frame (See Figs. 20 and 21).

176   Disconnect horn wires at horn and terminal block and remove horn by running out the cylinder head bolt which holds horn to cylinder head (Fig. 25).

177   Disconnect switch to starting motor cable at starting motor (See "C" Fig. 35).

178   Disconnect spark plug wires and run out spark plugs, replacing them with pipe plugs.

179   Remove radiator apron by loosening the two fender iron bolts—side (See "B" Fig. 22) and slipping apron off over end of starting crank.

180   Remove fan and fan belt by running out fan bracket bolt (See "D" Fig. 22).

181   Run out the two crankcase front bearing cap, cap screws (See "A" Fig. 24).

182   Disconnect commutator pull rod at commutator by withdrawing cotter key which holds rod to commutator case (See "B" Fig. 24).

183   Loosen commutator case spring bolt and lift off commutator case and loom (See "D" Fig. 24).

184   Disconnect ammeter to cutout wire at cutout (See "C" Fig. 24).

185   Disconnect headlamp wires at headlamps by withdrawing headlamp plugs.

186   Lift off hood blocks from frame, placing them to one side.

187   Loosen the four bolts and one cap screw which hold engine pans to crankcase (Figs. 26 and 27) and withdraw engine pans.

188   Run off nut on end of steering gear post and drive off ball arm (See "A" Fig. 33).

189   Run off nuts and withdraw steering gear bracket bolts and block (Figs. 34 and 35).

190   Run off nuts and remove the four steering gear tube flange bolts (See "B" Fig. 35).

191   Swing steering gear bracket cap to one side by removing one of the two steering gear bracket bolts and loosening the other bolt (Fig. 15).

192   Steering gear can now be drawn back through dash.

193   Lift out mat and floor boards.

194   Disconnect exhaust pipe from manifold by running off exhaust pipe pack nut (See "A" Fig. 30).

195   Disconnect magneto terminal wire at terminal post (See "B" Fig. 30).

196   Run off nuts on ends of the two universal ball cap bolts and withdraw bolts (See "A" Fig. 32).

Fig. 129

197   Run off nuts and withdraw crankcase arm bolts—side.  Crankcase arm blocks can now be lifted from channel of frame (See "A"
and "B" Fig. 31).

198   Run off nuts and withdraw the two crankcase arm bolts—top
(See "C" Fig. 31).

199   Engine can now be lifted from frame with lifting hooks and chain
falls as shown in Fig. 38 and disassembled on an engine stand.

## Disassembling the Engine

200   Remove exhaust, and intake manifolds together with carburetor
by running off the four manifold stud nuts (See "A" Fig. 129) and
withdrawing clamps.  Exhaust manifold "B" can then be removed
and intake manifold "C" with carburetor "D" attached, lifted from
cylinder block.

201   Remove the four inlet and exhaust clamp studs from cylinder
(See "A" Fig. 130).

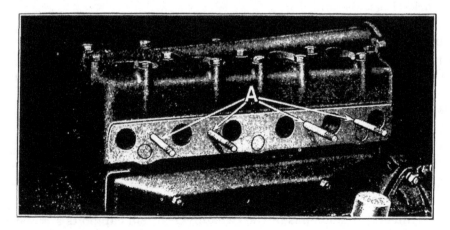

Fig. 130

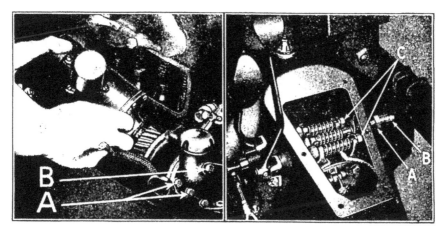

Fig. 131          Fig. 132

**202** Remove generator by running out the two generator mounting bolts (See "A" Fig. 131) and the commutator case spring bolt "B". Generator and generator gasket can now be lifted out of bracket.

**203** Remove transmission cover door (See "B" Fig. 299) and loosen transmission bands by loosening slow speed adjusting screw lock nut (See "A", Fig. 132) adjusting screw "B" and adjusting nuts "C".

**204** Remove crankcase and transmission cover by running out the bolts, nuts and cap screws which hold crankcase to cylinder block and transmission cover (See Fig. 133). Engine and transmission are now exposed as shown in Fig. 134, the transmission bands and ball cap can then be lifted off.

Fig. 133

**205** Disconnect transmission from engine by breaking wire (See "A" Fig. 135), and running out the four flywheel cap screws "B".

**206** Remove oil pipe (See "A" Fig. 136), and magneto coil assembly "B" by breaking wire and running out the four magneto coil screws "C".

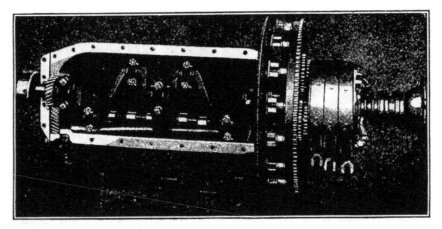

Fig. 134

**207** Remove valve cover, cylinder head and valves as described in Pars. 363 to 369. Remove pistons by running out the 8 connecting rod cap bolt nuts and lifting off caps (See Fig. 229). Pistons can then be withdrawn through top of cylinders (See Fig. 238). Remove fan pulley as described in "c" Par. 458. Remove commutator brush and shield and cylinder front cover as described in Pars. 454 and 455. The generator bracket can then be removed by running out the two cap screws which hold it to cylinder block. Run out the two cam shaft bearing set screws as shown at "A" Fig. 280. Before removing valves, each valve should be marked with a center punch to insure their being replaced in the same valve guides from which they were withdrawn. For example No. 1 valve (the valve nearest the time gears) is marked with one mark, No. 2 valve two marks, and so on up to No. 7 valve (See Fig. 137). It is unnecessary to mark No. 8 valve. When marking the valves be sure valves are firmly seated in cylinder block and not riding on the push rods.

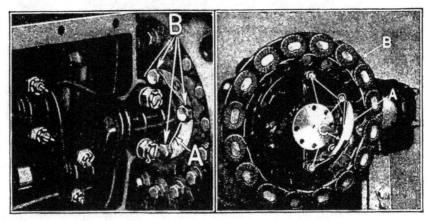

Fig. 135　　　　　　　　　　　　　　Fig. 136

Fig. 137

**208** Remove valve springs and seats by compressing springs and lifting seats off end of push rods (See "A" Fig. 138). The springs can then be lifted from valve guides.

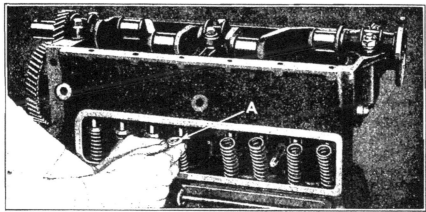

Fig. 138

**209** Remove camshaft by driving it out of cylinder block with a hammer and brass drift (See "A" Fig. 139). When performing this

Fig. 139

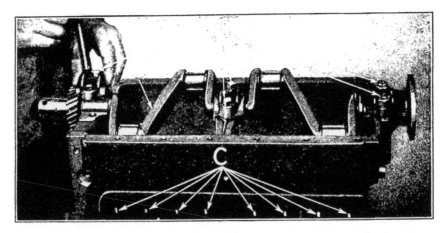

Fig. 140

operation make sure that heaas of push rods are seated in block in order to have sufficient clearance between camshaft and push rods when driving out shaft.

210   Remove main bearing caps and shims by running off the six crankshaft bearing bolts and nuts and withdrawing bolts. (See "A" Fig. 140).

211   Lift out crankshaft "B" and push rods "C" from cylinder block.

### Inspecting The Cylinder Block, Valves and Push Rods

212   Before re-assembling, all engine and transmission parts should be thoroughly cleaned and carefully inspected.

213   Check cylinders (See "A" Fig. 141) for being tapered, out of round or scored. Inspect valves and push rods, also valve stem guides "B" and push rod guides "C" for wear. Note whether valve seats "D" in cylinder block are pitted. Inspect all bolt and cap screw holes in cylinder block for stripped threads. Examine bearings "E" in cylinder block to see if babbitt is badly worn, loose, or cracked.

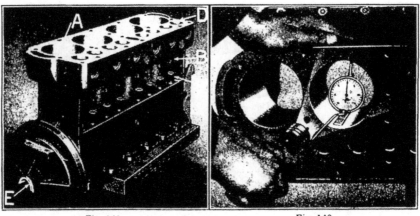

Fig. 141                    Fig. 142

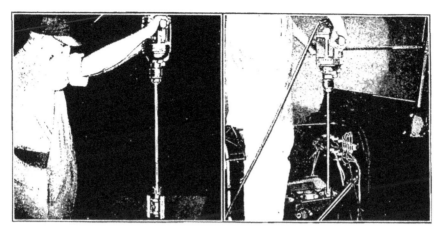

Fig. 143            Fig. 144

**214** A cylinder gauge graduated in one thousandth of an inch is used for checking cylinders for being tapered or out of round. The gauge is placed in the cylinder as shown in Fig. 142, and moved up and down the full length of the cylinder at different points around the bore. The amount the cylinder is out of round or tapered is indicated by the movement of the hand on the dial. Scores in the cylinder can be noted by visual inspection.

**215** If the cylinder is tapered or out of round more than .0025″ or is slightly scored, the cylinder can be reconditioned by honing. The hone is operated with an electric drill; an extension can be used with the hone so that No. 4 cylinder can be honed with cylinder block in car (See Figs. 143 and 144). When a cylinder is honed with the cylinder block in the car a cloth should be placed under the cylinder. This will prevent any cuttings getting into the crankcase. The hone is inserted into the cylinder and moved up and down the bore until the cylinder attains a smooth even surface. If the cylinder is deeply scored it will be necessary to rebore the cylinder block with a reboring fixture. The fixture is used in conjunction with a drill press (See Fig. 145).

**216** As there are a number of different makes of cylinder hones and reboring fixtures on the market it is important that the detailed in-

Fig. 145

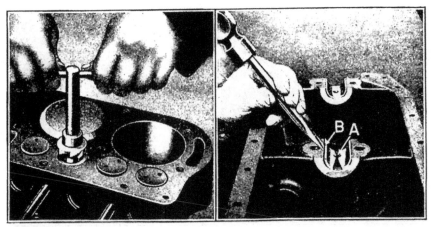

Fig. 146                                    Fig. 147

structions furnished by the manufacturer applying to the use of his particular equipment be carefully followed when honing or reboring a cylinder.

**217**  If valves are warped or pitted or the stems badly worn so that there is more than .008″ clearance between valve stem and valve guide, new valves should be installed.

**218**  If the push rod stems are worn so there is more than .006″ clearance between stem and push rod guides, or the ends of the stems are badly worn, new push rods should be installed.

**219**  Valve stem guides can be checked for wear by inserting a new valve in valve stem guide and checking the clearance. If there is more than .008″ clearance between stem and guide the valve guide should be reamed with a $\frac{21}{64}$″ reamer and valves with oversize stems (T-3052-B-424-AR) installed.

**220**  Push rod guides can be checked in the same manner, i.e. by inserting a new push rod into the guide and checking the clearance. If there is more than .006″ clearance between stem of push rod and push rod guide, the guide should be reamed with a $\frac{29}{64}$″ reamer and push rods with oversize stems (T-3058-B-426-AR) installed.

**21**  If valve seats in cylinder block are pitted, the pits can be removed with a valve reseating tool. The valve reseating tool is inserted into the valve seat in cylinder block as shown in Fig. 146, and sufficient metal removed from valve seat to clean up the pitted spots. If valve stem guides have previously been reamed oversize a reseating tool with an oversize pilot should be used. The valves are then ground as described in Par. 369, after which they are removed and all grinding compound washed from valves and cylinder block.

  Bolt or cap screw holes in which the threads have been stripped an be drilled and tapped. A cold rolled steel plug the outside diameter of which is threaded to the same size as the tapped hole, is nen screwed into the opening. To eliminate any possibility of the lug working loose, drill a $\frac{1}{8}$″ hole between edge of plug and cylinder ock and insert a small steel pin $\frac{1}{8}$″ x $\frac{1}{4}$″ driving the pin down tightbetween plug and cylinder block. The plug is then drilled and pped to the original size of the bolt or cap screw hole.

# Rebabbitting the Cylinder Block

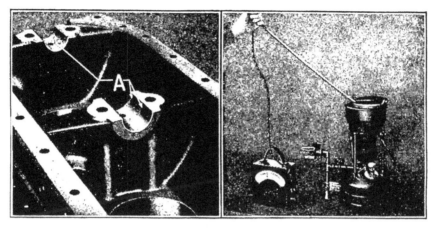

Fig. 148                                    Fig. 149

**223**   If the babbitt bearings in the cylinder block have become loose, cracked or badly worn, the cylinder block should be rebabbitted and the crankshaft run in.

**224**   In rebabbitting a cylinder block and running-in the crankshaft, the first operation is to remove the old babbitt. This is done by cutting out a strip of the babbitt at the bottom of the bearing, a chisel is used for this purpose (See "A" Fig. 147), the two remaining pieces of babbitt can then be driven out with the chisel as shown at "B". If any babbitt remains in anchor holes (See "A" Fig. 148) after the old bearings have been removed, it should be drilled out.

**225**   The success of pouring the babbitt depends largely on the next operation, viz. to provide a clean dry surface for the babbitt. If water or oil are present, even in the smallest quantity, there will be blow holes in the babbitt.

**226**   The babbitt is placed in a melting pot and heated. The temperature of the metal is very important. Perfect bearings can be poured only when the temperature of the babbitt is between 800° and 840° F. The temperature of the metal can be checked with a pyrometer (See Fig. 149). If no pyrometer is available an experienced repair man can estimate the temperature of the metal by its appearance. When the correct temperature is attained the metal has the appearance of quick silver and tarnishes slowly when the scum is scraped off; the coat of tarnish showing various colors. When cold the metal acts sluggish and the tarnish assumes a dull appearance.

**227**   The equipment for forming the bearings should be set up according to the instructions of the manufacturer.

Fig. 150

**228**    If the pouring bar is not equipped with plugs with which to plug the oil holes in the cylinder block while pouring the babbitt, it is necessary to fill the oil holes in the bottom of the bearings with asbestos waste before pouring the babbitt. This prevents the babbitt entering the oil holes.

**229**    While many equipment manufacturers advise heating the block and pouring bar, we have obtained best results by pouring into cold blocks; this success being due in a large measure to the cleaner condition of the parts. Heating with an open flame results in a deposit of carbon. During winter months, if blocks are stored where there is little or no heat the chill must be taken out of block before pouring the babbitt. If a torch is used for this purpose, the flame should not be directed on the bearings into which the babbitt is to be poured.

**230**    While heating the babbitt, the ladle used in pouring should be kept in the pot in order that it will be approximately the same temperature as the metal. When ready to pour, either two ladles or a two lip ladle should be filled with babbitt, pushing the scum on the babbitt back so that only clean metal is used for the bearings. The bearings should be poured rapidly from both sides at the same instant (See Fig. 150). Sufficient babbitt to more than form the bearings should be poured. As the babbitt sets quickly the bar may be removed immediately after the bearings have been poured.

**231**    The next operation is to cut off the surplus babbitt from top of bearings. When performing this operation the chisel should be inserted from the inside of the bearing as shown in Fig. 151.

Fig. 151

232   The bearings should now be peened to conform to the cylinder block.   This is done with a peening tool.   The tool is laid on the bearing and is tapped first on one side of the bearing and then on the other (See Fig. 152).

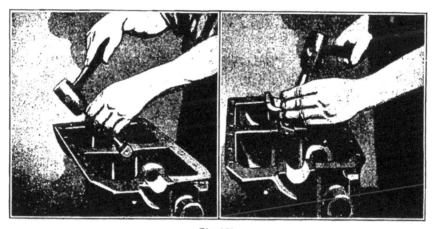

Fig. 152

233   Bearings are now ready to be line reamed.   This should be done according to the instructions of the manufacturer which accompany the machine or fixture, making sure, however, that the cutters in the bar are so adjusted that all bearings will be cut to exactly the same depth.

234   To insure bearings being cut to a uniform depth, a fixture which locates from camshaft holes in each end of cylinder block should be used.   An attachment is furnished so that the fixture can be operated with an electric drill.   If a drill is not available a hand crank can be used as shown in Fig. 153.

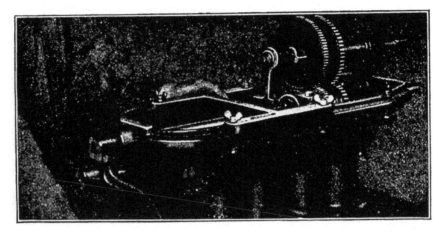

Fig. 153

**235** Before placing the fixture on the cylinder block, the surface of the block should be thoroughly cleaned in order that the fixture will seat squarely on block.

**236** After the bearings have been bored to size, the edges should be dressed off with a file at a 45° angle (See Fig. 154) and the ends of the babbitt bearings filed flush with the casting. The surfaces on

Fig. 154

which the bearing caps rest should be absolutely free from dirt, babbitt or burrs. A $\frac{3}{16}''$ radius should be formed on both ends of rear and center bearings and on the rear end of the front bearing. The tool used for reaming the bearings may be provided with a cutter for this purpose or the radius may be formed with a bearing scraper (See Fig. 155).

**237** Babbitt and waste are next drilled out of the oil holes in each of the three bearings, and the oil holes countersunk (See "A" Fig. 156).

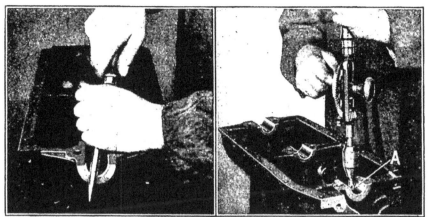

Fig. 155                    Fig. 156

If the boring bar is not equipped with a device for forming oil grooves in the center and rear main bearings, the grooves can be formed with a cape chisel (See Figs. 157 and 158). When cutting the grooves the chisel should be tapped very lightly to prevent any possibility of loosening the babbitt in the block.

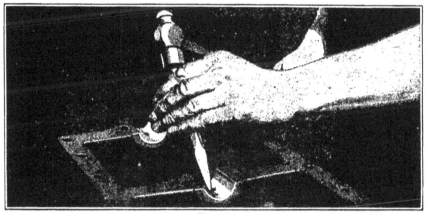

Fig. 157

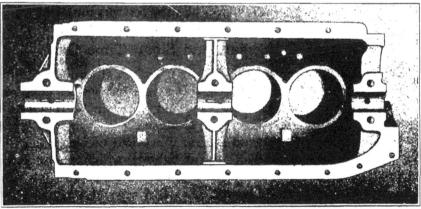

Fig. 158

Fig. 159

238  Check alignment of bearings by placing a thin coating of Prussian blue on a test bar. The bar is then placed on the bearings and slowly revolved (See Fig. 159), after which, it is removed and the bearings examined. If the Prussian blue is evenly distributed on all bearings the alignment of the bearings is O. K. If the blue shows only on one side or at bottom of bearings, or does not show at all, the bearings are out of alignment and they should be removed and the block rebabbitted.

239  When new bearings are out of alignment it is usually due to:-

(a) Cutters in boring fixture loose or not adjusted uniformly.

(b) Boring fixture not seating squarely on cylinder block, due to dirt or loose babbitt between fixture and block.

(c) Fixture not clamped down tightly on block.

(d) Locating plugs in fixture not entered or loose in cylinder block.

240  After rebabbitting, clean off any cuttings and loose babbitt from cylinder block; compressed air can be used for this purpose.

## Inspecting Crankshaft and Small Time Gear

241  Before installing crankshaft the shaft and small time gear should be carefully checked and inspected. If teeth are badly worn or chipped a new gear should be installed. The old gear can be removed by pressing it off of crankshaft with an arbor press as shown in Fig. 160. Examine shaft for cracks and scores; if cracked or badly scored, a new shaft should be installed. Burnt babbitt or light scores can be removed from bearings by oiling a strip of fine sandpaper and wrapping it around the bearing, and rotating the sandpaper back and forth with a narrow strap as shown in Fig. 161.

Fig. 160                              Fig. 161

**242** Check all bearings for wear or being out of round. This can be done with a pair of micrometers. If the main bearings show more than .001″ or connecting rod bearings more than .002″ out of round, the shaft should be changed. If bearings on shaft are O. K. the shaft is placed on centers and checked for being sprung (See Fig. 162); If the shaft is sprung less than .012″ it can be straightened on a press (See Fig. 163). If shaft is sprung more than .012″ a new shaft should be installed.

**243** When shaft is O. K. press small time gear onto shaft on an arbor press. Insert small time gear key into keyway on shaft, making sure that key fits tightly in keyway. Place crankshaft in arbor press resting shaft on point back of gear seat (not on flange end). Position gear over end of shaft with the side of the gear on which the script word "FORD" is stamped, facing outward. Line up keyway in gear with key in shaft and press gear onto shaft with a driver.

Fig. 162                              Fig. 163

## Installing Crankshaft and Bearing Caps

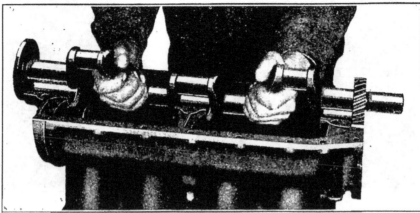

Fig. 164

**244** Position crankshaft on bearings in cylinder block (See Fig. 164). Inasmuch as all end play in the crankshaft is taken up by the rear main bearing and cap; the crankshaft should fit in rear main bearing

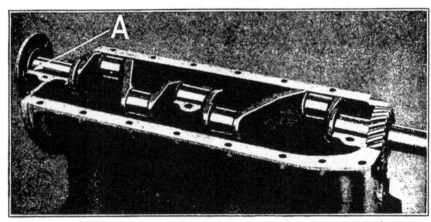

Fig. 165

Fig. 166          Fig. 167

Fig. 168

with but .002" to .004" end play between end of bearing and flange on crankshaft (See "A" Fig. 165), when shaft is moved back and forth in cylinder block. The end play is checked with thickness gauges (feelers) (See Fig. 166). After checking the fit of the shaft in the block, the bearing cap is assembled on shaft and the end play between cap and shaft checked in the same manner (See Fig. 167). If there is more than .004" play between cap and shaft, a $\frac{1}{64}$" oversize bearing cap (T-3031-405-AR) can be filed down to the correct size (See Fig. 168).

**245** To allow for expansion of crankshaft caused by heat generated in the engine, the center and front bearings are fitted with an end clearance of from $\frac{1}{32}$" to $\frac{1}{16}$".

**246** New caps should be used in assembling the crankshaft, sufficient shims being equally placed under each side of cap to allow the bearings .006" rock (See "A" Fig. 169); in other words there should be a gap of .003" between each side of cap and the top shim. This will allow .002" to .003" for burnishing in. The crankshaft bearing bolts are then inserted through bearing caps and nuts drawn down as tightly as possible without stripping the threads.

Fig. 169

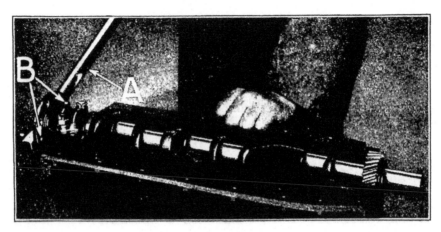

Fig. 170

**247**  Turn crankshaft over with a turning bar (See "A" Fig. 170). The bearing should hold the shaft so that it is necessary to use a turning bar 18″ to 20″ long in order to turn the shaft. When using a turning bar, make sure both pins in bar are inserted in cap screw holes "B" in flange on crankshaft (not in dowel pins or on the edge of the flange). After crankshaft has been turned over, remove bearing caps and shaft and examine bearing surfaces in cap and cylinder block. The spots, which appear bright, are the high points on the bearing surfaces and these spots should be lightly scraped with a bearing scraper. Crankshaft and bearing cap are then replaced and the above operations repeated until a 65% bearing is obtained on all bearings, after which the bearings are oiled, crankshaft positioned on block, caps replaced and crankshaft bearing bolts and nuts drawn down tightly, the castles on the nuts being lined up so that cotter keys can be inserted through bolts after crankshaft has been run in.

## Running In the Crankshaft

**248**  The next operation is to run in the crankshaft. This requires a running-in stand (See Fig. 171). With the crankshaft revolving at a speed of approximately 700 R. P. M. the bearings can be burnished in from one to two minutes. The bearings should smoke freely and be liberally oiled while being run in. If they do not smoke it indicates a loose fit and some shims should be removed from each side of bearing caps. Bearings should then be tightened and the running-in operation repeated.

**249**  When sufficiently run in, the shaft can be turned over with the hand wheel on the running-in stand (See "A" Fig. 171) or by means of a 20″ turning bar.

**250** When the shaft can be turned in this manner the rear bearing cap should be removed and inspected. There should be a bearing the entire length of the cap and covering at least 95% of the surface. If the cap does not meet these requirements it should be scraped and re-run, taking out one or more shims from each side of cap.

**251** While it is not necessary for an experienced operator to remove the center and front caps, it is advisable for the beginner to do so, so that he may be sure his work is correctly performed. When crankshaft has been properly run in, lock all bearing bolt nuts with cotter keys.

Fig. 171

## Inspecting and Assembling Pistons and Push Rods

**252** After a crankshaft is fitted and run-in, the pistons, piston pins, piston rings and connecting rods are checked and the pistons installed as outlined in Pars. 401 to 431. The connecting rod bearings are then scraped and burnished in on the running in stand in the same manner as the crankshaft bearings.

**253** Place a little oil on stems of push rods and insert them into push rod guides.

## Inspecting and Installing Camshaft, Camshaft Bearings and Large Time Gear

**254** Remove bearings from camshaft as described in Par. 477.

**255** Remove large time gear from camshaft by running off lock nut and dropping gear end of shaft on a wooden block. Inspect large time gear. If teeth of gear are badly worn, chipped, or web in gear is cracked or a new small time gear was installed on crankshaft, a new camshaft gear should be installed.

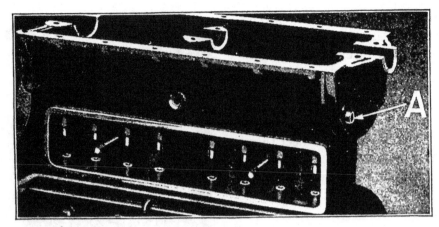

Fig. 172

**256**　Inspect camshaft bushing in cylinder block for wear (See "A" Fig. 172). This can be done by inserting a camshaft into the bushing and checking the clearance. If there is more than .004" clearance between shaft and bushing, a new bushing should be installed. The old bushing is removed by driving it out with a driver and a new bushing installed by driving it into camshaft hole in cylinder block with a bushing driver, and with the notched side of the bushing facing up. The bushing is driven in until the end of the notch is flush with end of block. The bushing is then line reamed so that shaft will fit in bushing with a clearance of from .0015" to .002".

**257**　Camshaft and bearings should now be inspected as described in Pars. 478 to 481. Bearings are then oiled and assembled to shaft and camshaft installed in cylinder block as described in Par. 482. The large time gear is then driven onto camshaft and lock nut run down and tightened as shown in Figs. 272 and 270. If new gears were installed, the clearance between the teeth of the gears should be between .0005" and .003"; if the old gears are installed a clearance up to .006" is permissible. The clearance should be uniform at all points around gear.

### Inspecting and Installing Valve Springs and Seats

**258**　The valve springs should next be checked for strength; when valve springs are installed in the car they are compressed to $2\frac{1}{8}''$ and at this height exert a pressure of 24 to 28 lbs. To check the strength of the springs compress them to $2\frac{1}{8}''$ and check the tension with a spring tension gauge. A pressure of 24 to 28 lbs. should register on the gauge.

**259**　Valve springs are next assembled in cylinder block by inserting the springs over ends of valve guides and positioning valve spring seats over ends of springs (See "A" Fig. 138). The springs are then compressed until the valve spring seats can be placed over ends of push rods.

**260**　The valves are replaced by positioning them in valve stem guides and compressing the valve springs sufficiently far to permit inserting valve spring seat pins into valve stems.

# Valve Timing

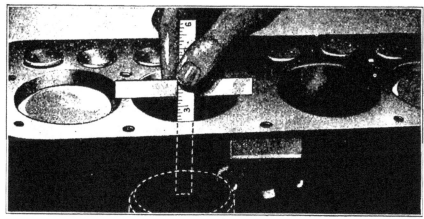

Fig. 173

**261** Valves should next be checked for opening and closing with respect of piston travel. The opening and closing of valves with respect to position of pistons is as follows: Exhaust valve opens when the piston reaches $\frac{5}{16}''$ before bottom center; this can be determined by measuring the distance from the top of the piston head to the top of the cylinder block; the distance between these points being $3\frac{3}{8}''$ (See Fig. 173). The exhaust valve closes at top center, the piston being $\frac{5}{16}''$ above face of cylinder block. The intake valve opens $\frac{1}{16}''$ past top center or when piston is $\frac{1}{4}''$ above top of cylinder block. The intake valve closes $\frac{9}{16}''$ past bottom center, the distance from the top of the piston to the face of the cylinder block being $3\frac{1}{8}''$.

**262** Should a valve open early and close late, a small amount of stock should be filed from the end of the valve stem. The valve should be held in a valve end squaring block when being filed. If the valve opens late and closes early the stem is too short, and a new valve should be installed.

**263** The intake valve should be timed accurately on the opening, and the exhaust valve timed on the closing as in an engine where the camshaft is worn it is not always possible to have both the opening and closing check accurately with the figures given.

**264** The method of determining when the valves open and close is as follows: With the spring assembled, close the valve. When it is closed, hold it with the fingers and twist back and forth on head of valve while slowly cranking engine (See Fig. 174). When checking the opening and closing of valves with engine removed from car a turning bar is used to turn crankshaft. The instant the valve will turn it has started to open. In the same way the valve may be checked for closing, the valve turning until it has seated.

Fig. 174

**265** After checking the opening and closing of the valves, replace cylinder head, valve cover and generator bracket as described in Pars. 373, 377 and 450. Replace cylinder front cover and commutator and check alignment of cover with camshaft as described in Pars. 466 to 469. Install fan drive pulley on crankshaft by driving it onto crankshaft with a driver. The pulley is locked in position on shaft by inserting the camshaft starting pin with the cotter pin hole end up (See Fig. 278) through the larger of the two holes in fan drive pulley and driving it through pulley and shaft. The pin is then locked in position with a cotter key.

## Disassembling the Transmission

**266** Compress clutch spring with a spring compressor and turn support until clutch spring support pin hole lines up with pin (See "A"

Fig. 175          Fig. 176

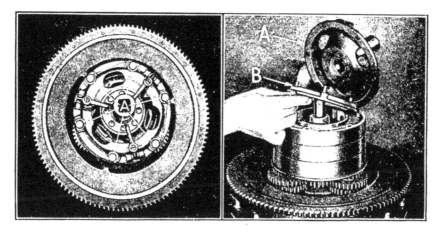

Fig. 177                    Fig. 178

Fig. 175). Pin can then be driven out with a drift, and the clutch spring support (See "A" Fig. 176) clutch spring "B" and clutch shift "C" lifted off of drive plate assembly.

**267** Break wire and run out the six drive plate cap screws (See "A" Fig. 177); drive plate assembly (See "A" Fig. 178) and clutch push ring "B" can then be removed.

**268** Remove the 13 large and 12 small transmission clutch discs by tilting transmission, allowing the discs to slip off of drums (See Fig. 179).

**269** Remove cotter pin (See "A" Fig. 180) and run out clutch disc drum set screw "B".

Fig. 179                    Fig. 180

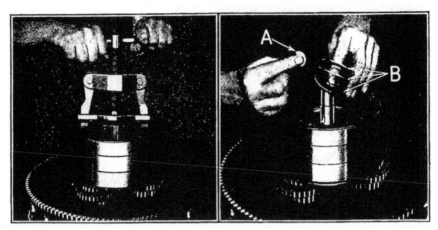

Fig. 181                    Fig. 182

**270**    Remove clutch disc drum with a puller as shown in Fig. 181.

**271**    Drive transmission clutch disc drum key out of gear shaft (See "A" Fig. 182) and lift out the three driven gear sleeve washers "B".

**272**    The brake, slow speed and reverse drums and driven gear together with the triple gears can now be lifted off of shafts as shown in Fig. 183.

**273**    Remove transmission gear shaft by tapping end of shaft with a brass hammer as shown in Fig. 184. Remove driven gear by holding brake drum stationary in a clamping fixture and withdrawing gear by means of a gear puller as shown in Fig. 185. Remove the

Fig. 183                    Fig. 184

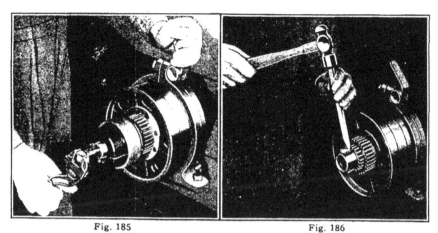

Fig. 185                    Fig. 186

two driven gear keys by tapping them out of keyway with a hammer and drift (See Fig. 186). The reverse and slow speed plate assemblies (See "A" and "B" Fig. 187) can then be lifted from brake drum assembly "C".

**274**   Triple gear shafts, magnets and flywheel ring gear should now be checked.

**275**   Triple gear shafts are inspected for wear by measuring the diameter of the shafts with micrometers. If the shafts show more than .002″ wear they should be removed and new shafts installed as described in Pars. 288 and 289.

Fig. 187

# Testing the Strength of the Magnets

Fig. 188

276    The magnets are checked for strength with a magnet tester. The tester is placed between the ends of the magnets so that the poles on the tester come in contact with both sides of the magnet (See Fig. 188). The operation is repeated until each magnet has been checked. If the magnets are at full strength a reading of 50 units or more should register on the dial. (With the transmission cover removed the strength of the magnets can be checked in the car in the same manner, turning the engine over with the starting crank about one-quarter turn at a time until all of the magnets have been tested. With the magnet clamps positioned directly between the magneto coil cores, a reading of 45 units or better should register on the dial when magnets are checked in the car. When magnets are removed from the flywheel and checked individually a reading of 35 units or better should be obtained).

277    If any of the magnets are weak or broken a set of new magnets should be installed.

278    The flywheel ring gear is inspected for badly worn or broken teeth.

279    If the magnets are O. K. but the triple gear shafts are worn under-size new shafts are installed as described in Pars. 288 and 289.

280    If the magnets are weak and the shafts are O. K. or if it is necessary to install a new set of magnets as well as new triple gear shafts, it is first necessary to remove all of the magnets.

# Removing and Installing Magnets

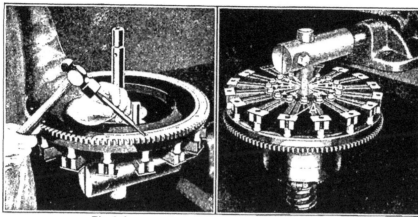

Fig. 189              Fig. 190

**281** To remove the old magnets, chip off the ends of the 16 magnet clamp screws (See Fig. 189). The screws can then be run out and the magnet clamps (See "A" Fig. 190) removed. (If the teeth of the flywheel ring gear are worn or broken, the gear can now be removed by tapping it off of flywheel with a lead or copper hammer and a new gear installed with the chamfered side of the teeth on the gear pointing towards transmission drums (See "A" Fig. 191). Run out the 16 magnet bolts and washers (See "B" Fig. 190) and lift out magnet supports and magnets.

**282** The old triple gear shafts can now be removed and new shafts installed as described in Par. 289.

**283** It is very important that the new magnets be assembled on the flywheel, so that all adjacent magnet ends have the same polarity. This can readily be determined by moving the magnets so that their sides come together, when in this position they should be free; if two or more magnets stick together they should be turned over or have their relative position changed until the sides of no two magnets are attracted to each other.

Fig. 191

Fig. 192

284　When new magnets are shipped from the factory they are placed on a board (See Fig. 192) and unless they have been disturbed they are in identically the same relation to each other as they should be when installed on the flywheel.

285　To assemble the magnets, place magnets on flywheel, position magnet bolt washers over end of magnet bolts and run down bolts but do not tighten.

286　As a final check to make sure that all adjacent magnet ends have the same polarity, move all the magnets back and forth on the flywheel and see that none of them stick when the sides of the magnets are placed together (See Fig. 193).

287　When the magnets are correctly positioned, install magnet supports under ends of magnets (See "A" Fig. 194). Place the magnet clamps "B" over the ends of the 16 brass screws (new screws should be used), and run the screws down through the magnet supports, flywheel and ring gear. Draw the brass screws and magnet bolts down tightly. (The ends of the brass screws are not peened until transmission is completely assembled and the magnet clamps have been checked for height and alignment as described in Pars. 316 and 317.)

Fig. 193　　　　　　　　　　　　　　　　Fig. 194

# Removing and Installing Triple Gear Shafts

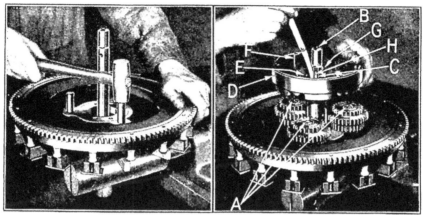

Fig. 195          Fig. 196

288   To remove triple gear shafts, when magnets test O. K., it is first necessary to remove the magnets, which prevent gear shaft being driven out (See Par. 281). Before removing the magnets they should be marked to insure their being replaced in exactly the same position on the flywheel.

289   The shafts are removed by driving them out from the inside of the flywheel, with a brass hammer as shown in Fig. 195; the new shafts being driven in from the opposite side. As the holes in the cast iron flywheel become slightly enlarged when the steel shafts are withdrawn, it is necessary to use T-3315-T-751-AR shafts, which are .003″ oversize on the section of the shafts which fits into the flywheel. The magnets are now assembled to the flywheel as described in Pars. 285 to 287, new magnet clamp screws being used.

# Assembling Transmission

290   Wash all parts thoroughly in kerosene. In addition to washing it is frequently necessary to scrape some of the parts such as the discs and drums in order to remove the formation of burnt oil which sometimes forms on them.

291   Examine triple gears, if the teeth are badly worn, or broken, new gears should be installed.

292   Check the triple gears on the triple gear shafts. If there is more than .005″ play between bushing and shaft (See "A" Fig. 196), new bushings should be installed in the gears. The bushings are then reamed (All new bushings installed in transmission drums and gears are reamed to a .002″ running fit. When the reaming operation is completed remove all cuttings.) When installing new bushings in triple gears, make sure that the flange face of the bushings project from .006″ to .010″ over side of gears (See Fig. 197.)

Fig. 197          Fig. 198

293  Examine transmission gear shaft (See "B" Fig. 196), also the keyway "C" in shaft, if the shaft is worn more than .002" undersize or if the keyway in the shaft has worn so that the key will not fit tightly a new gear shaft should be installed.

294  Examine brake drum at points "D", "E", "F" and "G" Fig. 196; if web is cracked, lugs badly worn, rivets loosened, keyways worn oversize or drum is scored, a new brake drum should be installed.

295  Place brake drum on gear shaft and check the clearance between shaft and bushings with a thickness gauge as shown at "H" Fig. 196. If there is more than .005" clearance between bushings and shaft, new bushings should be installed and reamed. The old bushings are pressed out of the drums and new bushings pressed in with a bushing driver on an arbor press as shown in Fig. 198. To prevent bending or cracking web in drums when removing and installing bushings, place drums on a drum support so that the pressure will be directed on the support rather than on edge of drums. It is important that the new bushings be accurately reamed; this can be done by placing drums in an alignment fixture when reaming the bushings (See Fig. 199).

Fig. 199

296 Examine slow speed and reverse drums and gears. If teeth are badly worn, web cracked, rivets loosened or drums scored, new drums and gears should be installed. If slow speed drum is O. K., place it over brake drum shaft and check slow speed gear bushing for wear. If there is more than .005" clearance between bushing and brake drum shaft, a new bushing should be installed and reamed.

297 If reverse drum is O. K., place drum over slow speed gear and check clearance between gear and bushing; if there is more than .005" clearance between reverse drum bushing and slow speed gear, press out old bushing (See Fig. 198) and install a new one. The new bushing is then reamed.

298 After the shafts, triple gears and drums have been inspected as outlined above, place oil on brake drum and slow speed shafts. The parts are then assembled by inserting slow speed drum gear over brake drum shaft and placing reverse drum gear over slow speed gear.

299 Clean the two keyways in brake drum shaft and insert the two driven gear keys.

300 Examine teeth on driven gear for wear, if teeth are O. K., place brake drum on a drum support and press gear over end of brake drum shaft. Gear should be pressed down on shaft until outer face of the gear is flush with end of brake drum shaft. The clearance between driven and slow speed gears should now be checked; there should be a clearance of approximately .006" between the gears.

301 After driven gear has been installed, check the drums to make sure they revolve freely, and that the bushing inside of brake drum shaft has not been distorted. Examine driving plate for loose rivets, if O. K. check bushing in driving plate for wear; this can be done by inserting driving plate over end of gear shaft and checking the clearance between bushing and shaft with thickness gauges. If there is more than .005" clearance a new bushing should be installed and reamed.

302 Position gear shaft on flywheel, making sure that dowel pins in flywheel enter dowel pin holes in flange on shaft (See "A" Fig. 200). The shaft is then seated in flywheel by tapping it into place with a copper or lead hammer. The shaft is held in position while drums and gears are assembled by the four flywheel cap screws which are run down through gear shaft flange into flywheel. If a fixture for holding the transmission similar to the one shown in Fig. 194 is not used, it is necessary to place spacer washers approximately ½" thick over ends of flywheel cap screws before inserting the screws in flywheel (See "B" Fig. 200). This prevents the screws protruding through the inside of the flywheel and coming in contact with the triple gears before crankshaft is connected to flywheel.

303 Place drums and driven gear assembly on bench with gear side of assembly up.

Fig. 200                    Fig. 201

**304** Mesh triple gears with driven gear, making sure that the punch marks (See "A" Fig. 201) between the teeth on triple gears mesh with teeth on driven gear. The first triple gear can be meshed at any point on driven gear. The second and third sets of triple gears are assembled in the same manner as the first triple gear, but at intervals of nine teeth or 120° apart on the driven gear.

**305** After triple gears are assembled on drum assembly, place oil on triple gear and transmission gear shafts then pick up the complete drum and gear assembly (See Fig. 202) and place it over transmission shaft, positioning the triple gears on the triple gear shafts. Drums and gears should now revolve freely on shafts.

**306** Examine the three driven gear sleeve washers for wear, if washers are O. K., oil them and insert over end of transmission shaft (See Fig. 182).

**307** Install transmission clutch disc drum key into keyway in transmission shaft (See "A" Fig. 203), making sure that key fits tightly in keyway. Examine keyway "B" in disc drum, if not worn oversize, drive disc drum down on shaft with a driver until there is .015" to

Fig. 202                    Fig. 203

Fig. 204                    Fig. 205

.022″ clearance between washers and brake drum. Drums should revolve freely. If the drums are tight they can usually be loosened by striking the end of the shaft with a lead hammer.

308    Run down clutch disc drum set screw until pilot on end of screw seats in transmission shaft. Lock screw in position by inserting cotter pin through head of screw (See Fig. 180).

309    Inspect clutch discs for wear and cracks. If discs are O. K. oil thoroughly and assemble them in brake drum. There are 25 discs, 12 small ones and 13 large ones. When assembling discs in brake drum, start with a large disc (See Fig. 204), and alternate with a small and large one, ending with a large disc.

310    Inspect clutch push ring for loose or worn pins. If O. K. position clutch push ring on top of discs (See "B" Fig. 178).

311    Insert driving plate "B" Fig. 205 over end of transmission shaft; positioning driving plate on brake drum so that the ends of the adjusting screws "C" in clutch fingers come in contact with the three pins "A" on push ring.

312    Run in the six cap screws which hold driving plate to brake drum. Draw screws down tightly and wire them together two at a time (See Fig. 177).

313    Insert clutch shift, clutch spring and clutch spring support over end of driving plate sleeve (See Fig. 176).

314    Compress clutch spring until clutch spring support pin can be inserted through hole in support and driving plate sleeve (See Fig. 175), then turn the support until pin slips into slot.

315    Adjust the three clutch finger screws until there is a clearance of $13/16″$ between lower side of clutch shift and drive plate shaft flange (See Fig. 206). The adjusting screws are then locked in position by inserting cotter keys through fingers and screws.

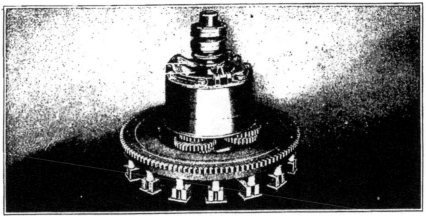

Fig. 206

## Alignment of Magnet Clamps

**316**　Check the magnet clamps for height and alignment. The distance between the face of the magnet clamps and the face of transmission shaft flange should measure between $13\frac{1}{16}''$ and $53\frac{1}{64}''$. The use of a gap gauge, which is adjusted to these dimensions is a considerable time saver in lining up the magnets.

**317**　To check the height of the magnets with a gap gauge, position the gauge on the flange of the transmission gear shaft and slowly revolve gauge (See Fig. 207). If there is any variation in the height of the magnets it can be readily detected. Magnets which are high can be set to the correct height by lightly tapping the magnet clamps with a copper or lead hammer. The magnet clamp screws should then be tightened. The ends of the brass screws are then peened and the screws carefully inspected to make sure they are all drawn down tightly.

Fig. 207

Fig. 208                  Fig. 209

**318** The oil tube should next be thoroughly cleaned, compressed air can be used for this purpose. After cleaning oil tube, position magneto coil on cylinder block and run in three of the four magneto coil cap screws which hold coil to cylinder block (See "A" Fig. 208). Insert end of oil tube "B" through hole in rear and center walls of cylinder, sliding the tube back until it enters hole in front wall of cylinder. The remaining magneto coil cap screw, which holds oil tube to magneto coil is then entered and run down.

**319** After magneto coil support is assembled to cylinder block, it should be adjusted so there will be a clearance (gap) of not less than .025 or more than .040" between magnet clamps and coil cores, when transmission is assembled to engine. The adjustment is obtained by placing shims between magneto coil support and cylinder block, until the distance from the face of crankshaft flange to the face of the coil cores on upper half of coil support measure approximately $27\!/\!_{32}"$ (See Fig. 209). As the weight of the flywheel and transmission tends to decrease the clearance between the magnet clamps and the lower half of the magneto coil support, the lower half of the support is fitted with a .006" to .010" higher clearance

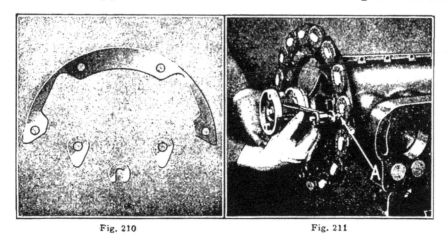

Fig. 210                  Fig. 211

than the upper half. Shims (See Fig. 210) are furnished in various thicknesses so that extremely close adjustments can be obtained in setting the gap. The shims are held in place between coil support and cylinder block by the four magneto coil cap screws which are inserted through them.

320 In addition to checking the height of the magnets, the use of a gap gauge is a time saver in obtaining the correct clearance between magnet clamps and coil cores.

321 With the coil support assembled to cylinder block, clamp the gap gauge to the face of the crankshaft. The gap between the end of the gauge and the face of the coils represents the thickness of the shims which should be inserted between coil support and cylinder block. With the shims installed, the gauge when revolved, should lightly touch the faces of all coils on upper half of coil support (See "A" Fig. 211), leaving a gap of .006" to .010" between end of gauge and face of coils on lower half of support to allow for the weight of transmission and flywheel. If there is any variation in the height of the cores the adjustment can be regulated by removing or installing additional shims between coil support and cylinder block. When the correct adjustment is obtained, the four magneto coil cap screws are locked in position by wiring them together with brass wire (See "C" Fig. 136).

## Assembling Transmission to Engine

322 Before assembling transmission to engine, see that the face of flanges on crankshaft and transmission gear shaft are free from dirt or burrs. The transmission is assembled to the engine by positioning it on crankshaft flange, making sure that flywheel dowel pins enter dowel pin holes in crankshaft flange, and running in the four flywheel cap screws. The screws should be drawn down evenly, after which they are tightened and wired together (See Fig. 135).

323 Check clearance between magnet clamps and coil cores by inserting feelers between magnets and face of coil cores. There should be a gap of .025" to .040" between magnets and coil cores.

324 Examine transmission band linings for wear, if worn install new linings in bands as described in Par. 515.

325 Position transmission bands over drums using a clip to temporarily hold them in place, as shown in Fig. 304.

## Inspecting and Installing Crankcase

326 Clean crankcase thoroughly; see that no parts of gaskets are sticking to flanges of crankcase.

327 Check crankcase for alignment by placing it on an aligning jig (See Fig. 212). The case should rest evenly on the fixture when

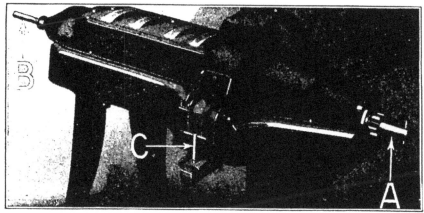

Fig. 212

locating plugs "A" and "B" are entered through crankcase, and fixture, and locating pin "C" is entered through both crankcase arms and fixture. If crankcase is only slightly sprung it can be straightened on the aligning jig. If badly sprung, a new case should be installed.

328 After checking crankcase, install new crankcase and transmission cover gaskets on case, placing a little cup grease on gaskets to hold them in place when assembling crankcase to engine.

329 Position crankcase on cylinder block and run down the two crankcase cap screws through cylinder front cover and into crankcase (See "A" Fig. 213). Place gasket on universal ball cap (See "A" Fig. 214), oil end of drive plate shaft and insert ball cap over end of shaft with oil hole "B" towards the top. The two ball cap, cap screws are then entered into ball cap and run down about half way into crankcase (See "A" Fig. 215). (The two cylinder front cover to crankcase cap screws and the two ball cap, cap screws are entered first, to insure correct alignment when assembling crankcase to cylinder block.) The remaining crankcase bolts are then inserted, and lock-washers and nuts run down and tightened.

Fig. 213            Fig. 214

Fig. 215                                    Fig. 216

330  Install transmission cover felt gasket on cylinder block (See "D" Fig. 304). After gasket is installed, insert a small piece of candle wicking underneath ends of gasket as shown at "E" Fig. 304. The transmission cover with starting motor attached, is installed by inserting clutch release ring into rear groove on clutch shift (See Fig. 305) and lowering cover over bands. The transmission band springs are then positioned between lugs on bands; the transmission band clip withdrawn and cover forced down onto crankcase as described in Par. 518. The 12 bolts, cap screws, lock washers and nuts which hold transmission cover to crankcase are run down and tightened as described in Par. 519. After installing cover, adjust bands and replace transmission cover door as described in Pars. 523 to 527.

331  The fit of the ball cap on drive plate shaft should now be checked by loosening the two ball cap, cap screws. If the crankcase and cylinder block are in correct alignment the ball cap can be moved freely on drive plate shaft. If ball cap does not move freely on shaft, insert a flat bar between cylinder block and transmission cover (See Fig. 553) and slightly pry the cover back until ball cap moves freely on shaft without the use of the bar.

## Completing the Assembly

332  Insert the four manifold clamp studs into cylinder block, drawing them down tightly. (See "A" Fig. 130). Position inlet and exhaust pipe gaskets on glands and insert glands into port holes in inlet and exhaust pipes. Position exhaust pipe (See "B" Fig. 129) and inlet pipe "C" with carburetor attached onto cylinder block, making sure that the gaskets on the exhaust and intake pipes fit tightly against cylinder block. Place the four inlet and exhaust pipe clamps "A" over ends of studs and run down the four manifold stud nuts.

333  Pour one gallon of a light high grade engine oil into crankcase through breather pipe.

334  The complete assembly is now placed on a running-in machine, and run in for a period of at least 20 minutes and carefully checked for oil leaks, and knocks which might possibly develop due to incorrect assembly of parts (See Fig. 216).

335  After completing the running-in period and inspection, the assembly should be operated under its own power by connecting it up with the attachments on the stand, and again checked for correct

operation, making sure there is sufficient oil in the crankcase and that water is flowing freely through the water jackets. Engine is now ready for installation in car.

## Installing Engine in Car

336 (a) Mount engine in frame.
   (b) Enter universal joint into drive plate assembly.
   (c) Install crank case arm bolts and blocks.
   (d) Connect axle to transmission.
   (e) Connect magneto terminal wire to terminal post.
   (f) Connect exhaust pipe to manifold.
   (g) Connect front radius rod to crank case.
   (h) Install crank case front bearing cap.
   (i) Assemble engine pans (right and left) to engine.
   The above operations are described and illustrated in Pars. 96 to 107 inclusive.

337 Install radiator apron by slipping apron over starting crank handle and positioning ends of apron between frame and fender irons. Tighten fender iron bolt nuts and lock them with cotter keys (See Fig. 90).

338 Install steering gear, steering gear bracket and steering gear block by running in the three bolts and nuts which hold bracket and block to frame (See Fig. 97).

339 Connect steering gear tube flange to dash by inserting the four flange bolts through flange and dash and running down lock washers and nuts on ends of bolts (See Fig. 99).

340 Install commutator case and ammeter to cutout wire as described in Par. 119.

341 Install steering gear ball arm as described in Par. 124.

342 Connect commutator pull rod to commutator case by inserting end of rod through lever on case, and locking the rod in position with a cotter key. (See "B" Fig. 24) the commutator is then checked for correct setting as described in Par. 126.

343 Install carburetor pull rod by slipping rod through hole in valve cover and inserting ends of rod through carburetor throttle and throttle rod lever, the rod is then locked in position by inserting cotter keys through ends of rod (See "A" Fig. 28).

344 Install carburetor hot air pipe as described in Par. 113.

345 Connect priming wire to carburetor butterfly valve by inserting end of wire through lever and bending the wire as shown at "E" Fig. 92.

346 Connect carburetor adjusting rod to carburetor by inserting forked end of rod into head of needle valve and locking rod in position with a cotter key. (See "C" Fig. 92).

347 Connect feed pipe to carburetor by running down feed pipe pack nut (See "A" Fig. 29).

348 Install fan, fan belt, radiator, horn, and carburetor priming rod as described in Pars. 127 to 129.

349 Position hood blocks on frame, making sure that headlamp wire bushings enter holes in hook blocks (See "A" Fig. 112). Insert the four engine pan bolts (two to a side) through hood block, frame and engine pans. (See "B" Fig. 112). Place lock washers over ends of bolts and run down nuts.

350 Connect headlamp plugs by pressing plugs into headlamps and turning the plugs clockwise.

351 Install spark plugs and connect spark plug wires to plugs (See "B" Fig. 106).

352 Connect switch to starting motor cable by positioning cable on starting motor terminal and running down lockwasher and nut (See "C" Fig. 35).

353 Insert horn wires through hole in dash as shown at "B" Fig. 99; slipping terminal of the shortest of the two wires under head of screw "C" (Fig. 99) on terminal block. The other wire is connected to the horn as shown at "A" Fig. 25.

354 Install steering post bracket cap (See "A" Fig. 15) by running down the two screws which hold cap to bracket.

355 Install floor boards and mat.

356 Turn on gasoline by opening cock on sediment bulb underneath gasoline tank (See "C" Fig. 12).

357 Install hood; checking fit of hood on dash and radiator shell as described in Par. 145.

358 Close drain cock in bottom of radiator and fill radiator with clean water.

## 359 Time Study

### Engine and Transmission Overhaul

| | | Hrs. | Min. |
|---|---|---|---|
| 1 | Install car covers on front fenders, running board, steering wheel and upholstery | | 5 |
| 2 | Remove engine from chassis | | 38 |
| 3 | Wash engine | | 10 |
| 4 | Disassemble engine and wash all parts | | 40 |
| 5 | Ream valve and push rod guides | | 22 |
| 6 | Reseat valve seats in cylinder block and grind valves | 1 | 10 |
| 7 | Rebore cylinder block | | 55 |
| 8 | Rebabbitt cylinder block and bore out bearings | | 35 |
| 9 | Fit crankshaft, run in bearings | | 45 |
| 10 | Fit pistons, connecting rods, push rods, camshaft and gears, run in | 1 | 55 |
| 11 | Assemble valves and springs, and check timing of engine | | 20 |
| 12 | Overhaul transmission, including checking and replacing magnets | 1 | 50 |
| 13 | Assemble magneto coil, feed pipe, transmission to cylinder block | | 18 |
| 14 | Replace cylinder head, valve cover, cylinder front cover and fan pulley | | 30 |
| 15 | Install crankcase, transmission cover, intake and exhaust manifolds and block test | 1 | 40 |
| 16 | Install engine in chassis | | 42 |
| | | 12 | 35 |

With the exception of removing and installing the engine, in which two men are used, all of the above operations are performed by one man.

# CHAPTER IV

# Clean Carbon and Grind Valves

Fig. 217            Fig. 218

**360**   Drain water by opening pet cock under radiator.

**361**   Lift off hood.

**362**   Remove carburetor pull rod (See "A" Fig. 28).

**363**   Remove cylinder valve cover and gasket by running off the two cylinder valve cover stud nuts (See "A" Fig. 217).

**364**   To prevent damaging spark plugs it is advisable to remove them by disconnecting spark plug wires at plugs and running out the plugs.

**365**   Run out the two cylinder head outlet connection screws (See "A" Fig. 218). Remove horn by running out cylinder inlet connection screw "B" and cylinder head bolt "C". Run out the remaining 14 cylinder head bolts "D" from cylinder block and lift off cylinder head and gasket.

**366**   In removing carbon from the pistons and block, care must be taken to prevent any carbon getting into the cylinders, water jacket holes, cap screw holes or underneath the valves.

**367**   Turn engine over with starting crank until No. 2 and No. 3 pistons arrive at top center and the intake and exhaust valves of these cylinders close. Place cloths in No. 1 and No. 4 cylinders, and scrape carbon from top of cylinder block, heads of pistons and valves (a flat scraper or small putty knife can be used for this purpose) (See Fig. 219). Blow off any loose carbon with compressed air. (If the valves are to be ground time can be saved by removing carbon from valves with a buffing wheel.) When the carbon is removed from No. 2 and No. 3 pistons, turn engine over until No. 1 and No. 4 pistons are at top of cylinder and place cloths in No. 2 and No. 3 cylinders and repeat the carbon cleaning operation until all pistons

Fig. 219

and valves are clean. With the end of a small screw driver, loosen any dirt or carbon in the bottom of the cylinder head bolt holes and blow out the carbon with compressed air. This is done to permit cylinder head bolts being drawn down tightly and eliminate the possibility of water and compression leakage after cylinder head is installed.

368    Carbon can be removed from the cylinder head by means of a small circular wire brush inserted into an electric drill (See "A" Fig. 220). Any loose carbon which remains in combustion chamber or enters spark plug holes can be removed with compressed air.

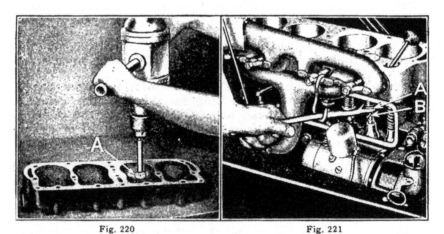

Fig. 220                    Fig. 221

## Grinding Valves

369    Remove valves by inserting a valve lifter under valve spring seat (See "A" Fig. 221) and compressing valve spring until valve spring seat pin "B" can be withdrawn from valve stem. Valve can then be lifted from cylinder block. Examine valves, if a valve is warped, pitted or badly worn on the stem, a new valve should be installed.

Fig. 222            Fig. 223

370  Examine valve seats—

(a) If seats are burned or pitted, they should be refaced with a re-seating tool. The valve reseating tool is inserted into the valve seat in cylinder block as shown in Fig. 146, and sufficient metal removed from valve seat to clean up the pitted spots.

(b) To grind the valves, place a small amount of grinding compound on the bevel face of the valve (See Fig. 222).

(c) Position the valve on the valve seat and rotate it back and forth with a grinding tool about a quarter of a turn, then lift the valve slightly from its seat, turning it another quarter turn, and continue the rotation until both valve and seat have been ground. To facilitate lifting valve when grinding, insert a spring over end of valve (a starting crank spring can be used for this purpose) (See "A" Fig. 223). The valve should not be turned through a complete revolution at one time, as this is apt to cause scratches running around the entire circumference of the valve and seat.

371  The ideal seat for valves in an internal combustion engine is a hair-line bearing. The nearest practical approach to such a

Fig. 224

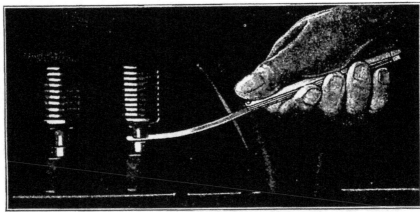

Fig. 225

bearing is probably the straight face of the valve making contact with a radial seat (See "A" Fig. 224). The advantages of a narrow valve seat are that a complete bearing is obtained all around together with the fact that the continual operation of the valve has a tendency to form a better bearing. Where the seat on the cylinder block is cut straight as shown at "B", there is a greater possibility of carbon getting between valve seat and cylinder block.

(d) When the grinding is completed the valve should be removed and carefully washed in kerosene. The valve seat should also be cleaned thoroughly. Extreme care should be taken that no abrasive substance gets into cylinders or valve guides. This can be avoided if the grinding compound is applied sparingly to the bevel face of the valve.

(e) When replacing a valve after grinding, place a little oil on stem of valve and position it in valve guide. The valve spring is then compressed sufficiently far to permit inserting valve spring seat pin into valve stem. If for any reason more than one of the valves have been withdrawn at one time be sure to replace the valves in their original valve stem guides.

Fig. 226

Fig. 227

**372**  After grinding the valves, the clearance between ends of push rods and valves should be checked.  This can be done by inserting thickness gauges (See Fig. 225) between ends of valves and push rods.  The clearance should not be greater than $\frac{1}{32}''$ or less than $\frac{1}{64}''$.

**373**  Replace cylinder head by inserting the 14 cylinder head bolts into cylinder head (See Fig. 226).

(a)  Position gasket over ends of bolts with the large slot in gasket placed towards rear of cylinder head as shown at "A".

(b)  Turn motor over until No. 1 and No. 4 pistons are on top (this prevents shifting of cylinder head gasket).

(c)  Position cylinder head on cylinder block (See Fig. 227).

(d)  Run down the 14 cylinder head bolts; running down the bolts at the front and rear of the cylinder head first.  The bolts are then tightened, starting with the bolts in the center and working toward both ends of cylinder head until all of the bolts are drawn down evenly.

**374**  Install horn by running in the two bolts which hold horn to cylinder inlet connection and cylinder head (See "B" and "C" Fig. 218).

**375**  Insert cylinder head outlet connection gasket between cylinder head and outlet connection and run in the two screws which hold outlet connection to cylinder head (See "A" Fig. 218)

**376**  Screw in spark plugs and connect spark plug wires.

**377**  Replace cylinder valve cover and gasket by positioning gasket and cover on the two cylinder valve cover studs and running down the two nuts over ends of studs (See "A" Fig. 217).  Before installing gasket make sure it is in first-class condition.

**378**  Install carburetor pull rod by inserting it through throttle rod lever and throttle lever assembly, and locking it in position with cotter keys.

**379**  Install hood.

**380**  Close radiator drain cock and fill radiator with clean water.

381

# Time Study

## Clean Carbon and Grind Valves

(One man doing the job)

|  |  | Hrs. | Min. |
|---|---|---|---|
| 1 | Drain water, install car covers, lift off hood, remove cylinder head and valve cover.............................. | | 18 |
| 2 | Clean carbon off cylinder and pistons................... | | 8 |
| 3 | Mark valves, take out pins and valves, clean and inspect valves and seats................................. | | 12 |
| 4 | Grind valves, wash compound off valves and seats in cylinder block................................. | | 32 |
| 5 | Replace valves, assemble pins, check gap between valves and push rods, and install valve cover................. | | 20 |
| 6 | Clean cylinder head, inspect gasket, install cylinder head, run down and tighten bolts......................... | | 18 |
| 7 | Install hood, fill radiator with water, remove car covers... | | 8 |
|  |  | 1 | 56 |

If necessary to reseat valve seats, add 24 minutes to the above time.

# CHAPTER V

# Taking up Connecting Rod Bearings

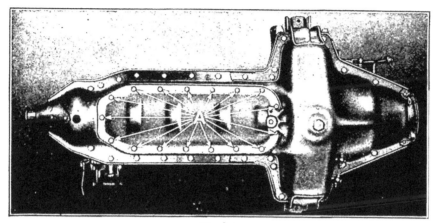

Fig. 228

382 Remove crankcase lower cover and gasket by running out the 17 crankcase lower cover screws which hold cover and gasket to crankcase (See "A" Fig. 228). Turn engine over with starting crank until No. 1 and No. 4 rods are at bottom center. (If the car is equipped with the old design crank case, see "f" Par. 399).

383 Remove connecting rod bearing caps (See "A" Fig. 229) from No. 1 and No. 4 rods by running off the two nuts which hold each cap to rod. Before removing the caps examine both rods and caps to make sure they are plainly marked. When connecting rods and caps are assembled in new engines, they are marked with a file mark which corresponds to the number of the cylinder into which they are fitted. For instance No. 1 rod and cap which are fitted into No. 1

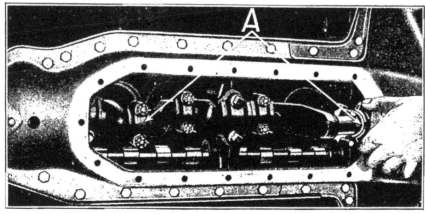

Fig. 229

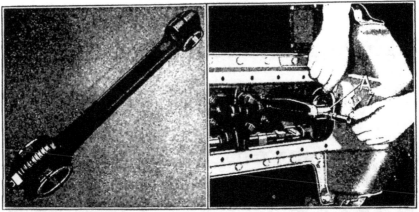

Fig. 230                                    Fig. 231

cylinder (the cylinder nearest radiator) are marked with one file mark, No. 2 rod and cap carry two file marks, and so on up to No. 4 rod, which carries four marks (See Fig. 230). When replacing a cap, the markings on the cap should be made to correspond with the markings on the rod. The markings on the rod and cap should be on the same side as the connecting rod clamp screw.

384   Check pin bearings on crankshaft with a micrometer to see that bearings are not out of round (See "A" Fig. 231).   Take the measurement across several different points.   If the crank pin shows more than .002" out of round, the shaft should be changed.   If the shaft is O. K. and the babbitt in the rod and cap have not been damaged, the cap should be filed with a large mill file as shown in Fig. 232, filing about .002" from face of cap. (If the babbitt has been burned out, see Par. 389.)   The repair man must exercise considerable care to hold the file squarely on the cap.

385   When the cap has been dressed down sufficiently, check the cap on a surface plate to make sure that the face of the cap has been filed evenly.   (See Fig. 233.)

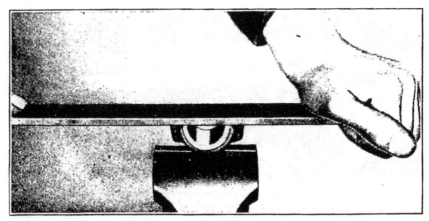

Fig. 232

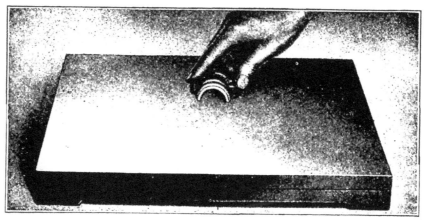

Fig. 233

**386** The rod should be fitted to crankshaft so that it will move slightly on the shaft when the side of the bearing cap is tapped with a small brass hammer. The movement of the rod on the shaft can be detected by placing a finger on one side of the cap while tapping opposite side (See Fig. 237). The clearance between connecting rod and piston pin bushings should next be checked. If the clearance is less than $\frac{1}{32}''$, remove the rod and lightly file end of piston pin bushing. This necessitates removing the piston and piston pin, as described in Pars. 399 and 413. When the filing operation is completed, clean piston with compressed air, assemble rod to piston and install piston and connecting rod assembly in cylinder. When correct adjustment is obtained, lock the two connecting rod cap bolt nuts with cotter keys.

**387** When No. 1 and No. 4 bearings have been adjusted, turn motor over with starting crank and repeat the operation on No. 2 and No. 3 bearings.

**388** After taking up the connecting rod bearings, examine crankcase lower cover gasket to make sure it is in good condition. Replace cover by running in the 17 screws which hold cover to crankcase (14 screws on the old style cover). If oil has been drained from crankcase, pour in a gallon of fresh oil through breather pipe.

**389** If the babbitt has been burned out, a new rod should be substituted. This necessitates removing piston and piston pin as explained in Pars. 399 and 413. When installing a new rod in place of one that has been burned out, make sure that the pin bearing on crankshaft is free from any babbitt left by the burned out rod. If any babbitt remains on the pin bearings it can be dressed off by oiling a strip of fine sandpaper and wrapping it around the bearing, and rotating the sandpaper back and forth with a narrow strap as shown in Fig. 161. It is also a good plan to drain the oil and remove any loose babbitt from the crankcase.

**390** Before installing a rod, it should be carefully checked to see if rod is twisted or sprung as a rod which is out of alignment will cause excess wear and knocking.

Fig. 234                                    Fig. 235

**391**   The alignment of the rod can be checked by inserting a piston pin through end of rod and placing the rod in an alignment fixture (See Fig. 234).  If alignment is O. K., piston pin will fit snugly against fixture at points "A" and "B"; if rod is sprung or twisted there will be a clearance at one of these points.

**392**   If a rod is slightly sprung or twisted it can be straightened with a connecting rod straightening iron as shown in Fig. 235.  When rod is O. K. it is assembled in piston and checked for alignment as described in Pars. 418 to 420.

**393**   In fitting a new rod on an old shaft the pin bearings on crankshaft are usually worn undersize.  This not only necessitates removing the two paper shims from between cap and rod, but it is frequently necessary to lightly file the face of both the cap and rod in order to properly fit rod to shaft.  Before removing cap from rod, the cap and rod should be marked as described in Par. 383, to insure their being correctly assembled.  If the pin bearing is badly undersize, in addition to filing cap and the rod, it is necessary to scrape the bearing in until at least a 50% bearing is obtained on both cap and rod.

**394**   To scrape a bearing in—

(a)   Assemble cap and rod to crankshaft by installing piston and connecting rod assembly in cylinder as described in Par. 431 and forcing the piston down until the bearing end of the rod rests on the crankshaft.  The connecting rod bearing cap is then assembled to the rod by inserting it over the ends of the two connecting rod cap bolts and running down nuts tightly on ends of bolts.

(b)   Turn engine over with starting crank.

(c)   Remove cap and rod from crankshaft and examine the bearings.

(d)   The spots on the bearing which have come in contact with the shaft, will appear bright.  These are the high points and they should be removed with a bearing scraper (See Fig. 236). Scrape very lightly as a deep hole is hard to smooth out.

**395**   When a bearing of approximately 50% is obtained on both rod and cap, place a little oil on cap and rod and assemble rod to crank-

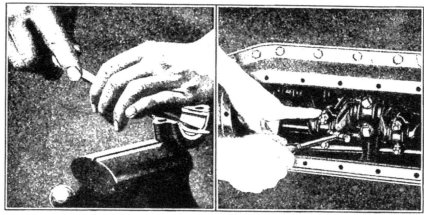

Fig. 236                    Fig. 237

shaft by installing cap and running down nuts on ends of connecting rod bolts, drawing nuts down tightly and locking the nuts with cotter keys.  The crankcase lower cover is then replaced as described in Par. 388.

# Time Study

396

## Taking Up Connecting Rods

### (One man doing the job)

|     |                                                                | Hrs. | Min. |
|-----|----------------------------------------------------------------|------|------|
| 1   | Install car covers.................................            |      | 5    |
| 2   | Remove No. 1 and No. 4 caps, file, replace caps and test for tightness................................... |      | 32   |
| 3   | Turn engine, remove No. 2 and No. 3 caps, tighten and test     |      | 32   |
| 4   | Clean and install crankcase cover and remove car covers..      |      | 10   |
|     |                                                                | 1    | 19   |

The above time applies to cars equipped with the new design crankcase (See Fig. 256).  On cars equipped with the old type case, add 15 minutes to the job.  If it is necessary to install a new rod owing to the babbitt having been burned out, add 45 minutes to the above time.

# CHAPTER VI

# Installing New Pistons and Rings

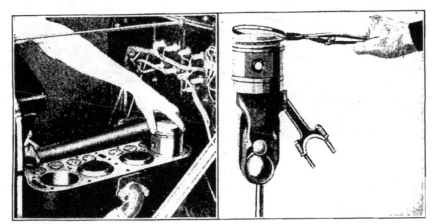

Fig. 238                    Fig. 239

**397**  The pistons and rings in an automobile engine act as a seal when compressing the gases and transmitting their energy to the crankshaft. It is, therefore, necessary that both pistons and rings fit the cylinder walls within comparatively close limits.

**398**  Due to heat generated in the engine resulting in expansion of pistons in cylinders it is necessary to fit the pistons in the cylinders with a clearance. As the head of the piston is subjected to greater heat than the lower wall or skirt, it is necessary to allow more clearance at the top of the piston than at the bottom. This is taken care of in manufacturing, the piston being .010 smaller at the head than at the skirt.

**399**  To remove pistons from engine—

(a) Drain water from radiator.

(b) Lift off hood.

(c) Remove cylinder head as described in Par. 365.

(d) Turn engine over with starting crank until No. 2 and No. 3 pistons are at top of cylinder; this will bring No. 1 and No. 4 connecting rods into position so that caps can be removed.

(e) Remove crankcase lower cover and connecting rod bearing caps as described in Pars. 382 and 383.

(f) To facilitate running off the nuts on No. 4 connecting rod bearing cap, on cars equipped with the old design crankcase, turn the engine over until No. 4 piston reaches a point approximately 1″ before bottom center; this brings one of the No. 4 bearing cap bolt nuts into the position where it is most easily removed. Next, turn the engine until the piston is approximately 1″ past bottom center and run off the other nut.

(g) Remove No. 1 and No. 4 pistons by pushing them up in cylinder until bottom ring clears top of cylinder. Pistons can then be withdrawn (See Fig. 238).

(h) Turn engine over half a turn with starting crank; this will bring No. 2 and No. 3 connecting rod caps in position so they can be removed and the pistons withdrawn.

**400**  After withdrawing pistons, the cylinder bores should be inspected for being scored, tapered or out of round.

**401**  The pistons should next be inspected for scores, leaks and wear. A piston, if not too badly scored can be dressed off with a mill file. This practice, however, is not recommended unless the mechanic is skilled in the use of a file. As a general rule it is better to install a new piston.

**402**  Leaks in pistons can be found by pouring about 1″ of gasoline into the interior of the piston, after piston rings have been removed with a ring extractor as shown in Fig. 239, and the oil wiped out of the grooves. If there is a leak, the gasoline will seep through.

**403**  Pistons can be checked for wear by inserting them into cylinders and measuring the clearance between piston and cylinder wall (See "A" Fig. 240). Thickness gauges (feelers, See Fig. 166) can be used for this purpose. If there is more than .006″ clearance, the old pistons should be discarded after removing the piston pin and connecting rod as described in Par. 413 and new oversize pistons installed.

**404**  New pistons are fitted with .003″ to .004″ clearance between piston and cylinder wall. When checking pistons, the feelers should be tried at several points between the piston and cylinder bore. especially around sides of the two oil pockets on the pistons (See "B" Fig. 240). Pistons can be checked for being out of round by inserting the feeler between piston and cylinder and holding the feeler stationary while the piston is turned and checked a quarter of a turn at a time. If the piston shows out of round, remove piston and lightly tap it with a rawhide mallet on the greatest diameter of the skirt, to true it up.

**405**  When installing new pistons, select pistons which will insure all four of them being approximately the same weight. This can be done by weighing the pistons on a scale as shown in Fig. 241.

**406**  Before installing the old pins and rods in the new pistons they should be checked for wear and alignment.

**407**  Piston pins are checked for wear by measuring the diameter of the pin with micrometers. The diameter of new piston pins is $\frac{.740}{.741}$; if the old pin is worn down .001″ or more below the low limit a new pin should be installed.

**408**  Piston pins are fitted and installed as described in Pars. 415 and 418.

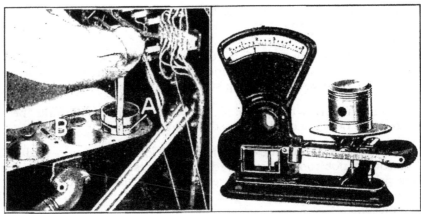

Fig. 240                    Fig. 241

409   The connecting rods should be checked for being sprung or
      twisted as described in Pars. 391 and 392, also for worn or cracked
      babbitt in both cap and rod.   If babbitt is badly worn or cracked
      a new cap and rod should be installed.

410   After checking the pistons for wear, the piston pin and piston
      pin bushing should be inspected to see that there is no play between
      pins and bushings.

411   To check the play between piston pins and bushings hold the
      piston with the piston pin perpendicular to the bench and move the
      connecting rod back and forth in such a manner as to cause the pin
      to be forced against first one side of the bushing and then the other
      (See Fig. 242).

412   If there is .002″ or more play a new pin should be fitted.   If this
      does not overcome the trouble it will also be necessary to install new
      bushings.

413   The piston pin is removed by running out the connecting rod
      clamp screw (See "A" Fig. 243), after which the pin can be pushed
      out.

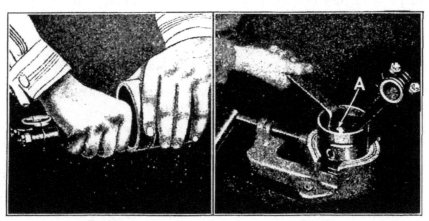

Fig. 242                    Fig. 243

Fig. 244                                    Fig. 245

**414** A piston clamp should be used for holding the piston while performing these operations, as the practice of holding the rod in a vise, invariably results in a twisted or sprung rod.

**415** The piston pins are fitted in the bushings by selective fit. A pin is tried in the bushing. If it turns freely another pin is selected until one is found which requires a fair amount of effort to force it in and turn it.

**416** The bushings can be removed on an arbor press. Care should be exercised when performing this operation to prevent distorting the piston. Driving the bushings out with a hammer invariably throws the piston out of round. The arbor press should be provided with a fixture for supporting the piston, and the driver provided with a pilot and sleeve. The bushing is pressed out by inserting the driver through side of piston and pressing the bushing out from the inside of the piston (See Fig. 244). When pressing in the new bushings it is important to have them line up properly with the hole in the piston, as a cocked bushing requires considerable more pressure to force it in, and as a result the piston is forced out of round.

**417** The bushing should be pressed in until about $\frac{1}{16}$ of an inch of the bushing shows on the inside of the piston or until the bushing is $\frac{1}{32}$ of an inch below the outside diameter of the piston. When the bushings are in place they should be line reamed to size with a .740″ diameter pilot type reamer. If a drill press is not available the bushings can be reamed by hand (See Fig. 245).

**418** After oiling both piston pin and bushings, position rod in piston and insert piston pin through piston and rod. Turn the pin until the groove in the pin lines up with the connecting rod clamp screw hole and insert the clamp screw (See "A" Fig. 246). Run down the screw with a speed wrench. Press the rod from one side of the piston to the other to see that the piston pin does not extend beyond the outside diameter of the piston (See "A" Fig. 247). If it does, remove the rod and pin and press the piston pin bushing in a little further. If it does not, tighten down the cap screw "B", with a connecting rod clamp screw wrench and lock the screw with cotter pin as shown at "C".

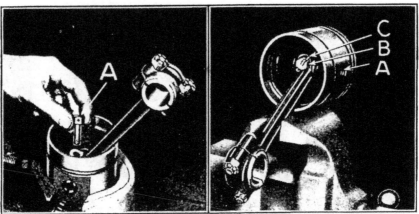

Fig. 246          Fig. 247

**419** The fit of the pin in the bushings can now be checked as shown in Fig. 248. The rod should drop gradually when the piston is held in both hands and given a quick shake.

**420** Piston and connecting rod assembly should next be checked for alignment by placing the assembly in an alignment fixture. As the diameter of the piston is .010 smaller at the top of the piston than it is at the bottom, there should be a clearance of .005" between top of piston and fixture at point "A" Fig. 249. The bottom of piston, point "B" should fit snugly against fixture without any clearance. If the assembly is slightly sprung or twisted it can be corrected by straightening the rod with a straightening iron as shown in Fig. 235 until the assembly checks accurately at points "A" and "B" on fixture (Fig. 249).

**421** Piston rings can now be fitted to pistons and the pistons installed in car as described below.

## Installing Piston Rings

**422** The piston ring is used to fill the gap between the piston and cylinder wall, preventing the gases escaping into the crankcase and excess oil working into the combustion chamber.

Fig. 248          Fig. 249

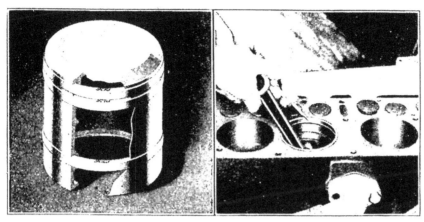

Fig. 250                    Fig. 251

**423**  Ford rings are machined .003″ taper on the face of the ring. This insures the ring wearing to conform to the cylinder wall in the shortest possible time and when assembled with the script word "FORD" up, as shown in Fig. 250, the ring presents a sharp edge to the cylinder wall on the down stroke, and an incline on the up stroke, the incline rides over the oil while the sharp edge pushes the oil before it, thus preventing the oil working into the combustion chamber.

**424**  Since the rings are softer than the cylinder walls against which they are tightly pressed and also present small wearing surfaces, they wear undersize in time. To insure maximum power, together with minimum oil and gas consumption, the rings should be renewed every 10,000 miles.

**425**  When a ring is worn undersize, or does not seat all the way around, it allows oil and gas to pass, and should be replaced. The rings are removed with a ring extractor as shown in Fig. 239. Any carbon in the ring grooves in the piston should be removed and the ring grooves thoroughly cleaned.

**426**  Before installing new rings, the gap between the ends of the ring should be checked. This is done by placing the ring into the cylinder in which it is to operate, and checking the gap between the ends of the ring with feelers (See Fig. 251). To insure the ring fitting squarely, insert a piston without rings into cylinder, place ring in cylinder and raise piston until ring fits evenly. The two top rings are checked at the top of the cylinder. In a car that has been in service for some time, it is advisable to check the bottom ring at the bottom of the cylinder, as the cylinders sometimes wear slightly taper. The ring gap clearance is .008″ to .012″ for the top ring, .006″ to .008″ for middle ring, and .004″ to .006″ for bottom ring.

**427**  If the gap is too small, the ends of the ring can be filed (See Fig. 252), until the correct gap is obtained. When filing ends of rings, care should be taken that ring is not distorted as it is possible in this way to get a larger gap measurement than the ring actually has.

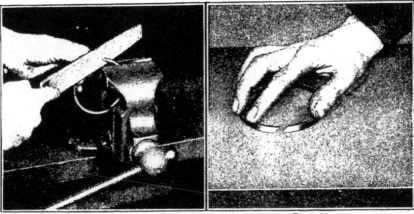

Fig. 252　　　　　　　　　　　　　Fig. 253

428　Rings should next be checked on a surface plate to make sure they have not been sprung (See Fig. 253). If alignment of ring is O. K. run the ring around the groove in the piston into which it is to be fitted (See Fig. 254). The ring should fit in the groove with a clearance of from .001″ to .002″. If the ring fits too tightly it can be dressed down by rubbing it on a surface plate covered with fine sandpaper.

429　The fit of the piston ring in the ring groove and on the cylinder wall are of vital importance in controlling oil pumping and leakage. If a ring has considerable up and down motion in the ring groove, it will act as a miniature oil pump, i. e. as the piston moves downward, the ring moves to the top of the groove. The oil in the cylinder wall then collects in the space under and in back of the ring. When the piston starts upward, the ring shifts to the bottom of the groove and the oil below and in back of the ring is forced around to the upper side. As the piston reaches the top of the stroke and starts downward, the ring again shifts to the top of the groove and the oil is deposited on the cylinder wall at a point above the top ring, and therefore, cannot be carried back with the piston on its down stroke. It will be seen that a large amount of oil can be pumped into the combustion chamber in this manner.

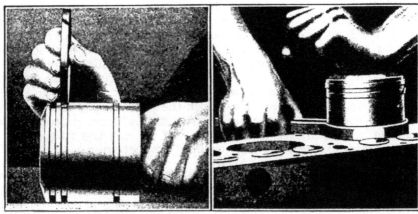

Fig. 254　　　　　　　　　　　　　Fig. 255

430 After pistons have been checked and rings correctly fitted, turn the rings in the groove so that the gaps in the rings will not be in line. The gaps should be approximately 120° apart.

431 Before installing pistons in cylinders place oil on sides of pistons and wipe out cylinder bores with a cloth free from lint. The pistons are then inserted into cylinder bore by pressing rings into piston grooves with a ring squeezer and tapping piston down into cylinder bore with the hand (See Fig. 255) until the bearing end of the rod rests on the crankshaft.

432 Place oil on surfaces of connecting rod caps and install caps by inserting caps over the ends of the connecting rod cap bolts and running down nuts tightly on ends of bolts (the rods should be fitted to the crankshaft as described in Par. 386). The nuts are then locked with cotter keys and the crankcase cover installed as described in Par. 388.

433 Install cylinder head gasket, cylinder head and horn as described in Pars. 373 to 376.

434 Install hood, close radiator drain cock and fill radiator with clean water.

435

# Time Study
## Fitting New Pistons
### (One man doing the job)

| | | Hrs. | Min. |
|---|---|---|---|
| 1 | Drain water, install car covers, remove hood and cylinder head.................................... | | 15 |
| 2 | Remove crankcase cover, connecting rod caps and pistons.. | | 20 |
| 3 | Fit new pistons, pins, assemble connecting rods and check for alignment, fit and install piston rings.............. | 1 | 06 |
| 4 | Install pistons and connecting rod caps................. | | 20 |
| 5 | Install crankcase cover, clean and install cylinder head.... | | 28 |
| 6 | Install hood, fill radiator with water, remove car covers... | | 8 |
| | | 2 | 37 |

436
## Changing Piston Rings
### (One man doing the job)

| | | Hrs. | Min. |
|---|---|---|---|
| 1 | Drain water, install car covers, remove hood and cylinder head...................................... | | 15 |
| 2 | Remove crankcase cover................................ | | 5 |
| 3 | Remove connecting rod bearing caps and pistons......... | | 15 |
| 4 | Remove rings, clean carbon from ring grooves and top of pistons............................................ | | 18 |
| 5 | Check alignment of rods and pistons, straighten if necessary | | 15 |
| 6 | Fit new rings, check rings in ring grooves and on surface plate. Install rings on pistons........................ | | 20 |
| 7 | Install pistons and connecting rod caps................. | | 20 |
| 8 | Clean crankcase cover, replace gasket, install cover, remove car covers........................................ | | 10 |
| | | 1 | 58 |

The above time applies to cars equipped with the new design crankcase (See Fig. 256). On cars equipped with the old type case, add 15 minutes to the job.

# CHAPTER VII

# Taking Up Main Bearings

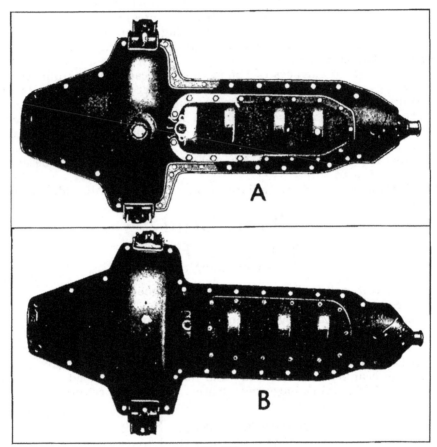

Fig. 256

**437** When not burned out or badly worn, all main bearings on cars equipped with the present design crankcase (See "A" Fig. 256), can be taken up without removing engine from car. (To take up No. 3 bearing on cars equipped with the old design crankcase "B" it is necessary to remove engine from car and remove the crankcase as described in Pars. 163 to 205.)

**438** To take up main bearings:

**439** Remove hood.

**440** Remove carburetor pull rod (See "A" Fig. 28).

**441** Remove cylinder valve cover by running off the two valve cover stud nuts (See Fig. 217).

**442** Remove crankcase lower cover (See "A" Fig. 228).

Fig. 257                    Fig. 258

**443**  Remove rear main bearing cap—

(a) Break flywheel cap screw wire (See "A" Fig. 257) and run out the flywheel cap screw "B" which prevents lifting bearing cap off of bolts.

(b) Withdraw cotter keys and run off the two crankshaft bearing bolt nuts "C".

(c) The heads of the rear main bearing bolts are machined flat on one side of head.  The flat side of head fits next to cylinder. This locks the bolt in position and prevents it from turning when running off nuts (See "A" Fig. 258).

(d) Lift bearing cap off ends of bolts; before removing bearing caps they should be marked to insure replacing them in their original positions.

(e) Withdraw one of the brass shims from each bolt (See Fig. 259). If shims have all been removed in making previous bearing adjustments it is necessary to file the cap in the same manner as the connecting rod cap (See Fig. 232).  As a general rule, however, by the time all shims have been removed, the babbitt in the block has become worn to such an extent that the block should be rebabbitted.

Fig. 259

Fig. 260

(f) Clean out any babbitt from oil grooves in bearing cap, and cover surface of bearing with oil.

(g) Replace bearing cap over ends of bolts making sure that cap is installed in its original position.

(h) Run down the two crankshaft bearing bolt nuts drawing them down tightly and lining up nut with cotter pin hole, so that cotter pin can be entered. In locating the cotter pin hole, never turn the nut back. If the cotter pin hole in the bolt does not line up with the nut, run the nut back sufficiently far to insure a new setting, then draw nut down tightly, taking care not to pass cotter pin hole.

(i) Test for tightness of bearing by turning engine over slowly with starting crank, a slight increase in resistance should be noted. If bearing cap is still loose it will be necessary to remove another shim from each of the two bolts, or lightly file face of cap. If the adjustment is too tight, replace a shim on one of the bolts.

(j) When correct adjustment is obtained insert cotter pins through crankshaft bearing bolt nuts.

(k) Run down and wire flywheel cap screw.

444 The center bearing is adjusted next while the front bearing is adjusted last. These two bearings are adjusted in the same manner as the rear main bearing, except that it is necessary to remove both the bearing bolts and nuts in order to remove caps and withdraw the shims. To remove the caps, one man holds a wrench on the two bearing bolt nuts, which on the center bearing are located between No. 2 and No. 3 cylinders (See "A" Fig. 260), while another man beneath the car runs out the bolts (See "A" Fig. 261). Front bearing bolt nuts (See "B" Fig. 260), are located in front of No. 1 cylinder.

445 When all the bearings have been adjusted it should be possible to turn the engine over at cranking speed with starting crank. If engine cannot be turned with starting crank, the bearings are adjusted too tightly and it will be necessary to loosen them by replacing shims. After bearings have been adjusted and nuts locked with cotter keys, replace crankcase lower cover gasket and cover, as explained

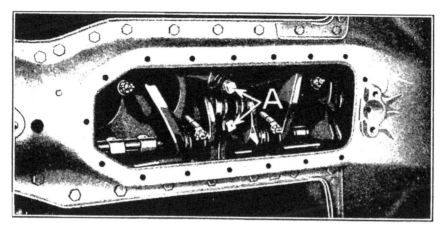

Fig. 261

in Par. 388. Position cylinder valve cover gasket and cover over valve cover studs and run down the two nuts which hold cover to cylinder block. Install carburetor pull rod. Connect starting switch cable to starting motor and replace hood.

### 446        Time Study

#### Taking up Main Bearings--Present Type Crankcase

|  |  | Hrs. | Min. |
|---|---|---|---|
| 1 | Install car covers | | 5 |
| 2 | Remove crankcase lower cover | | 5 |
| 3 | Remove flywheel cap screw, run off rear bearing bolt nuts, lift off cap and remove shims | | 40 |
| 4 | Install cap, run in flywheel cap screw | | 45 |
| 5 | Remove center and front bearing caps, remove shims, replace caps | | 30 |
| 6 | Clean and install crankcase cover and remove car covers | | 10 |
| | | 2 | 15 |

With the exception of removing center and front bearing caps and shims, and replacing caps, in which two men are used, all of the above operations are performed by one man.

# CHAPTER VIII
# Correcting Noisy Time Gears

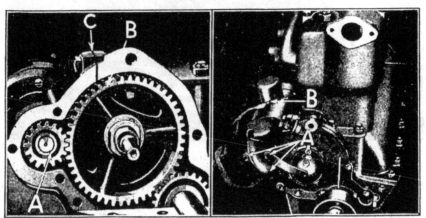

Fig. 262           Fig. 263

**447**  Noisy time gears usually result from—

  (a)  Excessively worn gears.

  (b)  Improperly fitted gears.

  (c)  Foreign matter getting between gears and raising a burr on the teeth.

  (d)  Failure to sufficiently tighten camshaft gear lock nut.

  (e)  Sprung camshaft or badly worn camshaft front bearing.

**448**  Noises which are attributed to time gears are sometimes due to the generator drive pinion (See "A" Fig. 262) not meshing properly with the large time gear "B". To determine whether the noise is due to generator pinion not meshing properly with time gear or whether it is in the large and small time gears; lift off hood and remove generator by running out the commutator case spring bolt and the two generator mounting screws (See "A" Fig. 263). Disconnect ammeter to cutout wire at cutout by running out cutout screw "B". Generator can then be lifted from bracket. Install a gear cover plate T-3017D-1773 on back of generator bracket by inserting plate over ends of generator mounting bolts and commutator case spring bolt and running down nuts on ends of bolts. The engine is then started.

**449**  If the noise is no longer heard the trouble is due to the generator pinion not meshing properly with large time gear. (If the noise is still heard see Par. 451.) The pinion should be meshed with the large time gear with a clearance of .002" to .004". The adjustment can be changed by varying the distance between generator bracket and cylinder block at point "C" Fig. 262. If pinion meshes too tightly with large time gear remove generator bracket by running out the four cap screws (See "A" Fig. 264), which hold bracket to

114

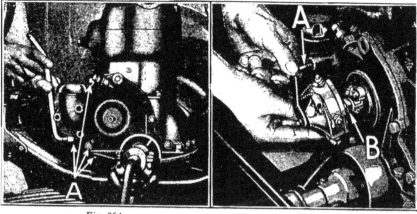

Fig. 264                              Fig. 265

cylinder block and crankcase and install an additional gasket at point "C" Fig. 262. If, however, there is too great a clearance between pinion and gear install a thinner paper gasket at point "C". If there is still too great a clearance, the trouble can be corrected by removing some of the metal from the generator bracket. This can be done by rubbing the joint surface of the bracket on a surface plate on which fine sandpaper has been attached.

450   The generator bracket is replaced by positioning generator bracket and gasket on cylinder block and running in the four cap screws which hold bracket to cylinder and crankcase. A lockwasher is placed under the bottom screw which is entered through crankcase into bracket. The generator is then positioned in bracket, the pinion being meshed with the large time gear. Commutator case spring is inserted over end of commutator case spring bolt and the bolt together with the two generator mounting screws are then entered and drawn down tightly. Ammeter to cutout wire is then connected at cutout, and the hood replaced.

451   If, when the generator is removed, the gears are still noisy the trouble lies in the time gears, camshaft or camshaft bearing, and they should be carefully inspected.

452   Noisy time gears can sometimes be corrected by simply changing the large time gear. On cars that have been in service for long periods, however, it is usually necessary to replace both large and small time gears.

453   To expose the time gears; remove radiator, and fan, as described in Pars. 14 and 16.

454   Remove commutator by running out commutator case spring bolt (See "A" Fig. 265), and lifting off commutator case. Run off commutator lock nut "B". Lift off commutator brush cap (See "A" Fig. 266) and withdraw pin "B". Commutator brush and shield can then be removed and felt ring lifted out of recess in cylinder front cover.

455   Run off the nuts on the ends of the two generator mounting bolts and lift off gear cover plate. The two generator mounting bolts

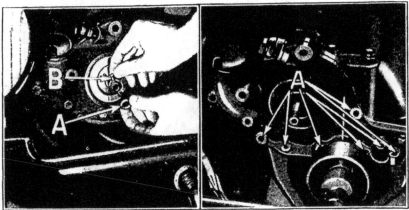

Fig. 266        Fig. 267

can then be withdrawn from the cylinder front cover. The cylinder front cover and gasket can now be removed by running out the seven remaining cylinder front cover cap screws and bolts (See "A" Fig. 267) which hold cover to cylinder block and crankcase. Front cover can then be lifted off over end of camshaft.

**456** Two brass bars about ¼" in diameter and 14" long, the ends of which are drawn out in much the same shape as a screw driver are used for checking the time gears for back-lash (space between the teeth) and the camshaft for a loose front bearing. Screw drivers should not be used for this purpose as they will form a burr on the teeth of the gears.

**457** New time gears are assembled with from .0005" to .003" back-lash (space between teeth). Jobs in which the old gears are again installed may have as high as .006". The experienced man may judge the back-lash by inserting the brass bars between the teeth of the gears and watching the movement of the large gear when it is moved back and forth with the brass bars (See Fig. 268). The accurate way of checking the gear is to hold the teeth to one side with a brass bar and insert a feeler between the free sides of the

Fig. 268        Fig. 269

Fig. 270          Fig. 271

teeth as shown in Fig. 269.   Try the gears at several points to find
any high spots, i. e., a spot where the gear is tighter than at other
points around the gear.   If a high spot is found, both gears should
be marked with a piece of chalk at that point and the large time gear
then removed.   The large time gear is removed from camshaft by
running off the locknut (See "A" Fig. 270) and withdrawing gear
from shaft with a gear puller as shown in Fig. 271.   Examine both
gears at points marked, for a burr (raised spot) on the teeth.   If
there is a burr on either gear, dress it off with a fine file and replace
the large gear in its original position by driving it onto the shaft
with a driver (See Fig. 272) then check the gears again.   If no burr
is found, replace gear on camshaft, turning it to a position opposite
to the one in which it was originally meshed with the small gear,
then check the play between the teeth of the gears.   If the high spot
still shows, the trouble is probably due to a sprung camshaft, and
it will be necessary to remove and straighten the shaft as described
in Chapter IX. If there is considerable play between the teeth
around the entire circumference of the gears, the camshaft should
be checked for a loose bearing; this can be done by inserting the
brass bars between each side of camshaft gear and cylinder block and

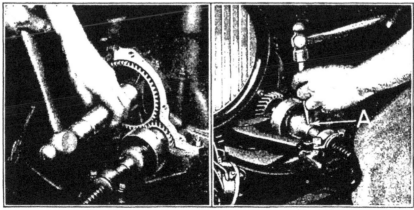

Fig. 272          Fig. 273

forcing the camshaft back and forth in bearing, at the same time noting whether there is any movement of the shaft. If there is play in the bearing it will be necessary to remove the camshaft and install new bearings as described in Chapter IX. If there is no play in the bearing, the trouble is undoubtedly due to worn gears and it will be necessary to install a new large and small time gear.

## Removing and Installing Small Time Gear

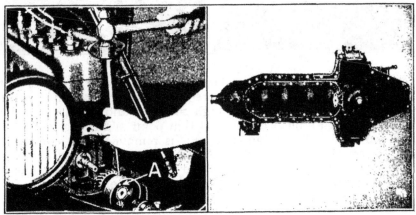

Fig. 274                    Fig. 275

**458**  To remove small time gear after large time gear and generator have been withdrawn:—

(a) Remove starting crank by withdrawing cotter key from starting crank ratchet pin and driving out pin with a drift (See "A" Fig. 273).

(b) Withdraw starting crank from ratchet and crankcase, and lift out ratchet.

(c) Remove fan drive pulley by withdrawing cotter key and driving out crankshaft starting pin (See "A" Fig. 274) through hole in fan drive pulley. Pulley can then be withdrawn from shaft.

(d) Remove carburetor pull and adjusting rods (See "A" and "B" Fig. 28). Remove hot air pipe by running off manifold stud nut (See "B" Fig. 29). Shut off gas at sediment bulb under gasoline tank and disconnect feed pipe at carburetor (See "A" Fig. 29). Lift out mat and floor board, disconnect exhaust pipe pack nut (See "A" Fig. 30). Run out universal joint bolts and screws as described in Par. 34.

(e) Run out the remaining 27 bolts and nuts which hold transmission and cylinder block to crankcase (See Fig. 275).

(f) Lift up front end of engine with chain falls and motor lifting hooks sufficiently high so that the small time gear can clear front wall of crankcase. Brace engine in that position by inserting two blocks of wood between cylinder and crankcase (See "A" Fig. 276).

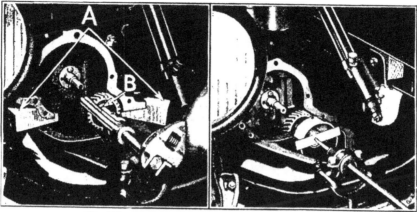

Fig. 276          Fig. 277

(g) Small time gear can then be withdrawn with a gear puller as shown at "B".

(h) The new gear is installed by slipping it over end of crankshaft with the script word "FORD" on gear facing out, lining up keyway in gear with key in shaft. The gear is driven onto shaft with a driver, in the same manner as the large time gear was installed (See Fig. 272).

(i) Replace large time gear by driving it onto camshaft with a driver as shown in Fig. 272, making sure that the tooth marked "FORD" on the small time gear meshes between the two teeth on the large gear at the point marked zero (0). After gear has been installed run down camshaft gear lock nut, drawing nut down tightly.

**459** Examine felt gasket in front wall of crankcase, if badly worn, a new felt should be installed.

**460** Remove blocks and lower engine onto crankcase making sure that crankcase gaskets are in position. Run down the bolts, screws, lockwashers and nuts which hold cylinder block and transmission cover to crankcase.

**461** Install fan drive pulley on crankshaft. This is done by placing a flat piece of stock across face of pulley and driving pulley onto crankshaft with a drift which is inserted through starting crank sleeve (See Fig. 277). Pulley is then locked in position on shaft by inserting starting pin, with the cotter pin hole end up (See Fig. 278) through the larger of the two holes in fan drive pulley and driving it through pulley and crankshaft. The pin is then locked in position with a cotter key.

**462** Replace starting crank by inserting it into starting crank sleeve and slipping starting crank ratchet over end of crank. Line up hole in ratchet with hole in starting crank and insert starting crank ratchet pin through ratchet and starting crank, driving the pin down through ratchet and crank and locking the pin with a cotter key.

**463** Replace universal joint ball cap by inserting the two bolts and two screws and running down nuts on the ends of the two bolts and

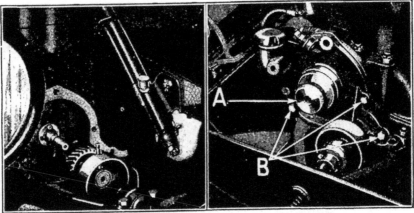

Fig. 278                               Fig. 279

locking the nuts with cotter keys. The two cap screws are locked in position by wiring them together (See "B" Fig. 32).

**464** Connect exhaust manifold to exhaust pipe by tightening exhaust pipe pack nut. Install floor boards and mat.

**465** Replace generator, carburetor hot air pipe, carburetor pull and adjusting rods, as described in Pars. 450, 113, 114 and 115. Connect feed pipe to carburetor by running down feed pipe pack nut onto carburetor inlet elbow (See "A" Fig. 29). Turn on gasoline at sediment bulb underneath gasoline tank.

**466** Place a little cup grease on cylinder front cover gasket and position it on cylinder block. Examine cylinder front cover felt in front cover. If felt shows effects of wear a new felt should be installed. Insert cylinder front cover over end of camshaft and position it against cylinder block.

**467** It is very important that the commutator case recess in cylinder front cover lines up accurately with camshaft. If these parts are not in exact alignment the commutator brush will not revolve centrally in the commutator case and as a result will cause an uneven spark, and possible damage to the engine.

**468** To check alignment of front cover with camshaft, place a cylinder front cover gauge into recess in cover provided for commutator case (See "A" Fig. 279). With the gauge in position insert and tightly draw down the three cap screws "B", which hold cover to cylinder. The gauge is then removed and the remaining cap screws, and bolts which hold cover to crankcase and cylinder are entered and drawn down tightly. After assembly is completed it is advisable to again insert gauge into recess to make sure that front cover has not been forced out of alignment in drawing down the cylinder cover to crankcase bolts.

**469** Position commutator felt over end of camshaft, seating it into recess in cylinder front cover. Position commutator shield over felt. Install commutator brush over end of camshaft. Insert commutator brush pin through brush and into shaft, positioning brush cap over end of pin. Run down commutator lock nut over end of shaft, drawing it down tightly against brush cap. The commutator case is then installed as described in Par. 119 and checked for correct setting as described in Par. 126.

470    Before installing fan and radiator, it is advisable to check the gears to make sure that they are correctly meshed. This can be done by starting the engine and noting whether the gears run quietly (do not run the engine more than a few seconds at a time with the fan and radiator removed). After checking the fit of the gears install fan and radiator as described in Pars. 127 and 128. Install hood; close drain at bottom of radiator and fill radiator with clean water.

471                            # Time Study
                        ## Noisy Time Gears

                    (One man doing the job)

| | | Hrs. | Min. |
|---|---|---|---|
| 1 | Install car covers, remove generator, install plate on bracket and test. . . . . . . . . . . . . . . . . . . . . . . . . . . . . . . . . . . . . . . . | | 15 |
| 2 | Remove radiator. . . . . . . . . . . . . . . . . . . . . . . . . . . . . . . | | 10 |
| 3 | Remove fan, front cover, check gear. . . . . . . . . . . . . . . . . | | 20 |
| 4 | Change large gear and check. . . . . . . . . . . . . . . . . . . . . . | | 15 |
| 5 | Install front cover, fan, generator, and radiator. . . . . . . . . | | 28 |
| 6 | Install hood, fill radiator with water, remove car covers. . . | | 8 |
| | | 1 | 36 |

If necessary to change small time gear add 45 minutes to this time, two men doing the job.

# CHAPTER IX
# Installing New Camshaft Bearings

Fig. 280                    Fig. 281

**472**   Lift off hood.

**473**   Remove radiator and fan as described in Pars. 14 and 16. Remove commutator, cylinder front cover and large time gear, as described in Pars. 454, 455 and 457. Remove carburetor pull and adjusting rods and hot air pipe as described in "D" Par. 458. Remove cylinder valve cover and gasket as described in Par. 363. Remove generator and generator bracket as described in Pars. 448 and 449.

**474**   Run out the two camshaft bearing set screws (See "A" Fig. 280).

**475**   Lift up push rods by inserting a valve lifter under valve seat pins (See Fig. 281). While valve is held up push rod can be raised with fingers until hole in rod is exposed. A pin is then inserted into the hole in each push rod (8d nails with the points filed off can be used for this purpose) and valve stems are allowed to rest on push rods as shown in Fig. 282.

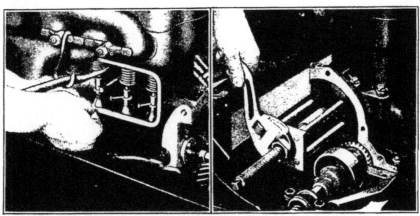

Fig. 282                    Fig. 283

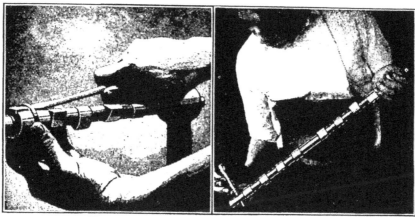

Fig. 284          Fig. 285

**476**  Withdraw camshaft from cylinder block with a puller (See Fig. 283).

**477**  Remove bearings from camshaft by inserting a screw driver under the circular springs which hold bearings to shaft, and prying off springs (See Fig. 284).

**478**  Before installing new bearings, check camshaft for wear, and alignment.  The shaft can be checked for wear by measuring the bearings (See Fig. 285), with a pair of micrometers the diameter of the bearings on the shaft is .748″.  If they are worn down more than .0025″ a new shaft should be installed.

**479**  The alignment of the camshaft is checked by placing it on centers as shown in Fig. 286.  Before placing shaft on centers inspect center holes in shaft to see that they are free from dirt or burrs. Scrape out any burr or dirt which may be in the center holes, as any foreign matter in the holes is likely to cause the shaft to run out. The amount the shaft runs out is measured by a dial indicator reading in one thousandths of an inch.  A ball point plunger rests on the bearings to be indicated; the shaft is then slowly turned, while the operator

Fig. 286

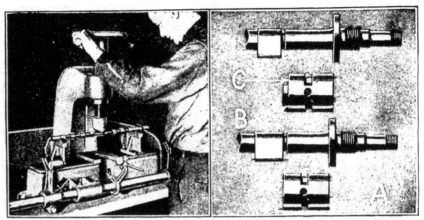

Fig. 287                                   Fig. 288

watches the dial. Any slight variation in the surface of the shaft is noted by the movement of the hand on the dial. The camshaft should run out no more than the limits given in Fig. 286. The high side of the shaft should be noted and the shaft straightened in a press as shown in Fig. 287. When straightening a shaft it is always advisable to first bend it far enough in the opposite direction to which it is bent, so that it will be distorted the other way. The shaft is then brought to normal from this side. This prevents any tendency of the shaft to spring out of line again.

480    After a camshaft has been straightened or when a new shaft is to be installed, the bearings are first positioned on the shaft. The center bearing is assembled to the shaft with the notch in the bearing pointing towards the rear end of camshaft. The front bearing is assembled with the radius on the end of the bearing (See "A" Fig. 288) set towards the front of the shaft. The old style front bearing with the 30° chamfer "B" and notch "C", is always assembled with the notch set towards the rear. This is to allow clearance for the head of push rod.

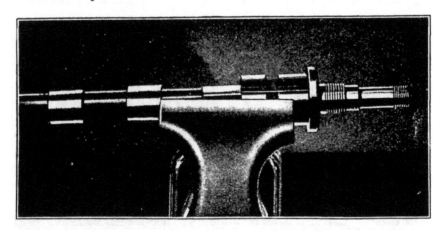

Fig. 289

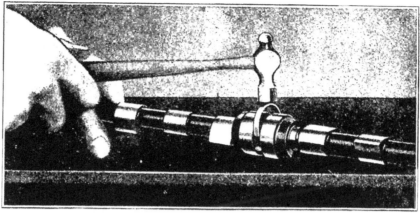

Fig. 290

**481** If the old bearings are to be installed, the fit of the bearings should be checked on the shaft. This can be done by positioning bearings on camshaft and placing shaft in vise (See Fig. 289). There should be very little movement between shaft and front bearing when shaft is moved up and down and back and forth. The front bearing should fit on shaft with not more than .004″ end play and .003″ side play. When placing shaft in vise do not draw vise tighter than is absolutely necessary to hold bearings in position. If camshaft is held tightly in vise it would, of course, be impossible to note any play. The center bearing is checked for side play only and should fit on shaft with not more than .003″ side play.

**482** To assemble the bearings oil and place them in position on the shaft, making sure that the two halves are properly fitted according to the break in the cast iron shell. Place the ring over the center of the bearing and tap it into position with a small hammer, as shown in Fig. 290. Position the two bearings on the shaft so that the set screw holes in bearings (See "A" Fig. 291) line up with the two

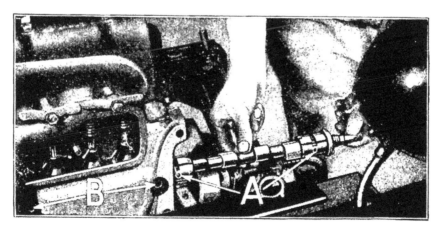

Fig. 291

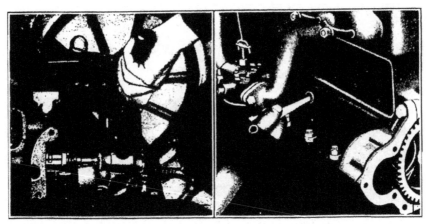

Fig. 292         Fig. 293

cam bearing set screw holes "B" in cylinder block. Insert shaft into engine, driving it into position with a driver and hammer; if a driver is not available a wooden or rawhide mallet can be used (See Fig. 292), taking care not to turn the shaft until the center bearing has started to enter bearing housing in engine; otherwise its position will be lost and it will be impossible to bring the set screw hole in the bearing to line up with the hole in the cylinder block. Drive the shaft in until the front bearing set screw hole lines up with the set screw hole in cylinder. The set screw hole in center bearing will then be at the edge of the set screw hole in the cylinder. As there is a clearance between center bearing and cam, it is impossible to drive bearing entirely into position. It is therefore necessary to insert a drift through the set screw hole in cylinder and draw the bearing into position as shown in Fig. 293. When the holes have been lined up, insert the two camshaft bearing set screws through cylinder block, drawing them down tightly.

483    Replace large time gear as described in "i" Par. 458. Replace generator bracket and generator as described in Par. 450.

484    Withdraw pins from push rods.

485    Replace cylinder valve cover gasket and valve cover, as explained in Par. 377, examining gasket to make sure it is in first-class condition.

486    Install hot air pipe and carburetor pull and adjusting rods as described in Pars. 113 to 115.

487    Install cylinder front cover and commutator as described in Pars. 466 to 469. Install fan and radiator as described in Pars. 127 and 128. Install hood; close drain cock at bottom of radiator and fill radiator with clean water.

488

# Time Study
## Installing New Camshaft Bearings
(One man doing the job)

|   |   | Hrs. | Min. |
|---|---|---|---|
| 1 | Drain water, install car covers, remove radiator.......... |  | 15 |
| 2 | Remove front cover, fan, generator, bracket, and camshaft bearing screws, lift valves and push rods............. |  | 40 |
| 3 | Remove gear and withdraw camshaft................... |  | 8 |
| 4 | Check shaft, fit new bearings, install shaft and gear, run in bearing set screws, lower push rods and valves........ |  | 28 |
| 5 | Install generator bracket, generator, front cover, fan and radiator........................................ |  | 32 |
| 6 | Install hood, fill radiator with water, remove car covers... |  | 8 |
|   |   | 2 | 11 |

# CHAPTER X

# Cleaning the Oil Line

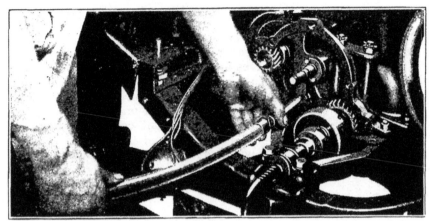

Fig. 294

**489** Lift off hood and remove radiator and fan as described in Pars. 14 and 16. Remove commutator, cylinder front cover and large time gear as described in Pars. 454, 455 and 457.

**490** Place nozzle of air hose in end of oil pipe (See Fig. 294) and blow out any foreign matter which may have accumulated in pipe. If no compressed air is available the feed pipe can be cleaned by forcing a small flexible cable through it.

**491** Turn motor over rapidly with starting crank to see that oil flows in an even stream out end of tube.

**492** Drain the old oil from crankcase and pour in a gallon of new oil.

**493** Replace time gear as described in "i" Par. 458. Replace cylinder front cover gasket and cover and commutator as described in Pars. 466 to 469. Install fan and radiator as described in Pars. 127 and 128. Install hood, close drain cock at bottom of radiator and fill radiator with clean water.

**494**

# Time Study
## Cleaning Oil Line
### (One man doing the job)

|   |   | Hrs. | Min. |
|---|---|---|---|
| 1 | Drain water, install car covers, remove radiator, fan, front cover and time gear | | 32 |
| 2 | Clean oil line, change oil | | 10 |
| 3 | Install gear, front cover, fan, radiator | | 28 |
| 4 | Install hood, fill radiator with water, remove car covers | | 8 |
| | | 1 | 18 |

# CHAPTER XI

# Stopping Oil Leak at Front End
# of Crankshaft

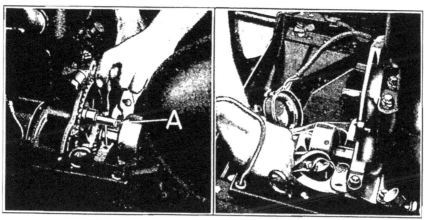

Fig. 295                              Fig. 296

**495**  After a car has been in service for a long period an oil leak will sometimes develop at the front end of the crankcase, due either to the felt gaskets around the crankshaft becoming worn, or if the car has been subjected to exceptionally hard usage, the solder around the crankcase front wall may have loosened.

**496**  To locate the trouble, wipe off all oil from front wall and end of crankshaft (back of pulley), then start the engine and note at which point the leak occurs. If the oil leak occurs around the crankshaft, it will be necessary to install new felt gaskets. If the leak occurs at the crankcase front wall see Par. 498.

**497**  To remove the old gaskets and install new ones, proceed as follows:

(a) Lift off hood and remove radiator and fan as described in Pars. 14 and 16. Remove commutator and cylinder front cover as described in Pars. 454 and 455.

(b) Loosen felt in crankcase by running a small screw driver around edges of felt and withdrawing it with a pair of pliers (See "A" Fig. 295). Felt in cylinder front cover can be removed in the same way.

(c) To install a new felt in crankcase, twist a piece of wire around one end of felt. Insert wire underneath crankshaft; grasp ends of wire with a pair of pliers (See Fig. 296) and pull felt into position.

(d) A new felt can be installed in cylinder front cover by positioning it in recess in cover and pressing it down tightly in cover with a screw driver.

(e) Cylinder front cover gasket, cover and commutator are replaced as described in Pars. 466 to 469. Replace fan and radiator as described in Pars. 127 and 128. Install hood; close drain cock at bottom of radiator and fill radiator with clean water.

498   If the oil leak occurs around the front wall, it will be necessary to solder the wall. To stop an oil leak around the front wall of the crankcase; lift off hood and remove radiator and fan as described in Pars. 14 and 16. Remove starting crank and fan drive pulley as explained in "a," "b" and "c," Par. 458. Thoroughly clean the metal around the leak and run on a little solder with a soldering iron. Care should be taken that the soldering iron is not too hot, as it will melt the solder in the seam between crankcase wall and crankcase. After soldering the leak, the fan drive pulley and starting crank are replaced as described in Pars. 461 and 462. The fan and radiator are replaced as described in Pars. 127 and 128. Install hood, close drain cock at bottom of radiator and fill radiator with clean water.

# Time Study

499

## Oil Leak at Front End of Crankshaft

(One man doing the job)

|   |   | Hrs. | Min. |
|---|---|---|---|
| 1 | Drain water, install car covers, remove radiator, fan and front cover. . . . . . . . . . . . . . . . . . . . . . . . . . . . . . . . . . . . . . . . . . . |  | 28 |
| 2 | Change felts in crankcase and cover, install cover, fan and radiator. . . . . . . . . . . . . . . . . . . . . . . . . . . . . . . . . . . . . . . . . . . . |  | 30 |
| 3 | Install hood, fill radiator with water, remove car covers. . . |  | 8 |
|   |   | 1 | 6 |

# Time Study

500

## Oil Leak at Crankcase Front Wall

(One man doing the job)

|   |   | Hrs. | Min. |
|---|---|---|---|
| 1 | Drain water, install car covers, remove radiator, fan and pulley. . . . . . . . . . . . . . . . . . . . . . . . . . . . . . . . . . . . . . . . . . . . |  | 22 |
| 2 | Solder wall, put on pulley, fan and radiator. . . . . . . . . . . . |  | 32 |
| 3 | Install hood, fill radiator with water, remove car covers. . . |  | 8 |
|   |   | 1 | 2 |

# CHAPTER XII
# Replacing Transmission Bands
## (Old Design)

Fig. 297

**501** When transmission band linings become worn to such an extent that their braking efficiency is impaired, the bands should be relined. (If the car is equipped with the new type bands see Par. 532.)

**502** To install new bands (one man doing the job).

**503** Lift off hood.

**504** Disconnect starting motor cable at starting motor (See "C" Fig. 35).

**505** Run out the four motor mounting screws which hold starting motor to transmission cover (See Fig. 297).

**506** Remove mat and floor boards.

**507** Disconnect manifold from exhaust pipe by running off pack nut (See "A" Fig. 30).

**508** Disconnect magneto terminal wire at magneto terminal (See "B" Fig. 30).

**509** Run out the two bolts from universal joint (See "A" Fig. 32).

**510** Run out the 12 bolts and cap screws that hold transmission cover to crankcase (See Fig. 298).

**511** Loosen transmission band adjusting screw (See "A" Fig. 299).

**512** Remove transmission cover door by running out the six screws "B" which hold it to transmission cover.

**513** Raise front end of transmission cover and insert a block of wood approximately 2″ thick between cover and crankcase (See "A" Fig. 300). This permits removal of starting motor and gasket "B" and bendix "C", which can be lifted out as one unit.

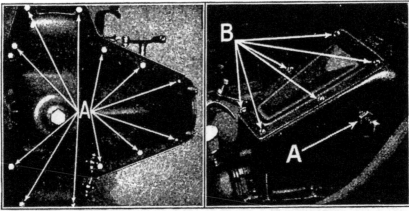

Fig. 298                                    Fig. 299

**514**  Lift off transmission cover (See Fig. 301); bands can now be slipped off of drums.   The reverse band (the band nearest flywheel) is removed first.   The band is positioned over edge of triple gears and turned until the lugs (See "A" Fig. 302) point downward.   The band can then be lifted off drum.   The slow speed and brake bands are removed in the same manner after first positioning them over reverse drum and edge of triple gears.

**515**  When installing new linings in bands much time will be saved by using a brake band riveting machine which cuts off the old rivets and rivets the new linings to the bands (See Fig. 303).   The new linings should be installed so that they conform exactly to the contour of bands and present a true circle to the drums; otherwise an unequal pressure will be exerted on the drums.   Best results will be obtained by soaking the linings in lubricating or Neats foot oil for at least eight hours.   This insures maximum life from the linings and an exceptionally smooth braking effect.

**516**  After the new linings have been riveted in the bands, they should be carefully inspected to see that the ends of the split rivets are

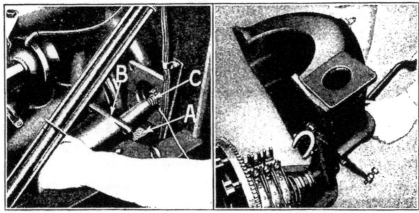

Fig. 300                                    Fig. 301

Fig. 302             Fig. 303

spread and are firmly imbedded in the lining. This prevents any possibility of scoring the transmission drums. The bands are installed one at a time by slipping them over the triple gears and edge of reverse drum, with the lugs downward; while in this position, the band is then turned until the lugs are on top. The first band installed is slipped to the rear (brake) drum; the second band to the center (slow speed) drum; while the third band is positioned on the third (reverse) drum (See Fig. 302). Bands must be turned so that the lugs are on top while the band is positioned over triple gears and edge of reverse drum, as there is not sufficient clearance between transmission drums and crankcase to permit installing the bands at any other point. To facilitate this operation turn flywheel so that one set of the triple gears is approximately 10° to the right or left of top center on flywheel. The bands are temporarily held in place on drums by means of a clip (See "A" Fig. 304).

517 Install transmission cover—

(a) Carefully examine ball cap gasket "B" and the cork and felt transmission cover gaskets "C" and "D" (Fig. 304). Unless these gaskets are in first-class condition they should be replaced with new gaskets; otherwise an oil leak will develop.

(b) If it is necessary to install a gasket on the top half of the ball cap, this can be done by cutting a ball cap gasket in half, and placing one of the halves on the upper section of the ball cap. Line up the holes in the gasket with the holes in the ball cap, making sure that the ends of the gasket extend down to the crankcase.

(c) When installing felt gasket a small piece of candle wicking "E" (Fig. 304) is inserted under end of felt gasket.

(d) Position the block of wood shown at "A" Fig. 300 on crankcase.

(e) Insert clutch release ring (See "A" Fig. 305) into rear groove "B" on clutch shift. Cover is then lowered until it rests on block of wood on crankcase.

(f) Examine motor mounting gasket (See "B" Fig. 300). If it has become hardened or torn install a new gasket.

(g) Run bendix gear back to end of bendix shaft (See "C" Fig. 300).

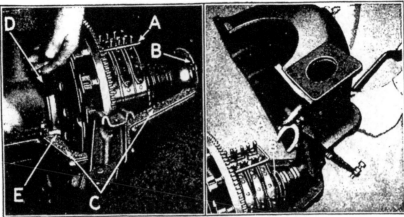

Fig. 304                          Fig. 305

(h) Position starting motor against transmission cover and run down the four motor mounting screws.

(i) Remove wooden block.

**518**  Compress transmission band springs (See "A" Fig. 306) with a screw driver until the springs are positioned between lugs on band with the transmission band washers "B" outside of lugs; the raised point on the washers should point outward so that they will fit into notch "C" on nuts.  Withdraw clip "D" and force the transmission cover down until the cover seats squarely on gaskets.

**519**  To prevent dropping any parts into the engine, it is a good plan to position the door on the transmission cover and run down one of the screws to temporarily hold it in place.  Run down the 12 bolts, cap screws, lockwashers and nuts which hold transmission cover to crankcase. (See Fig. 298).

**520**  Connect magneto terminal wire to terminal post (See "B" Fig. 30).

**521**  Run up exhaust pipe pack nut (See "A" Fig. 30).

**522**  Insert the two bolts in universal joint.  Run down nuts on ends of bolts and lock with cotter key (See "A" Fig. 32).

**523**  Remove transmission cover door, by running out the screw which was used to temporarily hold it in place.

**524**  Adjust low speed band by running in the adjusting screw (See "A" Fig. 307) on outside of cover and running down lock nut "B" tightly against cover.

**525**  The brake and reverse pedals are adjusted by tightening adjusting nuts "C" on pedal shaft.

**526**  After adjusting, examine bands to make sure they are not adjusted too tightly so that they drag on drums when pedals are released.  When bands drag on drums it causes premature wear of the linings and exerts a braking effect on the drums, which tends to overheat the engine.  The correct procedure is to adjust the bands as loose-

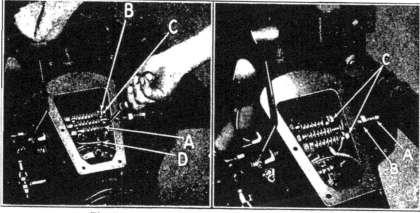

Fig. 306          Fig. 307

ly as possible without causing them to slip on the drums, then after the car has been driven for one or two days, tighten the adjustment.

**527** The transmission cover door and gasket can now be installed by running in the six screws which hold them to transmission cover (See "B" Fig. 299).

**528** Install floor boards and mat.

**529** Connect switch to motor cable at starting motor (See "C" Fig. 35).

**530** Install hood.

**531**

# Time Study

## Changing Bands (old design)

### (One man doing the job)

| | | Hrs. | Min. |
|---|---|---|---|
| 1 | Install car covers, lift out mat and floor boards, run off exhaust pipe nut, disconnect magneto wire............ | | 11 |
| 2 | Disconnect starter cable and run out starter screws, run out transmission cover bolts and screws and remove starter.. | | 25 |
| 3 | Lift off transmission cover, remove bands, clean off old gaskets................................... | | 10 |
| 4 | Install new bands and gaskets........................... | | 10 |
| 5 | Replace cover and starter, and run in bolts and screws.... | | 34 |
| 6 | Adjust bands, put on cover door....................... | | 8 |
| 7 | Connect magneto wire, run on exhaust pipe nut, put in floor boards and mat, and test for oil leaks and adjustment on bands................................... | | 15 |
| | | 1 | 53 |

# CHAPTER XIII

# Installing New Type Transmission Bands

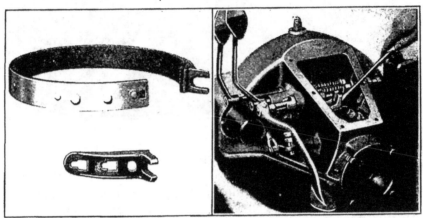

Fig. 308                     Fig. 309

**532**    The new type transmission band with detachable ear, shown in Fig. 308, considerably simplifies the work of changing bands and at the same time reduces the cost of operation. It is unnecessary to remove the transmission cover to change this type band as all of the operations can be performed through the transmission cover door.

**533**    Fig. 308 shows the band with the lug removed. The lug is held in place by means of studs in the band which protrude through the slots in the lug, the shoulder of the lug snapping over the end of the brake band and holding it securely in place.

**534**    To remove the lug, simply insert a tool through the end of the lug into the square hole in end of brake band, lift up on the tool forcing the brake band down and the lug back (See Fig. 309).

**535**    To remove the new type bands, remove transmission cover door (See "B" Fig. 299). Run off the nuts and lockwashers from the ends of the pedal shafts, run out slow speed adjusting screw and remove the springs.

**536**    "EXTREME CARE SHOULD BE EXERCISED TO PREVENT DROPPING ANY PARTS INTO THE TRANSMISSION."

**537**    The reverse pedal and brake pedal should then be pulled out as far as they will conveniently go (See Fig. 309) and the lugs removed as explained in Par. 534. The bands can then be withdrawn from the right side (See Fig. 310), permitting them to follow close to the cover to prevent their being distorted.

**538**    To replace the bands, insert end of band from which lug has been removed into right side of the transmission (See Fig. 311), forcing the band around until it is possible to reach the square hole with the hooked tool shown in Fig. 315. When the end of the band has

Fig. 310                    Fig. 311

been pulled around as explained above, the lug can be slipped over the stud and forced back into the locked position; if necessary it can be forced back with the hooked tool as shown in Fig. 312.

**539** The first band replaced should be positioned over the first or reverse drum; the second over the brake drum and the third band over the slow speed drum.

**540** The springs are then slipped over the ends of the shafts and the lugs drawn into place, holding them against the compression of the spring with the hooked tool as shown in Fig. 313.

**541** The lockwashers and nuts may then be replaced and the bands adjusted as outlined in Pars. 524 to 526.

**542** It is important that the lockwasher be assembled to the shaft with raised point on the washer facing out so as to engage with the slots in the nuts as shown in Fig. 306.

**543** To install the new type bands in a car which is equipped with the old type bands. It is necessary to remove the transmission cover and

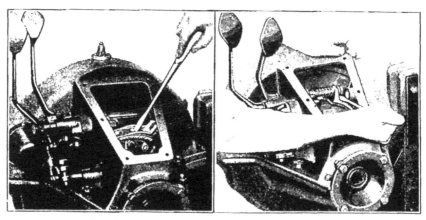

Fig. 312                    Fig. 313

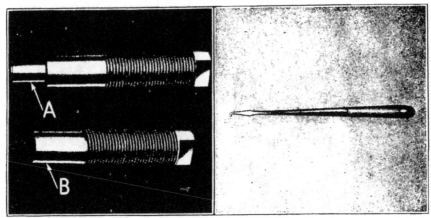

Fig. 314                              Fig. 315

bands as described in chapter **XII**. While it is possible to remove the old bands without removing transmission cover, it is very likely to cause trouble to the owner at a later date, as the slow speed shaft must be sawed off about ⅞" from the shoulder and unless the cover is removed, there is a possibility of the steel cuttings falling into the transmission case and shorting the magneto.

544    A new type slow speed adjusting screw (See "A" Fig. 314) must be installed with the new type bands in place of the old type adjusting screw "B". With the exception of sawing off the slow speed shaft, the first installation of these bands should be performed in the same manner as the old type.

545    The only special tool actually required is the one shown in Fig. 315. It is made by bending over the end of a screw driver approximately one quarter of an inch and can easily be made in the dealer's shop.

546

# Time Study
## Changing Bands (New Design)

(One man doing the job)

|   |   | Hrs. | Min. |
|---|---|---|---|
| 1 | Install car covers, lift out mat and floor boards, remove transmission cover door | | 8 |
| 2 | Remove adjusting screw, adjusting nuts and washers, remove springs and pedals | | 10 |
| 3 | Remove bands and install new bands | | 10 |
| 4 | Connect pedals, adjust bands, install transmission cover door, floor boards and mat, remove car covers | | 12 |
|   |   | 0 | 40 |

# CHAPTER XIV
# Replacing Transmission Clutch Spring

Fig. 316

**547** Lift up rear end of car with chain falls and lifting hooks (See Fig. 364).

**548** Remove the two rear spring hangers by running off the four spring hanger nuts "B" and lifting off the two spring hanger bars "C" (Fig. 364). If hangers cannot be withdrawn readily they can be removed by tapping them with a hammer and drift.

**549** Break wire and run out the two universal joint bolts and two cap screws (See Fig. 32). Disconnect brake rods from control shaft (See Fig. 52).

**550** Axle assembly can now be disconnected from transmission by withdrawing the assembly and lowering drive shaft tube onto a horse (See "A" Fig. 316).

**551** Run out the six transmission cover door screws and lift off door. (See "B" Fig. 299).

**552** Withdraw ball cap from end of drive plate shaft. (See "B" Fig. 316).

**553** The clutch spring is then compressed by inserting a piece of pipe (an old radiator outlet pipe with a notch cut in the end can be used) over the drive plate shaft, forcing the spring support in and turning it until the clutch spring support pin lines up with holes in spring support; then with a hammer and drift, drive the pin about two thirds of the way out. (The pin should not be driven out any further than this, as it is liable to drop into the crankcase). Turn the engine over one half turn with the starting crank and withdraw the pin with a pair of pliers.

**554** The new clutch spring is installed by positioning clutch spring (See "A" Fig. 317) and clutch spring support "B" over drive plate shaft against clutch shift "C" and lining up the hole in support with hole in drive plate shaft; compress the spring and support with a spring compressor until the pin hole in the drive plate assembly is in line with hole in support. The clutch spring support pin can now be

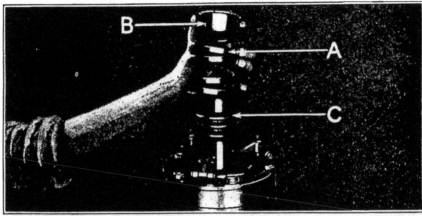

Fig. 317

entered and driven into place with a small hammer and drift. Turn transmission clutch spring and support until pin slips into recess in support.

**555** Replace transmission cover door gasket and door by running down the six screws which hold door in place (See "B" Fig. 299).

**556** Install ball cap front by slipping cap over end of drive plate assembly with oil hole towards top (See "B" Fig. 214). Before installing ball cap make sure that ball cap gasket "A" (Fig. 214) is in place and in good condition.

**557** Insert universal joint into transmission drive plate (See Fig. 85).

**558** Run in the two bolts and the two cap screws which hold ball cap to engine, locking the bolts with cotter keys and the caps crews with wire (See Fig. 32).

**559** Connect rear spring to perches as described in Pars. 663 to 665.

**560** Connect brake rods to control shaft as described in Par. 75.

**561** Install floor boards and mat.

**562**

# Time Study
## Changing Clutch Spring

| | | Hrs. | Min. |
|---|---|---|---|
| 1 | Install car covers, lift out mat and floor boards.......... | | 8 |
| 2 | Raise rear end of car, disconnect axle................... | | 15 |
| 3 | Remove transmission cover door and lift out ball cap..... | | 4 |
| 4 | Compress clutch spring, drive out pin, change spring, replace pin............................................ | | 10 |
| 5 | Install transmission cover door and ball cap............ | | 5 |
| 6 | Connect axle to car.................................... | | 15 |
| 7 | Install floor boards and mat, remove car covers.......... | | 5 |
| | | 1 | 2 |

With the exception of changing clutch spring and connecting axle, in which two men are used, all of the above operations are performed by one man.

# CHAPTER XV

# Overhauling Rear Axle

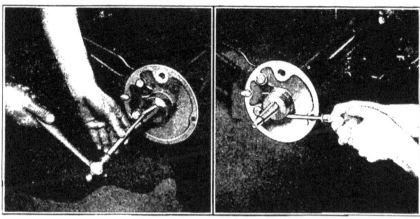

Fig. 318                                    Fig. 319

**563**  Remove rear axle as described in Pars. 34-56-57.

**564**  Place axle on axle stand.

**565**  Remove hub key by driving it out of keyway with a small hammer and drift (See Fig. 318).  Remove felt retainer by inserting a screw driver between retainer and housing and prying retainer off of housing (See Fig. 319).

**566**  Remove drive shaft by running off the two radius rod nuts from ends of rods (See "A" Fig. 320) and running out the six drive shaft roller bearing housing cap screws "B".  Drive shaft can now be lifted from axle housing as shown in Fig. 321.

**567**  Run off nuts on ends of the seven axle housing bolts and withdraw bolts (See Fig. 322).

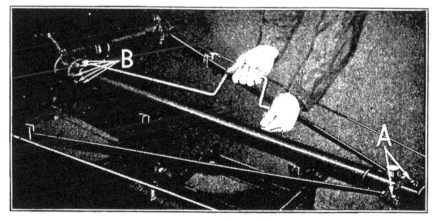

Fig. 320

Fig. 321

**568** Axle housings together with radius and brake rods and outer roller bearings can now be withdrawn as one unit from axle shafts (See Fig. 323).

Fig. 322

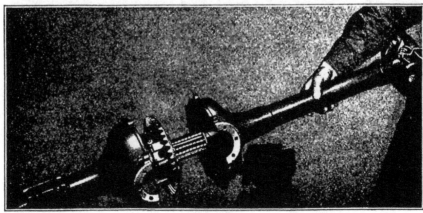

Fig. 323

Fig. 324

**569** Inner roller bearing (See "A" Fig. 324) differential thrust plates "B" and thrust washer "C" can be removed from each axle shaft by slipping them off over ends of shafts.

**570** Break wire and run out the 10 differential drive gear cap screws (See "A" Fig. 325). Break wire and run off nuts from ends of the three differential case bolts "B". The right and left differential cases can now be separated (See "A" Fig. 326) and the differential spider "B", pinion gears "C" and washer "D" lifted out. Differential cases right and left can then be withdrawn from axle shafts.

**571** Remove differential drive gear from differential case—left by tapping back of gear with a copper hammer (See Fig. 327).

**572** Remove inner and outer roller bearing sleeves from axle housings with a sleeve puller (See Fig. 328).

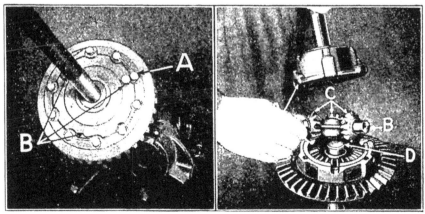

Fig. 325          Fig. 326

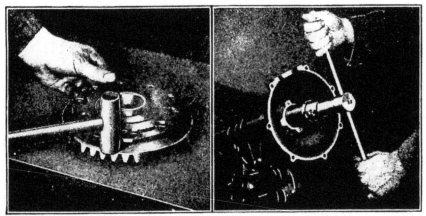

Fig. 327　　　　　　　　　　　Fig. 328

**573** Disconnect brake rod by removing cotter key and withdrawing clevis pin (See "A" Fig. 329). Remove radius rods by running off the two radius rod bolt nuts "B" and withdrawing bolts.

**574** If new axle shafts are to be installed the differential gears can be removed from the old shaft by positioning the gear into a gear support in arbor press and forcing the shaft down until the gear clears the lock ring. The shaft is then reversed and lock rings (See "A" Fig. 330) lifted out of recess in end of shaft, and the shaft pressed through gear.

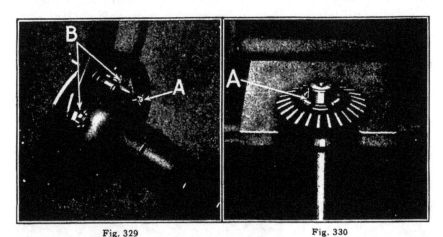

Fig. 329　　　　　　　　　　　Fig. 330

## Disassembling Drive Shaft

**575** Run out grease cup (See "A" Fig. 331) and the two joint housing plugs "B".

**576** Turn universal joint until ends of universal joint pin line up with holes in housing. Pin can then be driven out with a hammer and drift (See "A" Fig. 332), and the universal joint "B" withdrawn from end of drive shaft.

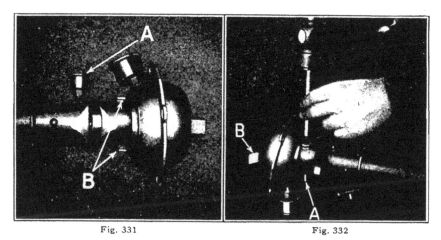

Fig. 331        Fig. 332

**577** Drive shaft, drive shaft pinion, thrust bearing assembly, roller bearing and bearing housing (See "A" Fig. 333) can then be withdrawn from drive shaft tubing.

Fig. 333

Fig. 334        Fig. 335

Fig. 336

**578** Withdraw cotter key and run off drive shaft castle nut (See "A" Fig. 334). Drive shaft pinion can then be withdrawn from shaft by means of a puller (See Fig. 335).

**579** Withdraw roller bearing and bearing housing from shaft (See Fig. 336).

**580** Remove drive shaft pinion key (See "A" Fig. 337) and withdraw drive shaft sleeve "B". The thrust ball retainer assembly and the two thrust bearing collars "C" can then be slipped off end of drive shaft. The drive shaft sleeve is withdrawn with a sleeve puller as shown in Fig. 338.

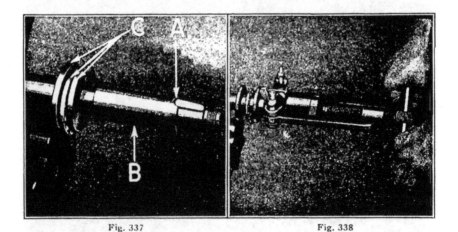

Fig. 337                    Fig. 338

**581** Remove drive shaft housing front bushing from housing with a puller as shown in Fig. 339.

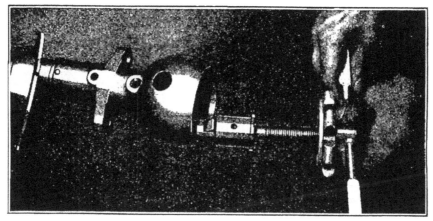

Fig. 339

## Assembling the Drive Shaft

**582**  Clean and examine all parts thoroughly.

**583**  Install drive shaft housing front bushing by driving it into the housing with a driver as shown in **Fig. 340**, making sure that the oil groove in the bushing is in line with the grease cup hole in drive shaft tubing.  As the greatest wear on the drive shaft assembly is on

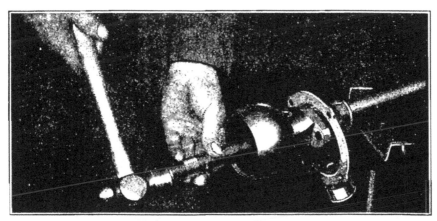

Fig. 340

this bushing, it is usually advisable to install a new front bushing when overhauling a rear axle assembly.  When a new bushing is installed, it is necessary to drill an oil hole in one side of the bushing through the grease cup hole in the drive shaft tubing (See Fig. 341); the bushing is then reamed and faced to fit the drive shaft with a .002 to .003" clearance.  This can be done with a combination reaming and facing tool (See Fig. 342). Remove any cuttings which remain in the housing.  Compressed air can be used for this purpose.

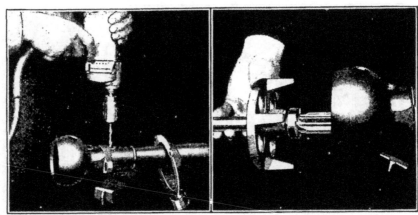

Fig. 341                    Fig. 342

**584**  Inspect the two drive shaft ball thrust collars and ball retainer. If the collars or ball bearings are cracked or chipped, new parts should be installed. Examine drive shaft to make sure shaft has not been sprung or that keyway or tapered end of shaft is not badly worn. If shaft is slightly sprung it can be straightened on a press. If badly sprung or the keyway or tapered end of shaft is badly worn a new shaft should be installed.

**585**  Place ball retainer between the two drive shaft ball thrust collars and insert retainer and collars over end of drive shaft (See "A" Fig. 343).

**586**  Inspect drive shaft sleeve for wear also examine it closely for cracks. If sleeve is O. K. press it onto drive shaft, as shown at "B" lining up the slot in the sleeve with the keyway in the shaft. The sleeve is pressed onto shaft sufficiently far to permit drive shaft pinion being drawn down tightly on tapered end of shaft. Install pinion key "C" into keyway in drive shaft, making sure that key is firmly seated in keyway.

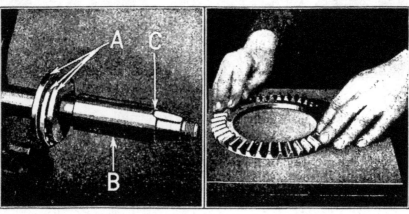

Fig. 343                    Fig. 344

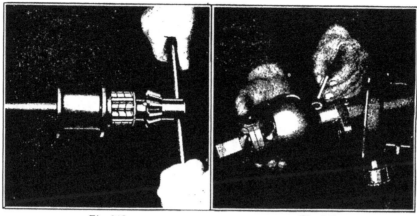

Fig. 345                    Fig. 346

**587** Inspect the drive shaft roller bearing for cracks and pits. As the bearings wear very slowly, it is seldom they need to be replaced for being undersize. If cracked, pitted, or badly worn a new bearing should be installed. If O. K. grease bearing and insert it over end of sleeve.

**588** Inspect bearing housing for cracks or pits. If cracked or pitted, install a new housing. If O. K. place bearing housing over top of bearing.

**589** Inspect differential drive gear for worn or chipped teeth. Check gear on a surface plate to see if it is sprung (See Fig. 344). If gear is sprung, teeth badly worn or chipped a new gear should be installed. If a new drive gear is installed, it will be necessary to install a new drive shaft pinion as described in Par. 590.

**590** Examine pinion for wear in keyway and on teeth. If teeth are badly worn or keyway is worn oversize, a new pinion should be installed. To install pinion insert it over tapered end of drive shaft, making sure that key in shaft enters keyway in pinion. The pinion is then drawn tightly on tapered end of shaft, by running on the drive shaft nut and drawing it tightly against pinion (See Fig. 345). The nut is then locked with a cotter key. After pinion is installed the drive shaft tube is positioned on drive shaft.

**591** Examine universal joint, making sure that the knuckles and rivets in joint rings are not loose. If there is over .006″ clearance between knuckles and rings a new universal joint should be installed. To install universal joint, insert joint over square end of drive shaft, forcing it back on shaft until pin hole in joint knuckle lines up with hole in drive shaft. If knuckle cannot be inserted far enough onto shaft to permit the pin holes lining up squarely it will be necessary to face off a little more stock from flange of drive shaft housing front bushing. There should be .002″ to .005″ end play between knuckle and bushing when pin is inserted. When holes have been lined up, insert joint knuckle pin through joint knuckle and drive shaft (See Fig. 346), driving the pin into position with a hammer and drift. The ends of the pin are then riveted through plug holes in universal joint housing (See Fig. 347).

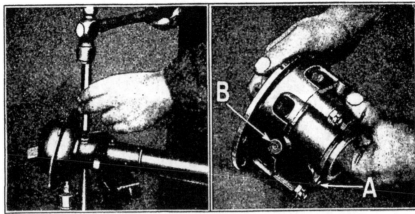

Fig. 347                         Fig. 348

**592**  Insert the two joint housing plugs (See "B" Fig. 331) into drive shaft tube.

**593**  Fill grease cup with grease and screw it into shaft (See "A" Fig. 331), then remove cup, again filling it with grease and screwing it down into shaft.    Drive shaft assembly is now completed.

## Assembling the Differential

**594**  Wash all parts thoroughly.

**595**  Examine axle shaft.  If shaft is badly worn or hub keyway is worn oversize, a new shaft should be installed.  If shaft is slightly sprung, it can be straightened in a press in the same manner as a camshaft is straightened (See Fig. 287).

**596**  Examine differential gears on end of axle shafts.  If gear is cracked, teeth badly worn or chipped, it will be necessary to remove gear from shaft as described in Par. 574.  The new gear is installed by positioning it over end of shaft, lining up the keyway in the gear with the key in shaft.  The gear is then pressed down on shaft sufficiently far to permit lockrings being inserted into grooves in shaft.  The gear is then pressed back on shaft until it fits tightly against lockrings.

**597**  Examine differential case—right and left.  See that web is not cracked, recesses, into which spider fits, are not worn oversize or that the interior of the cases where they come in contact with the gears are not badly worn and that thrust plate pin in cases (See "A" Fig. 348) fits tightly in case.  If pin is badly worn a new pin should be installed.

**598**  Check spider for wear by placing it in recesses in case.  The spider should fit solidly in recesses when cases are bolted together as shown at "B".

**599**  Install differential drive gear.  To install gear, position it over differential case—left lining up bolt holes in gear with bolt holes in case.  Insert the 10 differential drive gear bolts through case and draw them down tightly into gear. The bolts are then wired together, two at a time (See "A" Fig. 325).

600 Examine the differential pinions for wear and chipped teeth. If pinions are O. K. oil and position them over ends of spider.

601 Oil back and hub of differential gears. Insert differential case, right, over end of axle shaft positioning it against differential gear.

602 Install differential case—left on differential gear by inserting case over end of axle shaft positioning it against differential gear.

603 Place axle shaft washer on end of axle shaft (See "D" Fig. 326).

604 Position spider "B", together with differential pinions "C" into differential case—left, meshing the pinions with the differential gear.

605 Position differential case—right on differential case—left as shown at "A" Fig. 326, making sure that pinions mesh with differential gear in case.

606 Insert the three differential case bolts through differential cases running down nuts tightly on ends of bolts.

607 The assembly should now be tested to see that it revolves freely; this can be done by holding one axle shaft stationary in the axle stand and turning the opposite shaft with the hand. If assembly revolves freely, wire the three differential case bolts together (See "A" Fig. 349).

608 Inspect axle housings for cracks, loose rivets in flange and bell. Also check housing to make sure it has not been sprung. If sprung or badly cracked a new housing should be installed. Small cracks can be corrected by welding.

609 Examine both inner and outer roller bearing sleeves for wear. As considerable weight is directed on the outer bearing sleeve, it is subjected to greater wear than the inner sleeve. In an overhaul job it is usually advisable to install a new outer sleeve, unless the old sleeve is in first class condition. The sleeves are made in "rights" and "lefts" and are installed in housings as described in Par. 636, making sure that the raised point on the sleeves fits into hole in housing and that oil holes line up properly.

610 Examine radius rods to see if they are bent or cracked; if badly bent or cracked new rods should be installed. If only slightly bent the rods can be straightened. See that hub brake cam fits snugly in bushing but is not binding.

611 Install radius rods on housing by inserting the radius rod bolts through flange and forked end of radius rod, running down nuts tightly on ends of bolts and locking with cotter keys (See "B" Fig. 329).

612 Connect forked end of brake rod to cam shaft lever by inserting clevis pin through brake rod and lever and locking pin with cotter key (See "A" Fig. 329).

Fig. 349

**613**   Examine the four differential thrust plates and two washers for wear; if O. K. grease the parts and insert a thrust plate over end of each axle shaft, positioning them against differential cases (See "A" Fig. 350), making sure that dowel pin in case enters dowel pin hole in thrust plate.

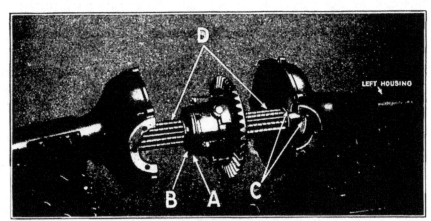

Fig. 350

**614**   Insert a differential thrust washer over ends of each case and position washer against thrust plates as shown at "B".

**615**   Position a thrust plate over the two dowel pins "C" in each housing.

**616**   Inspect roller bearings for cracks and pits as outlined in par. 587. If O. K. lubricate bearings with cup grease and insert a bearing over end of each axle shaft positioning the bearings against differential cases as shown at "D".

**617**   Place a little cup grease on axle case gasket and position it on bell of housing.  Insert housings over end of shafts, making sure that the left housing is placed over shaft on which differential drive gear is assembled (See Fig. 350).

Fig. 351

**618** Insert roller bearing into roller bearing sleeve in each housing, sliding the housings down on the shafts until the bells of the housings come together.

**619** Insert axle housing bolts through housings and run down nuts on ends of bolts (See Fig. 322), but do not tighten nuts until drive shaft assembly is installed. If cases do not fit together tightly do not try to force them into place by drawing up the nuts on the ends of housing bolts, as the trouble is no doubt due to one of the thrust plates slipping off the dowel pins in housings or differential cases, when the housings were installed.

**620** The assembly should now be checked to see that it revolves freely. This can be done by inserting the fingers, or a brass bar through opening in housing where drive shaft assembly is installed and turning the differential drive gear.

**621** Assemble drive shaft to housings:—

(a) Place a radius rod lockwasher over threaded end of radius rods and position it against lock nut which has been run down to end of threads on rods (See "A" Fig. 351).

(b) Place lockwashers over ends of the six drive shaft bearing housing cap screws which hold drive shaft to housing; insert the screws through drive shaft tube flange and bearing housing as shown at "B".

(c) Insert ends of radius rods into universal joint housing.

(d) Insert pinion end of drive shaft assembly "C" into axle housing, meshing pinion with differential drive gear and running down the six drive shaft bearing cap screws into axle housings.

(e) Run down radius rod nuts on ends of radius rods sufficiently far to permit entering cotter keys.

(f) Back up radius rod lock nuts tightly against universal joint housing (See Fig. 320).

(g) Draw down nuts tightly on ends of the seven axle housing bolts.

**622**  Install outer roller bearings, felt retainers and hub keys as outlined in Pars. 637 to 639.

**623**  Place 1½ pounds of high grade gear compound into differential housing.

## Connecting Rear Axle Assembly to Car

**624**  Lift up rear end of car with chain falls and lifting hooks (See Fig. 364).

**625**  Place axle on a rear axle installing truck and position axle underneath car.

**626**  Insert universal joint into transmission drive plate (See Fig. 85).

**627**  Run in the two bolts and two cap screws which connect axle to transmission, locking the bolts with cotter keys and the cap screws with wire (See Fig. 32).

**628**  Connect perches to axle; replace brake shoes; install rear wheels and connect and adjust brake pull rods as described in Pars. 72 to 76.

**629**  Lower car and remove lifting hooks.

**630**

# Time Study
## Rear Axle Overhaul

|   |   | Hrs. | Min. |
|---|---|---|---|
| 1 | Install car covers, lift out mat and floor boards | | 8 |
| 2 | Remove axle from car | | 25 |
| 3 | Overhaul rear axle, including washing and inspecting parts. | 2 | 30 |
| 4 | Connect axle to car | | 20 |
| 5 | Install floor boards and mat, remove car covers | | 5 |
|   |   | 3 | 28 |

With the exception of connecting axle to car, in which two men are used, all of the above operations are performed by one man.

# CHAPTER XVI

# Stopping Oil Leak at Rear Wheel

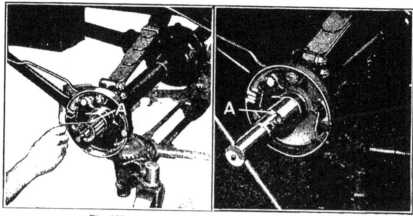

Fig. 352                    Fig. 353

**631** Jack up rear end of car and remove rear wheels as described in Par. 57. Remove hub key by driving it out of keyway with a small hammer and drift (See Fig. 318). With a fine file dress off any rough edges on keyway.

**632** Remove the old felt retainer by forcing it off end of housing with a screw driver. (See Fig. 319).

**633** Withdraw outer roller bearing by inserting a small wire hook over end of bearing; bearing can then be withdrawn from sleeve (See "A" Fig. 352).

**634** Withdraw outer roller bearing sleeve with a sleeve puller (See "A" Fig. 353).

**635** The new retainer is placed over end of axle shaft, with the neck part of retainer pointing towards differential (See Fig. 354). The steel washer (T-197-AR) is then positioned on shaft next to retainer, and washer and retainer driven down to end of machined part of shaft with a hollow driver or piece of pipe.

**636** The roller bearing sleeves are made in rights and lefts. When installing, make sure that the oil hole in sleeve (See "A" Fig. 355) is above slot "B" with the locking point "C" facing outer end of sleeve. To install the sleeve insert it into housing, making sure that the locking point (See "A" Fig. 356) on sleeve enters hole "B" in axle housing. This prevents any possibility of the sleeve turning or slipping in the housing.

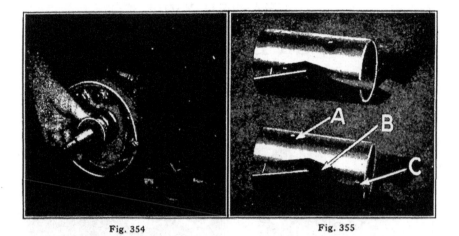

Fig. 354                    Fig. 355

**637** Place cup grease on roller bearing and slide it back in bearing sleeve until it rests against steel washer (See Fig. 357).

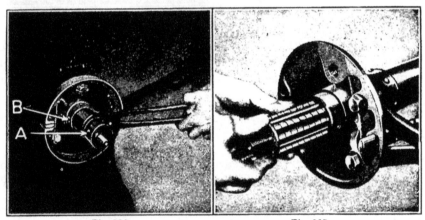

Fig. 356                    Fig. 357

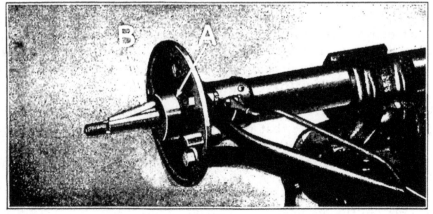

Fig. 358

**638**  Insert felt retainer over end of axle shaft positioning it over end of axle housing (See "A" Fig. 358).

**639**  The hub key is then inserted into keyway on axle shaft as shown at "B" and is forced into keyway by tapping it with a small hammer. When installing hub key the tapered end of the key should point toward axle housing as shown at "B".

**640**  Install wheel as outlined in Pars. 74 and 76, making sure that hub felt is in place on hub.

**641**

# Time Study
## Oil Leak at Rear Wheel

(One man doing the job)

|  |  | Hrs. | Min. |
|---|---|---|---|
| 1 | Install car covers | | 5 |
| 2 | Run off hub cap and axle shaft nut, lift car, remove wheel, remove hub key, felt retainer, roller bearing and sleeve | | 20 |
| 3 | Install oil retainer, sleeve, roller bearing, felt retainer, hub key and wheel; tighten axle shaft nut, put on hub cap, lower car, remove car covers | | 25 |
| | | | 50 |

# CHAPTER XVII

# Changing Rear Radius Rods

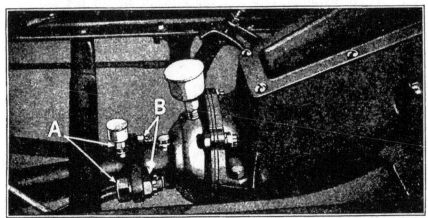

Fig. 359

## Removing Radius Rods

**642**  Loosen radius rod lock nuts (See "A" Fig. 359).

**643**  Remove cotter pin and run off the two radius rod nuts "B".

**644**  Remove rear wheel as described in Par. 57.

**645**  Remove brake rod from hub camshaft lever by withdrawing cotter key (See "A" Fig. 360) from clevis pin "B" and withdrawing clevis pin.

**646**  Run off nut "C" on brake rod support bolt and withdraw bolt. Brake rod support "D" together with brake rod can be lifted off of radius rod.

Fig. 360

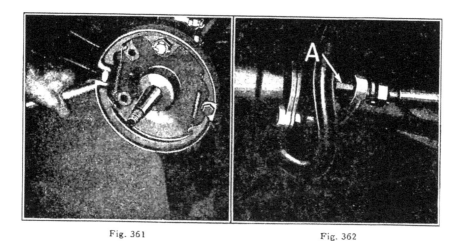

Fig. 361                                   Fig. 362

**647**  Run off nuts on ends of the two radius rod bolts (See "B" Fig. 329) and withdraw bolts from axle housing.

**648**  In order to remove the forked end of the radius rod, it is necessary to turn the hub camshaft lever in a horizontal position with the end of the lever pointing to the rear of the car.  When this is done, the cam assumes a vertical position as shown in Fig. 361.
Radius rod can now be removed.

## Installing Rear Radius Rod

**649**  Run down lock nut to end of thread on radius rods and position a lock washer over end of each rod next to lock nut and insert end of radius rod through universal joint housing as shown at "A" Fig. 362.

**650**  Insert the two radius rod bolts through axle housing plate and install forked end of radius rod over ends of bolts.  Run down the two radius rod bolt nuts (See "A" Fig. 363) and lock with cotter keys.

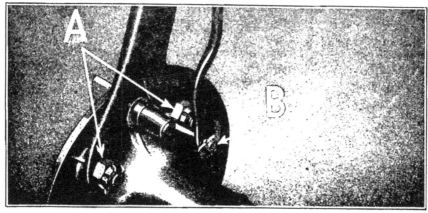

Fig. 363

**651** Turn hub camshaft lever to a vertical position (See Fig. 361).

**652** Run down radius rod castle nut sufficiently far to permit entering cotter pin (See "B" Fig. 359). This assures correct alignment of rear axle. Draw down radius rod lock nuts tightly against universal joint housing (See "A" Fig. 359).

**653** Install brake rod support (See "D" Fig. 360) on radius rod, approximately 18" from bolt holes in forked end of radius rod.

**654** Position forked end of brake rod on camshaft lever. Insert clevis pin and lock with cotter key (See "B" Fig. 360).

**655** Install rear wheel as outlined in Pars. 74 and 76.

**656**

# Time Study
## Changing Rear Radius Rod

(One man doing the job)

|  |  | Hrs. | Min. |
|---|---|---|---|
| 1 | Install car covers, lift out mat and floor boards, run off radius rod nut........................................ |  | 10 |
| 2 | Lift rear end of car, remove wheel, remove brake rod and support, remove radius rod bolts and radius rod........ |  | 20 |
| 3 | Install radius rod, install bolts and tighten nuts, run down radius rod nut, tighten lock nut, install floor boards and mat............................................. |  | 18 |
| 4 | Install brake rod, rear wheel and lower car, remove car covers.......................................... |  | 12 |
|  |  | 1 | 0 |

# CHAPTER XVIII

# Changing Rear Spring

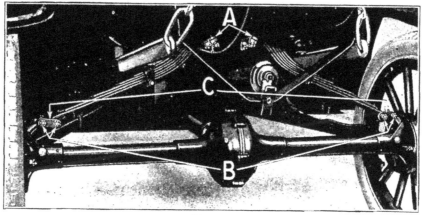

Fig. 364

## Removing Rear Spring From Car

**657** Lift up rear end of car with chain falls and lifting hooks (See Fig. 364).

**658** Run off the four nuts on the ends of the two spring clips and remove spring clip bars "A".

**659** Run off the four nuts "B" on ends of spring hangers lifting off the spring hanger bars "C" and drive the hangers out of spring and perches as shown at "A" Fig. 365.

**660** Spring can now be removed from cross member by tapping the spring with a brass or lead hammer. If spring fits tightly in cross member, it can be pried out with a pinch bar.

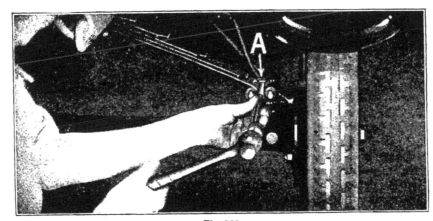

Fig. 365

Fig. 366

## Installing Rear Spring

**661**   Insert spring into rear cross member making sure that head of tie bolt enters the hole in rear cross member (See Fig. 66).

**662**   Insert the two spring clip bars over ends of spring clips and run down the four nuts which hold them in place, locking three of the nuts with cotter keys and the fourth nut with the wire on the tail lamp bushing assembly (See "B" Fig. 67).

**663**   Connect rear spring to perches by inserting hanger through end of spring and perch slipping spring hanger bar over ends of hanger and running down the two nuts which hold it in place.   Lock the nuts with cotter keys.

**664**   To facilitate lining up spring with perch so that hanger on opposite side can be installed a block of wood is placed under each end of the spring allowing the weight of the car to rest on the blocks (See "A" Fig. 366).

**665**   Remove blocks from underneath springs, lower car and remove lifting hooks.

**666**

# Time Study
## Changing Rear Spring

(One man doing the job)

|   |   | Hrs. | Min. |
|---|---|---|---|
| 1 | Install car covers. . . . . . . . . . . . . . . . . . . . . . . . . . . . . . . . . . . . . . . . |   | 5 |
| 2 | Lift rear end of car, run off spring hanger nuts and remove hangers. . . . . . . . . . . . . . . . . . . . . . . . . . . . . . . . . . . . . . . . . |   | 12 |
| 3 | Run off spring clip nuts, remove clip bars and spring. . . . . |   | 15 |
| 4 | Install spring, tighten clip nuts. . . . . . . . . . . . . . . . . . . . . . |   | 22 |
| 5 | Connect spring hangers and lower car, remove car covers. . |   | 20 |
|   |   | 1 | 14 |

# CHAPTER XIX

# Front Axle Assembly Overhaul

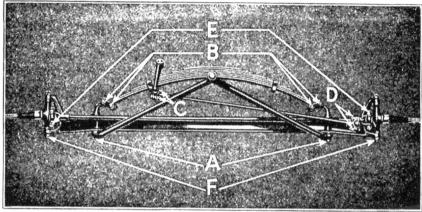

Fig. 367

## Removing Front Axle Assembly from Car

**667** Break wire and run off the two radius rod stud nuts. Radius rod ball cap springs and ball cap can now be withdrawn from studs (See Fig. 37).

**668** Run off nut on end of steering gear post and drive off steering gear ball arm (See Fig. 33).

**669** Raise front end of car with lifting hooks and remove front wheels as described in b, c, and d, Par. 60.

**670** Run off the two nuts from ends of spring clip and lift off license bracket and spring clip bar (See Fig. 59).

**671** Axle can now be removed from car and placed on axle stand.

## Disassembling Axle

**672** Remove radius rod by running off the two spring perch nuts (See "A" Fig. 367) and withdrawing rod from ends of perches.

**673** Remove spring hanger bars by running off the four spring hanger nuts "B" and lifting bars from ends of hangers. Hangers can then be withdrawn from spring and perches.

**674** Remove steering gear ball arm by running out the two ball socket bolts; this is done by loosening nuts "C" on ends of bolts, and holding the nuts stationary while running out the bolts.

**675** Remove steering gear connecting rod by running out the two ball socket bolts "D" in the same manner as those which hold ball arm. The connecting rod and ball socket cap can then be lifted off spindle connecting rod yoke ball.

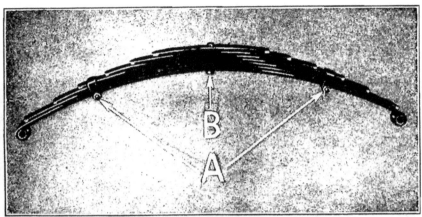

Fig. 368

**676**  Remove spindle connecting rod by running off the nuts on the two spindle connecting rod bolts "E" and running out the bolts. Spindle connecting rod can then be lifted from spindle arms.

**677**  Remove spindles by running off the two nuts "F" on the two spindle bolts and running out the bolts. Spindles can then be withdrawn from axle. If the spring perches have been sprung they can be removed by pressing them out of axle on an arbor press.

## Inspecting and Assembling Axle

**678**  Clean and examine all parts. Check alignment of axle. If slightly sprung the axle can be straightened on a press. If badly sprung or twisted, a new axle should be installed. Examine spindle bolt threads in ends of axle. If threads have been stripped it will be necessary to install a new axle.

**679**  Examine spring for broken or twisted leaves. The spring is disassembled by running off the nuts on the two spring clamp bolts (See "A" Fig. 368) and withdrawing bolts and clamps. The spring is then placed in a vise and the tie bolt nut "B" run off and bolt withdrawn from spring. If spring leaves are cracked, twisted or broken new leaves should be installed.

**680**  Before assembling spring, polish and graphite all leaves.

**681**  The spring leaves are assembled by lining up the bolt holes and inserting the tie bolt through the leaves. The nut is then drawn down tightly on the end of bolt. Position spring clamps over spring and insert clamp bolts through ends of clamps running down nuts on ends of bolts. The spring is held in a vise while performing these operations.

**682**  Examine bushings in spring and perches for wear. If bushings are worn they should be replaced. The old bushings are removed by driving them out with a driver and the new bushings installed by driving them in (See Figs. 377 and 378).

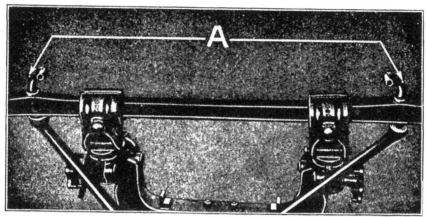

Fig. 369

**683** When installing new bushings, make sure that the oil holes in the bushings line up with the oil holes in spring and perches.

**684** Examine spring hangers and bars for wear. If parts show effects of wear, new parts should be installed. Examine radius rod for being sprung, cracked or badly worn on ball end. If slightly sprung the rod can be straightened. If cracked or the ball is badly worn, a new rod should be installed. If radius rod is O. K. insert spring perches through axle. Perches are made in rights and lefts; in addition to the "T" numbers which are stamped on them, (the right perch is stamped T-274-B; the left perch T-275-B), the perches can also be distinguished by the raised point or boss on the perch. The perches are assembled to the axle with the raised point on the inside edge of the perch (See "A" Fig. 369). Position radius rod over ends of perches, running down the perch nuts with the fingers, but not tightening the nuts until spring and hangers have been assembled.

**685** Assemble spring to perches by inserting the hangers through ends of spring and perches; position spring hanger bars over ends of the hangers and run down and tighten the hanger nuts, locking them with cotter keys (See "B" Fig. 367). Draw spring perch nuts down tightly and lock with cotter keys.

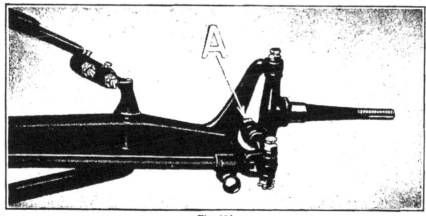

Fig. 370

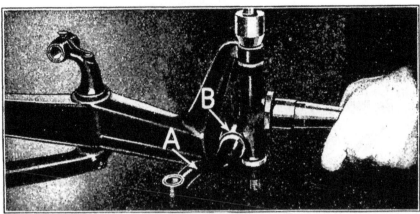

Fig. 371

**686** Examine spindles and spindle arms for alignment and wear. If arm is sprung or badly worn where it fits into spindle, a new arm should be installed. To remove arm from spindle, run off spindle arm nut (See "A" Fig. 370). If the arm cannot be removed from spindle by tapping it with a lead or copper hammer, it should be pressed out on an arbor press. Spindles and spindle arms are made in rights and lefts (the spindle arm right is stamped T-280; spindle arm left is stamped T-281). The arms are assembled to the spindles with the offset in the arm (See "A" Fig. 371) facing up and pointing in. The spindle body is assembled to the axle with the spindle pointing outward and the chamfered side of the arm hole "B" facing rear of car.

**687** If spindles and arms are O. K., examine the spindle and spindle arm bushings for wear. If the bushings are worn, new bushings should be installed. The spindle arm bushings are removed by driving them out of the arms with a bushing driver; the new bushings can then be driven in. The spindle bushings are removed by screwing a bushing extractor into the bushing and tapping the end of the extractor on a wooden block or bench (See Fig. 372). The bushings

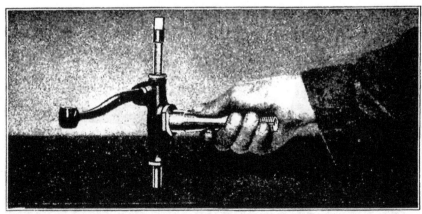

Fig. 372

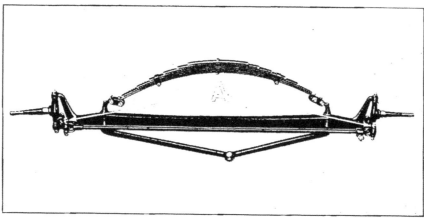

Fig. 373

are then pressed into spindles on an arbor press and line reamed to $\frac{.504}{.504}$ . The ends of the bushings are then faced so that the spindle fits in axle with not more than .002″ clearance.

688 Examine the spindle bolts for wear or stripped threads. If bolts are worn more than .003″ or the threads are stripped, new bolts should be installed. When the old bolts are installed, the oil hole in the bolts should be thoroughly cleaned.

689 Position spindle on axle, oil spindle bolt and insert it through axle and spindle, running the bolt down into lower side of axle (See Fig. 371). The bolt is then drawn down until the correct tightness is obtained; this can be checked by turning the spindle back and forth by hand. A slight resistance should be felt when moving the spindle. When the correct adjustment is obtained run on the spindle bolt nut, drawing it down tightly against axle, and locking the nut with a cotter key.

690 Examine steering gear and spindle connecting rods, yoke, and yoke ball for wear and worn or stripped threads. The rods are also checked for alignment. If parts are worn, or threads stripped, new parts should be installed. If the rods are sprung but otherwise O. K. they can be straightened and used again.

691 Examine spindle connecting rod bolts, if bolts show more than .003″ wear or the threads are stripped the bolts should be replaced; when the old bolts are used, make sure the oil hole in bolt is clear.

692 Position spindle connecting rod over ends of spindle arms with the yoke ball towards right side of axle (See"B" Fig. 373), insert spindle connecting rod bolts, running them down into forked end of rod and yoke, run down nuts on ends of bolts (See "A" Fig. 373) drawing them down tightly and locking with cotter keys.

693 Place a little cup grease in the ball sockets on each end of steering gear connecting rod and assemble rod to yoke ball by placing a ball socket cap over yoke ball (See Fig. 374), and assembling cap to socket by inserting the two bolts through cap and ball socket. When

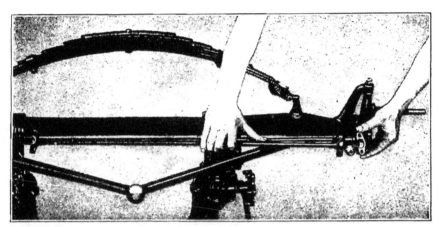

Fig. 374

the bolts have passed through the socket, the nuts can be started on ends of bolts and run down in the same operation. When bolts have been run in and tightened, the nuts are drawn down but not locked with cotter keys until the fit of the ball arm and yoke ball have been checked as described in Par. 694. The steering gear ball arm is then placed in socket on opposite end of rod and the ball cap assembled in the same manner (See Fig. 375).

**694** Check ball arm and yoke ball for being loose in sockets. If loose remove rod and lightly file face of ball socket caps. Care should be exercised not to file too much stock from caps as it will cause the sockets to bind on the spindle connecting rod yoke ball and steering gear ball arm after checking fit of ball arm and yoke ball lock the four ball socket bolt nuts with cotter keys.

Fig. 375

**695** Broken oilers can be withdrawn from oiler holes with a pair of pliers and new oilers installed by tapping them into place with a small hammer.

## Installing Axle Assembly In Car

**696** Place axle on jacks, position spring pad on spring and lower front end of car until spring enters cross member, making sure that head of tie bolt enters hole in front cross member (See Fig. 63). Place spring clip bar and license bracket over ends of spring clip (See Fig. 59), and run down the two spring clip nuts drawing them down tightly and locking with cotter keys. Place a little cup grease in radius rod ball socket and position ball on end of radius rod into socket. Place ball cap and springs over ends of studs, the two stud nuts are then run down on studs and locked by wiring them together as shown at "A" Fig. 379.

**697** Examine key in steering gear post, making sure it fits tightly in keyway (See Fig. 98). Drive steering gear ball arm on end of shaft, run down nut on end of steering gear post, drawing nut down tightly and locking it with a cotter key as shown at "A" Fig. 33. The front wheels are then installed as described in Par. 66.

**698** Lower car and remove lifting hooks.

**699** Front axle and wheels should now be checked for alignment as described in Pars. 146 to 154.

**700**

# Time Study
## Front Axle Overhaul

(One man doing the job)

| | | Hrs. | Min. |
|---|---|---|---|
| 1 | Install car covers | | 5 |
| 2 | Remove front axle from car | | 30 |
| 3 | Overhaul front axle | 1 | 25 |
| 4 | Install front axle, check alignment of wheels and axle, remove car covers | | 35 |
| | | 2 | 35 |

CHAPTER XX

# Changing Front Spring

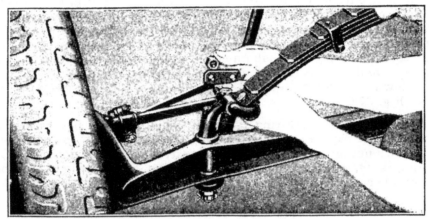

Fig. 376

## Removing Front Spring from Car

**701**  Raise up front end of car with lifting hooks. Run off the two spring hanger nuts from ends of each hanger and lift off hanger bars (See Fig. 376) and withdraw hangers.

**702**  Run off the two nuts from ends of crank case front bearing and spring clip, and remove license bracket and front spring clip bar (See Fig. 59). Front spring can now be removed.

**703**  ## Installing Front Spring

    (a)  Place spring pad over head of tie bolt in spring as shown in Fig. 62.

    (b)  Position spring in front cross member making sure that head of tie bolt enters hole in cross member (See "A" Fig. 63).

**704**  Insert spring clip bar and license bracket over ends of spring clip (See Fig. 59), running down the two spring clip nuts and locking them with cotter keys.

**705**  Insert one of the two spring hangers through perch and end of spring. To facilitate installing the other hanger place a block of wood approximately 2″ thick under each end of spring in the same manner as the rear springs were blocked (See Fig. 366). This will line up spring with perches so that hanger can be readily inserted.

**706**  Position spring hanger bars over ends of hangers and run down the two spring hanger nuts tightly (See Fig. 376) locking the nuts with cotter keys.

**707**  Remove the two blocks of wood from under ends of spring.

**708**  Lower car and remove lifting hooks.

**709**  Check alignment of axle as described in Pars. 147 and 148.

710

# Time Study
## Changing Front Spring
(One man doing the job)

Hrs. Min.

| | | Hrs. | Min. |
|---|---|---|---|
| 1 | Install car covers........................................... | | 5 |
| 2 | Run off spring hangers nuts, lift front end of car, remove hangers................................................ | | 12 |
| 3 | Run off spring clip nuts, remove spring................. | | 10 |
| 4 | Install spring, run on clip nuts......................... | | 15 |
| 5 | Connect hangers, lower, car, remove car covers......... | | 18 |
| | | 1 | 0 |

# CHAPTER XXI

# Rebushing Front Spring and Perches

Fig. 377          Fig. 378

**711**  Lift front end of car and remove spring hanger bars and spring hangers as described in Par. 701.

**712**  Drive spring perch bushings out of spring and perches with a bushing driver (See "A" Fig. 377).

**713**  The new bushings are inserted into spring and perches and driven into place with a driver as shown in Fig. 378. When installing bushings, make sure that oil hole in bushing (See "A" Fig. 378) lines up with oiler "B" in both spring and perches.

**714**  Install spring hangers and spring hanger bars as described in Pars. 705 to 707.

**715**  Lower car and withdraw lifting hooks.

**716**  The rear spring and perches are rebushed in the same manner as the front spring and perches.

**717**  Check alignment of axle as described in Pars. 147 and 148.

**718**

# Time Study

## Rebushing Front Spring and Perches
(One man doing the job)

|   |   | Hrs. | Min. |
|---|---|---|---|
| 1 | Install car covers........................................ | | 5 |
| 2 | Run off spring hanger nuts, lift front end of car, remove hangers................................................ | | 12 |
| 3 | Remove old bushings, install new ones.................. | | 15 |
| 4 | Connect hangers, lower car, remove car covers.......... | | 18 |
|   |   | | — |
|   |   | | 50 |

# CHAPTER XXII

# Changing Front Radius Rods

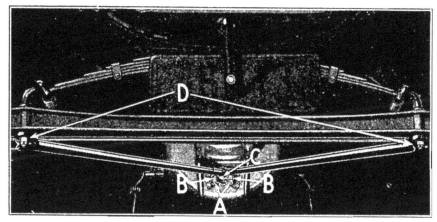

Fig. 379

## Removing Front Radius Rods from Car

**719** Break wire and run off the two radius rod ball cap stud nuts (See "A" Fig. 379), lift off springs "B" and ball cap "C".

**720** Run off the two spring perch nuts "D" on ends of spring perches. Radius rod can now be removed from car.

## Installing Radius Rods

**721** To install the new radius rod, the procedure is reversed. Before installing the new rod, place plenty of cup grease in ball socket.

**722** Check alignment of front axle as described in Pars. 147 and 148.

**723**

# Time Study
## Changing Front Radius Rod
### (One man doing the job)

| | | Hrs. | Min. |
|---|---|---|---|
| 1 | Install car covers | | 5 |
| 2 | Run off perch nuts, remove stud nuts, springs and ball cap | | 12 |
| 3 | Install radius rod, run on perch nuts, put on ball cap, springs, nuts and wire, remove car covers | | 18 |
| | | | 35 |

# CHAPTER XXIII
# Changing Front Axle

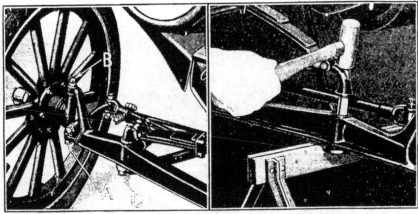

Fig. 380                    Fig. 381

## Removing Axle from Car

**724**  Raise front end of car with lifting hooks. Run off the two spindle bolt nuts (See "A" Fig. 380), and run out spindle body bolts "B".

**725**  Run off spring perch nuts "C" from ends of the two spring perches and withdraw perches by tapping axle with a lead hammer.

## Installing Front Axle

**726**  To install a new front axle, position the axle on horses which are placed underneath car. Insert ends of spring perches into axle, then lower car with the chain falls until weight of car rests on axle and horses (See Fig. 381). Perches can then be seated in axle by tapping them with a lead hammer.

**727**  Insert ends of radius rods over ends of spring perches and run down the spring perch nuts locking them with cotter keys. (See "D" Fig. 379).

**728**  Insert spindle body bolt through axle and spindle (See "B" Fig. 380); run down the threaded end of the bolt as far as possible and install nuts on ends of bolts. Draw nuts down tightly and lock with cotter keys (See "A" Fig. 380). It is very important that the spindle body bolt nuts be drawn down tightly.

    Lower car and remove front end lifting hooks.

**729**  Check alignment of axle as described in Pars. 147 and 148.

**730**

# Time Study
## Changing Front Axle
### (One man doing the job)

| | | Hrs. | Min. |
|---|---|---|---|
| 1 | Install car covers | | 5 |
| 2 | Run off perch nuts, lift front end of car, run out spindle bolts, remove axle | | 30 |
| 3 | Place axle on horses, lower car and connect perches | | 12 |
| 4 | Run in spindle bolts and nuts, check axle, remove car covers | | 24 |
| | | 1 | 11 |

# CHAPTER XXIV

# Replacing Front Hub Bearing Cup and Bearing

Fig. 382                Fig. 383

**731** Jack up car and remove front wheel as described in b, c, and d, Par. 60.

**732** Remove front hub dust cap assembly by driving it out of hub (See Fig. 382). Inside cone and roller assembly can now be lifted out of hub (See "A" Fig. 383). Drive out front hub bearing cup—inner (See "A" Fig. 384). The front hub bearing cup—outer is removed in the same manner.

**733** New bearing cups—inner and outer—are installed by positioning them in hub and forcing the cups into the hub with a cup inserter (See Fig. 385).

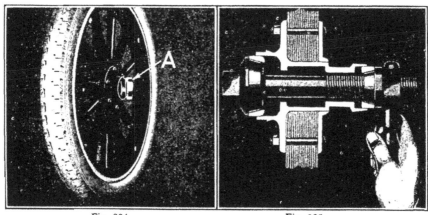

Fig. 384                Fig. 385

**734**    Place a little grease on inside cone and roller assembly and position it into bearing cup—inner. Front hub dust cap assembly is positioned in hub and driven into place with a driver.

**735**    Wheel hub is packed with grease and wheel is installed as outlined in Par. 66.

**736**

# Time Study
## Changing Front Hub Bearing Cups
### (One man doing the job)

|  |  | Hrs. | Min. |
|---|---|---|---|
| 1 | Install car covers | | 5 |
| 2 | Lift front end of car, take off front wheel | | 8 |
| 3 | Remove dust cap, bearing and bearing cups, clean hub and bearings | | 10 |
| 4 | Install new bearing cups, grease hub, put in bearing and dust cap | | 15 |
| 5 | Install and adjust front wheel, remove car covers | | 12 |
| | | | 50 |

# CHAPTER XXV

# Steering Gear Overhaul

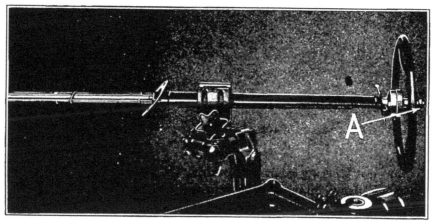

Fig. 386

## Remove Steering Gear from Car

**737**  Run off steering gear post castle nut (See "A" Fig. 33).

**738**  Drive off steering gear ball arm with a brass or lead hammer (See "B" Fig. 33). Steering gear ball arm key can then be withdrawn from keyway in shaft.

**739**  Lift off hood.

**740**  Disconnect carburetor pull rod at throttle rod lever (See "A" Fig. 28).

**741**  Remove cotter key, and disconnect commutator pull rod at lead rod lever (See "B" Fig. 24).

**742**  Drive out lead rod lever pin (See "C" Fig. 33) and slip lever off end of rod.

**743**  Disconnect horn wires at horn and terminal block (See Fig. 218).

**744**  Swing steering gear bracket cap to one side by removing one of the two steering gear bracket bolts and loosening the other bolt. (See "A" Fig. 15).

**745**  Run off nuts on ends of the four steering gear flange screws and withdraw screws from flange (See "B" Fig. 35).

**746**  Steering gear can now be withdrawn through dash.

## Disassembling the Steering Gear

**747**  Run off steering wheel nut (See "A" Fig. 386) and withdraw steering wheel with a wheel puller as shown in Fig. 14.

**748**  Remove steering gear drive pinion key (See "A" Fig. 387) by tapping it out of keyway in shaft with a small hammer and drift.

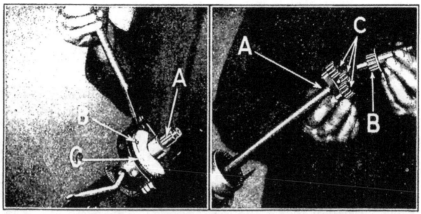

Fig. 387                    Fig. 388

**749** Run out steering gear cover screw "B" and remove steering gear cover "C" from internal gear case with a babbitt lined wrench.

**750** Withdraw steering gear post (See "A" Fig. 388) from steering gear tubing and lift out steering gear drive pinion "B". The three steering gear pinions "C" can then be lifted from pins on steering gear spider.

**751** Remove throttle rod lever by driving out throttle rod lever pin, (See "A" Fig. 389) and slipping lever off over end of rod.

**752** Remove lead and throttle rod guide "B" by slipping it off over ends of throttle and lead rods.

**753** Remove lead and throttle rod springs by compressing springs and withdrawing the two pins "C"; spark and throttle rod collars and springs "D" can then be slipped off over ends of rods.

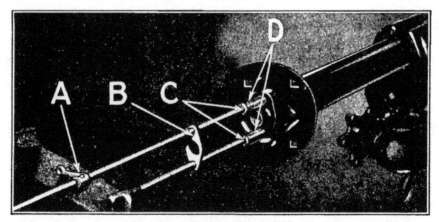

Fig. 389

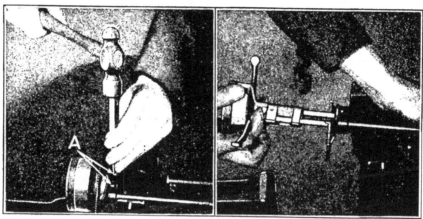

Fig. 390                    Fig. 391

**754**  Drive out the two internal gear case pins (See "A" Fig. 390).

**755**  Steering gear internal gear case and lead and throttle rods can now be withdrawn from steering gear tubing (See Fig. 391).

**756**  Steering gear case is removed from rods by spreading ends of rod guides (See "A" Fig. 392).

**757**  Steering gear is now completely disassembled.

## Assembling Steering Gear

**758**  Before assembling the steering gear, inspect steering gear tube for cracks around internal gear case pin holes.

**759**  Check internal gear case for play between case and steering gear post, by inserting case over end of post. There should not be over .006″ clearance between post and case; examine teeth in case for wear.

**760**  Examine lead and throttle rods for cracks at lever pin holes. If O. K. insert lead and throttle rods into guides in gear case, bending the ends of the guides tightly against rods; gear case and rods are then inserted into steering gear tubing as shown in Fig. 391. (If a new gear case is installed it will be necessary to drill holes into which the two internal gear case pins are inserted.)

**761**  Insert the two internal gear case pins through tubing and case. When replacing pins in an old gear case it is advisable to use No. 2 taper pins (See "A" Fig. 393) as the pin holes in both tubing and case wear slightly oversize and sometimes become enlarged when driving out the old pins.

**762**  Insert the two lead and throttle rod springs over ends of lead and throttle rods positioning springs against end of tubing as shown at "D" Fig. 389. Insert lead and throttle rod collars over ends of rods and position them against springs.

**763**  Compress collars and springs until lead and throttle rod pins can be inserted through rods (See "C" Fig. 389).

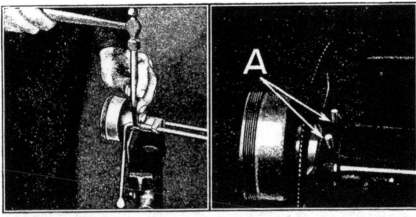

Fig. 392                          Fig. 393

**764**  Position lead and throttle rod guide on rods as shown at "B" Fig. 389.

**765**  Insert throttle rod lever on throttle rod. Line up pin hole in lever with pin hole in rod and insert pin through lever and rod; the ends of the pin are then riveted (See "A" Fig. 389).

**766**  Inspect steering gear post for alignment and wear, also make sure that the three steering gear pinion pins are tight in spider. See that key in tapered end of post fits tightly in keyway. If pin holes or keyway are worn oversize it is advisable to install a new post.

**767**  The post is installed by inserting the tapered end through internal gear case bushing and tubing making sure that pin, which protrudes through spider on steering gear post (See "A" Fig. 394) enters slot in internal gear case (See "A" Fig. 395).

**768**  Inspect steering gear pinions for wear; if pinions are badly worn, replace with new ones.

Fig. 394                          Fig. 395

**769** The pinions are installed by inserting them over the ends of the three pinion pins. The steering gear drive pinion is then inserted into end of steering post and meshed with the three pinions (See Fig. 388).

**770** Pack internal gear case with grease and install steering gear cover on case, drawing the cover down tightly on internal gear case with a babbitt lined wrench. Run down the steering gear cover screw through cover and into case (See Fig. 387).

**771** Insert steering gear drive pinion key into keyway in steering gear drive pinion (See "A" Fig. 116), making sure that key fits tightly in keyway. Position steering wheel on end of steering gear drive pinion, inserting key in pinion into keyway "B" in steering wheel. Force wheel onto pinion with a driver as shown in Fig. 117. Run down and tighten steering wheel nut on end of drive pinion.

## New Design Steering Gear Ratio

**772** Steering gears of "5 to 1" ratio, are now being used as standard equipment in all cars regardless of tire equipment. A new steering wheel, 17 inches in diameter, is also used with the new design steering gears.

**773** The pinions used in the new "5 to 1" steering gear are not interchangeable with the old "4 to 1" design and it is important that mechanics are thoroughly familiar with the difference.

**774** The installation of a "5 to 1" driving pinion in a set of "4 to 1" driving gears would very likely cause a serious accident due to locked gears, as the new style driving pinions are considerably smaller than the old design (See Fig. 396).

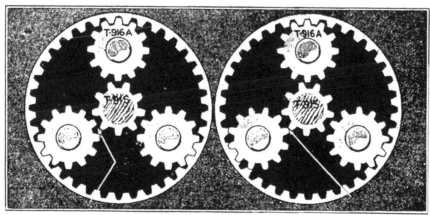

Fig. 396

Incorrect Assembly Dangerous          Locked Gears Dangerous

Fig. 397

Correct Assembly

**775** The steering gear tubing assembly T-3512-C is the only part which is interchangeable in the "4 to 1" and "5 to 1" gear assemblies. The following parts are used with the "4 to 1" ratio only, and must not be used in the "5 to 1" assembly:

    Part No. T-3516-D Steering gear post
           T-3517     Steering gear pinion
           T-3519     Steering gear drive pinion.

**776** The following parts are used in the "5 to 1" ratio only and must not be used in the "4 to 1" ratio assembly:

    Part No. T-3516-E Steering gear post
           T-3517-B Steering gear pinion
           T-3519-B Steering gear drive pinion.

**777** T-3517 the "4 to 1" ratio pinion has 12 teeth; T-3517-B the "5 to 1" ratio pinion has 13 teeth. The "5 to 1" ratio driving pinion has 9 teeth while the "4 to 1" ratio driving pinion has 12 teeth. Precaution should be taken not to mix old and new style pinions.

**778** Fig. 397 shows both the new and old style gears correctly assembled.

## Installing Steering Gear in Car

**779** Insert steering gear post through hole in dash, positioning end of post through steering gear bracket.

**780** Install lead rod lever on lead rod by slipping lever over end cf rod and locking it in position by driving lead rod lever pin through lever and rod. The ends of the pin are then riveted. (See Fig. 96).

**781** Connect steering gear tube flange to dash by inserting the four flange screws through flange and dash and running down lock washers and nuts (See "A" Fig. 99).

**782** Insert horn wires through hole in dash (See "B" Fig. 99). Connect wires to horn and terminal block.

783 Install steering gear bracket cap (See "A" Fig. 15) by running down the two screws which hold cap to bracket.

784 Connect carburetor pull rod to throttle rod lever and install steering gear ball arm key and ball arm as described in Pars. 122 to 124.

785 Connect commutator pull rod to lead rod lever as described in Par. 126.

786 Install hood.

787

# Time Study
## Steering Gear Overhaul

(One man doing the job)

|   |   | Hrs. | Min. |
|---|---|------|------|
| 1 | Remove steering gear from car |  | 15 |
| 2 | Overhaul steering gear | 1 | 0 |
| 3 | Install steering gear in car |  | 20 |
|   |   | 1 | 35 |

# CHAPTER XXVI

# Repairing the Radiator

Fig. 398

**788** Before going into the methods of repairing the radiator, information on the tools, equipment and the process of soldering will be in order.

## The Solder

**789** The first thing to consider is the solder. There are several types used in building the radiator. For repairing, however, only one type need be used. What is known commercially as 50-50 solder is adapted for all repair work and can be obtained from Ford Branches in either wire or bar form, as well as the special washer solder which is used when soldering the headers to the body.

## The Iron

**790** The second consideration is the soldering iron. The soldering iron should be heavy enough to convey sufficient heat to the work. The iron should be tapered to a flat point for getting into the corners. The cleanliness of the iron is most important as the solder cannot be drawn evenly unless the iron is clean. When the iron becomes so dirty that it cannot be cleaned with the sal ammoniac it should be heated and hammered to take out any low spots and the surfaces should be dressed with a fine file. At the factory, we even polish the copper, having found that the smoother the iron the better the work it will do and the longer it will last.

**791** Be careful to file all surfaces squarely as the more surface you have against the work at one time, the quicker the metal will be brought to heat. When the surfaces of the iron have been properly dressed, chamfer the edges to $\frac{1}{32}$ of an inch.

**792** After the iron has been dressed in this manner, it is necessary to "tin" it. This is done by heating the iron, dipping it into acid and rubbing it on a piece of sal ammoniac, at the same time touching a bar of solder to the iron (See Fig. 398). The iron should be turned over from one surface to the other until all sides of the taper are properly coated. Another way is to dip the hot iron into acid for a second and then dip it into a pot of molten solder. This latter method is the best if a pot of solder is available.

793 Solder oxidizes readily in heat; therefore, the iron should never be allowed to become red hot as the coating of solder will burn off. Each time that the iron comes from the fire, it should be dipped for an instant into a solution of water and sal ammoniac. Granulated or powdered sal ammoniac should be used in making this solution. The exact proportion of sal ammoniac to water is unimportant. However, a saturated solution or a solution with an excess of sal ammoniac is preferable. If dipping the iron into the solution does not clean it sufficiently, rub the iron on a block of sal ammoniac and if necessary re-tin it.

## The Torch

794 The torch should be of a type which can give either a concentrated or a flooding flame. The combined gas and air type of torch gives good results. The air must be of low pressure. Care must be taken in using the torch that the metal, particularly the fins, is not subjected to the heat for too long a period as it will cause the metal to burn. To overcome this, the torch should be kept moving. The torch is a very dangerous tool in the hands of a careless or inexperienced workman. The inexperienced man should experiment on a scrap radiator before attempting an actual repair. He will probably experience some of the following troubles.

(a) The pilot light—if one is provided on the torch, may be turned on so full that carbon (soot) is deposited on the material before the solder joint is made. The flame should not be over ½″ long.

(b) The work may be brought to heat so slowly that the acid is dried before the solder runs, which causes a very poor joint, having no holding strength.

(c) The flame may be directed on one part of the metal for too long a time, causing it to burn. Sometimes the metal is completely burned away. At other times a thin skin will be left which will break through under the strain of ordinary road conditions.

## The Acid

795 The acid used at the plant is commercial muriatic cut with zinc. By cut, we mean that zinc is placed in the acid, and left in it until the action (boiling) stops. This acid is used both in cleaning the surface and as a flux in soldering. Do not attempt to keep acid in a metal container. Keep it in a glass bottle or stone crock. A cone-shaped metal top with a hole in it set over the crock will prevent the acid or sal ammoniac solution from flying out when the iron is dipped into it and at the same time protect the operator's eyes and clothes. (See Fig. 398.)

796 The soldering acid should be kept clean; do not use the same container for both cleaning and soldering acid. The crocks should be cleaned once a week. The soldering acid may be poured into the cleaning acid and new acid used for soldering. If too much cleaning acid accumulates, strain the soldering acid through a cloth and use it again as soldering acid.

797 If a large quantity of acid is made at one time it is advisable to store it in a corked bottle as it has a tendency to become weak when exposed to air.

## Miscellaneous

798 A small horsehair brush for applying the acid and another for cleaning, are a necessary part of the equipment. To prevent a leak developing the repairman should guard against hairs coming out of the brush and lodging in the joints.

799 A fiber brush (See tool No. 21, Fig. 403), is used to scrub the parts with water after they have been cleaned with acid.

800 The oven for heating the irons may be obtained from any hardware dealer.

801 The repairman should wear a pair of canvas gloves to protect his hands from burns and the effects of the acid; the gloves should occasionally be rubbed with powdered chalk to absorb the moisture and counteract the acid. When working at the test tank rubber gloves should be worn.

## Soldering

802 Consider that we have two old pieces of metal to be soldered together. The first thing to do is to clean the surfaces of the metal carefully. Any dirt left on the surface has a tendency to expand and will cause a leak in the completed work. To clean the surface, heat it with the torch, dip the acid brush into the acid, and rub the heated surface with the brush. When all dirt is loose, take the parts to the test tank and wash them with a scrubbing brush and water. It is positively essential to have clean surfaces in order to run a seam of solder, and the repairman will save time and perform more efficient work by putting in a little extra time when cleaning the parts.

803 Next fit the two surfaces together. The closer they fit together, the easier the task of soldering and the less solder necessary to run a tight seam. The object of soldering is to hold the surfaces together and not to build up a wall of solder at the edge. It should be borne in mind that solder flows only on well heated surfaces, and that it will not flow up-hill. Fig. 399 shows the improper method of applying the iron. Here the iron is cocked against the edge of one surface, which prevents the solder from flowing between the surfaces and as a result considerable time is lost in running the seam. Fig. 400 shows the correct method. Here the iron is held flat against the upper sur-

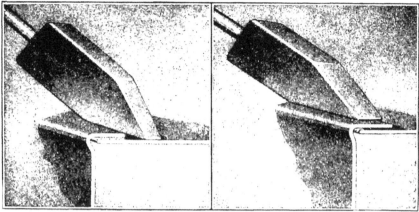

Fig. 399                Fig. 400

faces, transmitting the heat from the heel of the iron to the two surfaces, hence drawing the solder between them and making a strong joint with a minimum amount of solder in the shortest space of time. Always draw the iron so that the heel heats the metal before the point arrives. The point gives a good clean draw to the seam after the heel has warmed the surfaces and flowed the solder.

804   In using the torch, always solder in the direction of the flow of the flame as shown in Fig. 401. The reason for this is two fold. First, it preheats the surfaces saving time in soldering, and, second, it gives the solder a chance to cool after it has flowed into place. Use plenty of acid. Acid applied after the soldering operation is started, while necessary in a number of cases, is never as effective as though enough were put on in the first place. The acid should be used when soldering with the iron, also when soldering with the torch. The iron is used to best advantage in soldering two parallel surfaces. In all other cases the torch is the most efficient.

805   For removing soldered parts, a torch with a flood flame is usually used.

Fig. 401

# Equipment

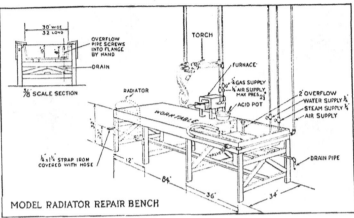

MODEL RADIATOR REPAIR BENCH

Fig. 402

806   The equipment necessary for repairing a radiator, while numerous is not expensive. The largest item of expense is the bench and test tank. The bench and frame for test tank may be built by the repairman and the tank and covering of the bench can be installed by a tinsmith although many service stations have performed their own work. Fig. 402 shows a good arrangement of bench and test tank, giving the necessary dimensions. The work table should be covered with sheet metal and the test tank should be given a coat of white enamel to keep the acid from attacking the metal and to make the water transparent. The steam pipe running into the test tank is for heating the water or if the operator wishes he may work in cold water.

807   **There should be check valves in the gas and air lines to prevent a combustible mixture forming in either of the lines due to unequal pressure. A serious accident may result from neglect of this precautionary measure.**

808   The hose covered strap irons shown at the left can be set to the proper height for the man who is to work on the bench. The radiator may be supported on these brackets as shown, or at any convenient angle. The pipe line leading to the front of the test tank and designated as air supply is used in testing the repaired radiators, a pressure of 5 to 8 lbs. being carried.

809   Fig. 403 shows the tools used in repairing the radiator. They will be referred to as their need arises.

# Index to Fig. 403

1  Dent puller or tube holder.  Can be made by a repairman if a forge is available.

2  12″ Mill file.

Tools 3 to 7 inclusive used in testing the radiator

3  Outlet air connection to which the hose is attached.
4  Outlet test plug.
5  Inlet test plug.
6  Filler flange plug.
7  Inlet air connection.  Screws into petcock hole in the radiator.

8  Scratchall.  Made from $\frac{3}{16}$″ to $\frac{1}{4}$″ stock.

9  Dent puller.  Made from $\frac{3}{16}$″ to $\frac{1}{4}$″ stock.

10  Hacksaw for cutting tubes.  Made by soldering a piece of tube to a broken hacksaw blade.

11  Weight for holding overflow tube down while soldering.

12  Soldering iron.

13  $\frac{1}{4}$″ rat-tail file.

14  10″ square nose pliers.

15  Fin spacer.  Drill and saw out a piece of sheet metal $\frac{3}{16}$″ thick to fit between the tubes.

16  Tube spreader, right angle, made of $\frac{3}{16}$″ to $\frac{1}{4}$″ stock.

17  Tube cleaner, $\frac{1}{8}$″ stock.  Fin spreader, $\frac{1}{4}$″ stock for holes in fin.

18  Acid brush.  Made by inserting horsehair into a copper tube, flattening the tube and trimming the rough ends of the hair.

19  Weaver's pliers.

20  Fin comb.

21  Fiber brush.

22  Tube regulator.

23  Tube cutter—sharpened piece of hacksaw blade on which a handle has been soldered can be used.

24  Rivet bucker.

25  Fin and header bar.  Made of $\frac{1}{2}$″ stock and flattened on the end.

26  Cold chisel.

27  Small tinner's hammer.

28  Acid jar.

29  Sal Ammoniac jar.

30  Radiator block, 8″ square, 4″ deep, made of wood with radius to fit radiator top tank.

31  $\frac{1}{16}$″ punch.

32  8″ shears.

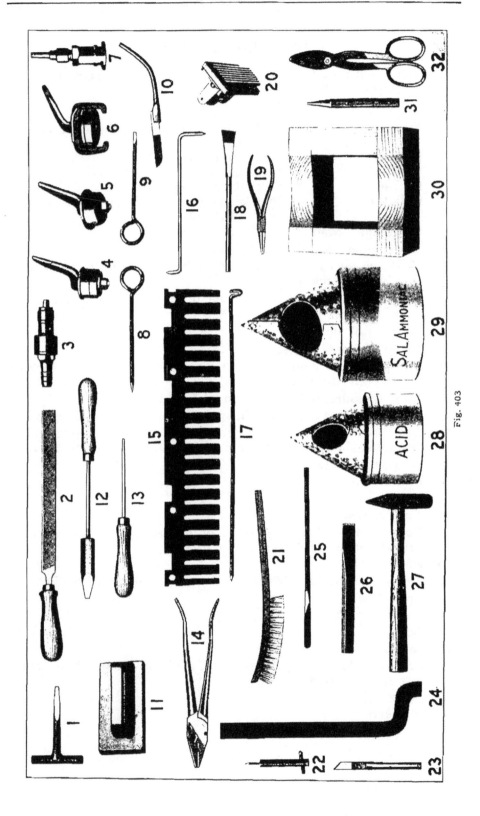

Fig. 403

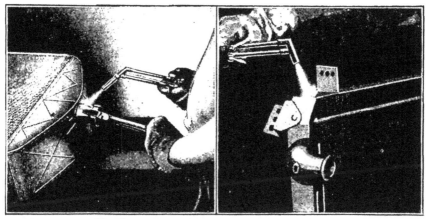

Fig. 404                    Fig. 405

## Removing the Radiator

810   Practically all radiator repairs require the removal of the radiator and shell. To remove the radiator (a) lift off hood. (b) Disconnect priming wire and remove radiator rod and stud nuts as described in "a", "c" and "d" Par. 14. (c) Loosen the cylinder head outlet hose clips and the radiator outlet hose clips (lower). (d) Radiator can now be lifted from car. The radiator shell is removed by running out the four screws which hold shell to radiator.

## Removing and Installing Filler Neck

811   To remove the filler neck of the radiator, cut it out with a chisel as shown in Fig. 404. Melt the solder then spread the neck and pull it off. Clean the old solder from the tank and bend the collar up so that the new filler neck will slip over it. Do not try to bend the metal while it is hot, as it is very brittle at this time.

812   Before positioning filler neck on top tank, dip the base of the filler neck into the acid. Set the filler neck in position on top tank and run in wire solder with the torch until the groove around base of neck is filled.

## Removing Bottom Tank

813   The bottom tank as considered here, will include the tank, reinforcements, and outlet connection. The first thing to do in removing the lower tank is to detach the overflow pipe. The overflow pipe is loosened from the lower tank by heating the solder at the point where pipe is connected to tank. Next, detach the reinforcements from the radiator support. The support and the reinforcements are spot-welded. The welds may be broken by driving a cold chisel between them; if the parts do not come apart readily, they can be heated with the torch. Next heat the surface of the reinforcement attached to the lower tank, brush off the solder and swing the reinforcement out of the way (See Fig. 405). In the same way detach the other reinforcement.

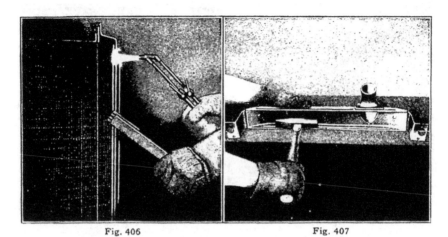

Fig. 406                                           Fig. 407

814    Place the radiator on its side (See Fig. 406) and apply the heat
to the side seam, commencing at the point where outlet connection
is soldered to side seam.   With a brush remove the heated solder
as it flows from the joint.   Do this on all four seams.   When the
joints show that most of the solder has been removed, bring all the
tank to heat at once by moving the torch rapidly over it.   Grasp
the outlet connection with a pair of pliers and remove the tank,
applying heat to any point that may be sticking.

## Replacing Bottom Tank

815    Removing the tank disturbs the solder around the tubes in the
header.   It is therefore advisable to heat the inside of the header,
brush off the old solder and rust and reset the tubes before replacing
the tank (See Fig. 401).

816    The torch should be adjusted to give a full flame of light blue
color, and should be held at such an angle that the flame will cover
from three to four of the five tube rows working from right to left.
Keep the torch moving in a small semi-circle, while the solder, which
is held in the left hand, is touched to the tube to see if it is warm
enough to flow.   As soon as the solder will flow touch each of the
five tubes in the first row with the wire solder, making sure that the
solder flows all the way around each tube.   Be careful not to get the
header too hot as the solder will flow through between the header
and the tubes.   As soon as the first row has been flowed, move on
to the second, watching the flame carefully to see that it does not
melt the solder around the first row to the point where it will flow
through header.

817    In replacing the lower tank, care should be taken that it fits
the header as closely as possible.   Stand the radiator bottom side up
on bench hangers, flare the edges on the header out a little and
spread the tank to fit.   Examine edges of tank to make sure they
are perfectly even.   Any indentations can be removed by tapping
the edges with the flat side of a hammer (See Fig. 407).   Clean

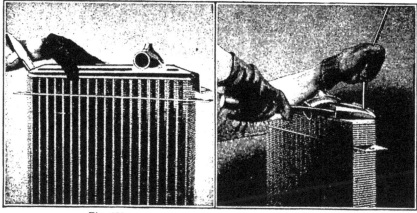

Fig. 408                    Fig. 409

the surfaces to be soldered with heat and acid, and insert the tank into the header. The tank is installed by positioning it on header and tapping down the corners until tank seats squarely on header (See Fig. 408). The joints are then soldered.

**818** First solder the ends, drawing the solder around the corners about ½ to ¾″. The radiator should be placed bottom side up for this operation (See Fig. 409). Next place radiator in a level position and solder both sides where tank and header are joined (See Fig. 410). When soldering around outlet connection a little extra time and care is necessary to make a good joint. It is a good plan to run all around the outlet connection with the iron to insure a tight seam.

**819** Next, stand the radiator bottom side up on the bench hangers shown in Fig. 402, swing the reinforcement into place and solder it to the support (See Fig. 411). When this joint has set, solder it to the tank. To insure a strong joint, flow the solder well under the reinforcement clear down to end of tank.

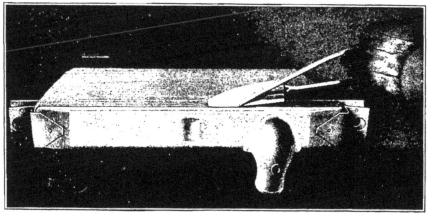

Fig. 410

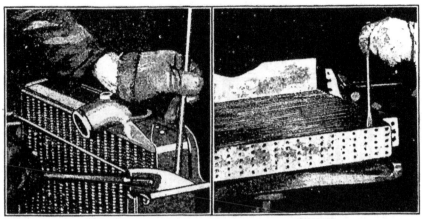

Fig. 411                    Fig. 412

## Removing Bottom Header

820    To remove the bottom header, it is first necessary to remove the bottom tank, as described in Pars. 813 and 814.   The header is removed by heating it and brushing off the solder from around the tubes.   Then heat the header by moving the torch over it rapidly and forcing it off by inserting the fin and header bar (See tool 25, Fig. 403) between header and the first fin (See Fig. 412).

## Replacing Bottom Header

821    Place the radiator on its side.   Heat all the tubes, brushing them with acid; when sufficient heat has been directed on the tubes to melt any solder which may be on or in the tubes, pick up the radiator and give it a quick downward shake to remove the surplus solder.

822    With a tube regulator (See tool 22, Fig. 403) straighten any of the tubes which may be out of line, using a radiator support as a gauge for lining up the tubes (See Fig. 413), draw the tubes into position with the regulator.   When all the tubes fit properly into the support, remove support and position the header.

Fig. 413

823  Place the new header in position, making sure that all the tubes are entering the holes, then tap header into position with a hammer, a tube regulator is used to facilitate entering the tubes through the holes in the header.  The header should be located about $1^{15}/_{16}''$ from the radiator support.  Wipe the tubes and header with acid and set the tubes as explained in Pars. 815 and 816.

## Removing Rear Wall

824  In removing the rear wall, it must be remembered that there are three rivets which hold the water inlet connection to the top tank header.  The rear wall is removed with this inlet assembled to it.  With a chisel, shear the heads from the rivets which hold the inlet connection to the header.  Heat the washer which holds the rear wall to the radiator rod support and remove it.  Clean the solder from the joints by applying heat and brushing off the heated solder.  Then drive the top of the rear wall off the tank to allow sufficient room to insert a rivet-bucker (See tool 24, Fig. 403).

825  Next, heat the water inlet connection at the point where it is soldered to the top header and drive out the rivets with a scratchall (See .tool 8, Fig. 403).  Insert the rivet-bucker through opening already made and buck the top header near the rivet that is being driven out.  When the three rivets have been removed, use the flood flame to heat the lower seam and water connection and pull the rear wall off by grasping the water connection with a pair of pliers.

## Replacing Rear Wall

826  In replacing the rear wall, first heat and brush off all excess solder from both the wall and the edges of the top tank assembly.  Tap out the edges of the tank to insure it fitting closely against rear wall.  Insert three new rivets in the header and tack them in place with a touch of solder on the inside of the tank.  Fit the inlet connection onto the rivets.  If the holes in the connection are too small for the rivets, clean them out with a scratchall (See tool 8, Fig. 403).  Insert the rivet-bucker through the opposite side and peen the rivets (See Fig. 414).  Fit the wall to the assembly and tack it at the ends of the header and at two or three points on the top tank top.  Then solder the washer in place around the radiator rod support.

827  Run the solder seams between the rear wall and the tank with the iron and bar solder.  As the excessive heat applied to the header has a tendency to warp the metal, it is necessary to exercise a little care in soldering the inlet connection and the header, particularly at the point where the header, rear wall and inlet connection come together.  It is good practice to clean the joints between the inlet connection and rear wall and re-run this seam also.

828  If there is too large an opening at any point in the joint, solder the dent puller (See tools 1 or 9, Fig. 403) to the top near the rear wall as shown in Fig. 415.  Using this as a handle, hold the top up

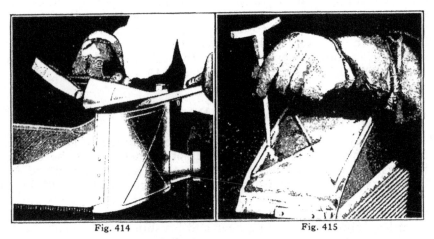

Fig. 414          Fig. 415

to the flange of the rear wall, closing the opening while tacking it with solder at the center of the gap.

## Removing Front Wall

**829**  The top tank of the radiator is so constructed that the front wall slips inside the break on the top header and over the top. To remove the front wall, it is necessary to heat the seams; brush off the excess solder and tap the top of the wall off with the back of the brush or a hammer.

## Replacing Front Wall

**830**  Before replacing the front wall, it is usually necessary to reset the tubes. Clean the tubes in the header with acid and a brush; using an oil can to hold the acid, facilitates the operation (See Fig. 416). The radiator is then set on the bench hangers and solder is flowed on the tubes in the same manner as the bottom header is reset (See Pars. 815 and 816).

Fig. 416

Fig. 417

831  Because the top tank assembly, which is in position, confines the heat, care must be taken not to melt the seams which have been run. Some repairmen lay cloths soaked in water over the tank to help keep it cool.

832  When the tubes have been properly set, the front wall may be assembled. Slip the front wall into position behind the break in the top header. Insert radiator support or any flat straight edge about 2″ or 3″ wide through the opening between the top of the top wall and the tank to hold the wall against the break while soldering the seam with the iron and bar solder. When the solder has set, tack the wall to the top at several points, and flow the seams. A little extra care is necessary to insure a tight joint at the corners of the front wall where the header turns back to meet the top. If necessary use the dent puller as explained in Par. 828.

## Removing Top Tank Top

833  The top tank top can be removed in two ways. The first method is used when the old top tank top is O. K. and is to be used again. The second method is used when the top section of the tank is beyond repair.

## First Method

834  To remove the top by the first method, remove the wall as described in Pars. 824, 825 or 829.

835  Remove the splash plate and the overflow pipe as described in Par. 843. Heat the joints between the top header and wall and brush off the solder as it runs out. Lay the radiator on the table and grasp the open end of the top with a pair of pliers (See Fig. 417). After heating the joints with a flood flame, tap the pliers with a hammer. When one side has started, start the other side. It is then a simple matter to drive the top off.

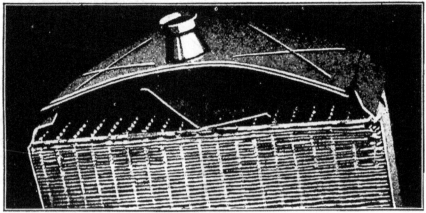

Fig. 418

## Second Method

836  To remove the top tank top by the second method, remove the front or rear wall as described in Pars. 824 or 829. Cut through the top with a hack-saw about one inch above the top and header joint, stopping at the flange of the remaining wall (See Fig. 418). Heat the joint between the top and the wall and brush off the solder as it flows out. Hit the top a sharp blow with a hammer at the corners, formed by cuts, to break it loose under the flange.

837  The top may then be brought to heat and removed by pulling it away from the wall and then raising it off the overflow pipe. As will be noted, it is unnecessary to remove the overflow pipe when this method is used. The two pieces of the top remaining attached to the header can now be removed by flowing out the solder and drawing them out with a pair of pliers.

## Replacing Top Tank Top

### First Method

838  When this method is used, the rear wall is already attached to the header.

839  Brush the excess solder from all the joints and bend the lips of the header out a little to insure room for those of the top. Start the header into the lips of the top tank top and force the top tank top in until it is in position against the wall.

840  The top should then be drawn up to fit the flange of the wall as closely as possible and tacked to it with a little solder on the iron at two or three points. Hold the rivet-bucker or some other piece of bar metal against the inside of the joint formed by the header and the top, and flatten the joint with a hammer as shown in Fig. 419. Flatten the other side in the same way; the top is then ready to solder.

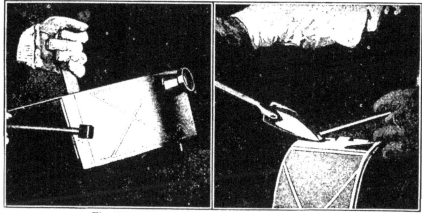

Fig. 419      Fig. 420

**841** Wipe the three joints with clean acid and flow tight solder seams with the iron and bar solder. When the top is securely fastened to the wall and header, lay the radiator on the bench with the exposed side of the tank up. Position the splash plate and tack it to the top with solder at three points on each side of the plate and install the overflow pipe as explained in Pars. 844 and 845. The tank is now ready for the last wall, which may be assembled as explained in Pars. 826 or 830.

## Second Method

**842** Brush the excess solder from all the joints and bend the lips of the header out a little to insure room for those of the top. Set the splash plate over the overflow pipe (if the one on the old header is intact, it may be removed, cleaned and used in making the repair). Next, fit the new top over the overflow pipe and, springing it under the lips of the header, force it into position under the flanges of the wall, then proceed as explained in Pars. 840 and 841.

## Removing Overflow Pipe

**843** The overflow pipe can be removed by detaching it from the core and lower tank, melting the solder setting in the header, and withdrawing the pipe. Because of the double curve in the pipe, it is necessary to exercise care when withdrawing it. First draw the pipe out until it binds, then turn it over to the other side of the radiator and withdraw it a little further. By turning back to the first position the pipe can be completely withdrawn. As it is practically impossible to get all the solder out of the setting, it is necessary to keep it hot with the torch during the operation of withdrawing. The pipe is very brittle while hot, and unless the repairman is careful it will be broken. Should it be broken, the top part can be withdrawn through the filler.

## Replacing Overflow Pipe

**844**   If the hole in the upper tank is too small for the pipe, clean it out with a rat-tail file. Insert the pipe and push it into position, reversing the action described in removing the overflow pipe. By looking through the filler, it is a simple matter to locate the hole in the splash plate through which the overflow pipe extends. When in position, solder it to the header and then to the core and lower tank.

**845**   The overflow pipe is assembled with a washer on the inside of the header. This washer usually drops out when removing the overflow pipe. As it is impossible to replace the washer unless one of the walls are off, it is necessary to have a well sweated in joint between the pipe and the header. It is also advisable to tack the pipe to the filler flange neck.

## Removing Top Header

**846**   To remove the top header, it is first necessary to remove the rear wall, front wall and top as described in Pars. 824, 829 and 833. The radiator is then placed on edge while the solder is removed from the tubes. Next lay the radiator on its back with the header extending over the edge of the bench. The top tank supports are then loosened from the header by brushing the hot solder from them and bending them out of the way. The header bar (See tool 25, Fig. 403) is then inserted between the tubes in the same manner as the lower header (See Fig. 412).

## Replacing Top Header

**847**   Before positioning the top header, heat the supports, brush off the excess solder, and bend the supports back into their original position. The tubes should next be inspected to see that they are clean, properly formed and in line for the holes in the header. Fit the header into position and tap it on with a hammer until it rests on the top tank supports; solder the header to the supports and line the header up with those two points. Stand the radiator upright on the bench hangers, wipe the tubes and the header with acid and flow the solder around the tubes, using the torch and wire solder. When the tubes have been properly set, proceed to assemble the remainder of the top tank as described in Pars. 838 to 840, 830 to 832 and 826 to 828.

**848**   Another way of making the assembly is to first asemble and solder the header front wall and top, which in turn is assembled to the core. The top is first assembled and soldered to the header. Next, position the front wall, tacking it to the header, then by drawing out the filler, the top will be drawn into contact with the flange of the front wall. While holding it in this position, tack it to the flange at five or six points. The tank can then be soldered as described in Par. 832. To aid in holding the wall to header, a support may be inserted through the opening in the back of the tank.

## Changing The Core

**849** Remove the lower tank as described in Pars. 813 and 814, remove front wall of the top tank (See Par. 829) and the overflow pipe (See Par. 843). The top tank can now be removed intact by brushing the solder from around the tubes in much the same manner as removing the header. The top tank supports should now be removed.

**850** Assemble the bottom tank to the new core as explained in Par. 815. Set the top tank onto the core, position the top tank supports against the back edge of the fins and the top tank header and solder then to the header (See Fig. 420). Draw down the header until the top tank supports rest on the radiator support and solder them together. Clean the tubes and solder as described in Par. 830. Replace the overflow pipe as described in Pars. 844 and 845 attach the front wall (See Par. 830) and the radiator is ready to test.

## Repairing a Broken Tube

**851** When a tube is broken in the core near one of the headers, cut the fins (with the 8-inch shears, (See tool No. 32 Fig. 403) along the tube and bend the fins back as shown in Fig. 421. Cut the tube a little above the rupture with a saw made from a piece of hack-saw blade (See tool No. 10 Fig. 403). Grasp the section with a pair of pliers and having heated the header and fins warm enough to let the solder run, draw it out. Next, warm the end of the tube and clean it with acid until both inside and outside of end of tube is entirely free from dirt. In the same way, clean around the hole in the header. Examine the tube and the hole to see that there is no excess solder to interfere with the insertion of the new section. If there is, heat and brush it off or file it out with a $\frac{1}{4}''$ rat-tail file (See tool No. 13 Fig. 403). Next, cut a section of tube about $\frac{3}{16}''$ longer than the gap to be filled. File the ends of the tube tapered so they will enter the header and the end of the tube in the core. Next, take the tube spreader (See tool No. 16 Fig. 403) and drive it into the end of the tube and into the hole in the header to give clearance for the new section. Dip the tube holder into the acid and solder it to the new section (See Fig. 422). Force the tube into the header; if necessary strike the holder (never strike on the section of the tube). Next, insert the free end into the tube, forcing it well in by lightly hammering the holder. Wipe the joints with acid and while heating with a torch apply wire solder. The radiator should be placed in a level position for all soldering operations; otherwise, the solder will run to end of tube where it will set, and stop the circulation.

**852** Bend the fins back into place with the flat-nosed pliers, and solder the fins to the tube with the torch and wire solder. If the repair was made on the front of the radiator, the fins should be supported by a strip cut from the edge of an extra fin to hold the edges of the

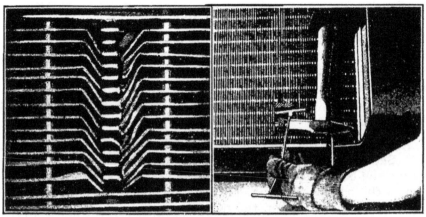

Fig. 421                                Fig. 422

cut fins together.  If it is necessary to remove a large section of the
fins, or to cut to the second or third layer of tubes, it is advisable to
cut away the fin and insert a patch as shown in Fig. 423.  The patch
straddles the tubes, and is tacked down by soldering with the iron
and bar solder.  The patch should be made to overlap the ends of the
fin and the edge should be turned down over the edge of the remaining parts of the original fin.  No support is necessary when the patch
is used.

**853**  If there is a leak between a number of the tubes and the header,
it is repaired by exposing the inside of the header, cleaning the surface and flowing new solder around all the tubes, as described in
Par. 816.

**854**  If there are a number of tubes badly damaged it is advisable to
remove the lower tank and one wall of the top tank and insert new
tubes the entire length. Remove the lower tank and wall as explained in Pars. 813, 814 and 829.  Heat the header around the
tubes to be removed and brush off the solder.  Repeat this operation
on the other header.   Next heat the fins the entire length of the tube

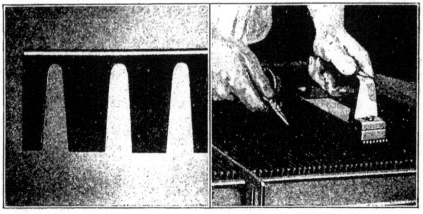

Fig. 423                                Fig. 424

and draw the tube out through the bottom header with square-nosed pliers. Clean the surfaces carefully and insert new tubes. Solder them by flowing solder on the inside of the headers with torch and wire solder and heat the fins along the tube to tack them in place. There is usually an excess of solder on the tubes, and in most cases this is sufficient for tacking the fins, if the fin surfaces have been properly cleaned. If the fins are not tacked properly, add a little more solder while applying the torch.

855 If there are one or two tubes broken near the center of the core, they may be repaired by cutting the damaged tubes above and below the rupture, and after thoroughly cleaning, inserting a new section (See Fig. 422) by entering it into one part of the tube and then into the other in much the same manner as described in Par. 851.

856 If there are a number of tubes broken or damaged near the lower header, it is advisable to expose the lower header, cut the tubes above the rupture and draw them out through the header in the same manner as described in Par. 854. The tubes may be spread with a tube cleaner (See tool No. 17 Fig. 403), inserted through the hole in the header—this prevents damaging the fins. The new section is inserted through the header and driven into place. When the tube is in position cut it off at the header, forcing the spreader into the tube until tube fits tightly into hole in header. Solder the tube connections with a torch and wire solder after having thoroughly cleaned them with acid.

## Cleaning the Tubes

857 The radiator tubes may be cleaned by removing the lower tank and forcing the tube cleaner (See tool 17, Fig. 403) through each tube. If any of the tubes are clogged, tap the cleaner with a hammer. If this does not remedy the trouble the tube should be replaced as described in Par. 854.

858 The radiator should then be flushed out with water, after which the lower tank may be replaced.

859 The radiator should be tested, as described in Par. 861, before replacing it on the car.

## Replacing Radiator Support

860 The radiator support is replaced by removing the lower tank and lower header, after which the fins below the support are heated and driven off, one at a time, with the bar, in much the same way as the lower header is removed. In a like manner, drive off the support and the first fin above it. Invert the radiator on the bench hangers and lay the fin spacer on the last fin. Put on a new fin, the bell end of the taper in the holes extending down, drive on the new radiator support and add one more fin. Solder these parts to the tubes with wire solder and the torch. Next, set the fin spacer on top of

Fig. 425

this assembly and place the next fin in position, starting all the fins on the tubes from the bell end of the taper in the holes. Move the spacer into position for the next fin and continue to add fins until the required number are in position. They should then be tacked to the tubes with the solder and torch. When they have been properly secured, replace the lower header and tank.

## Testing Radiators

861 When the radiator has been repaired it is taken to the test tank. The hose connections, filler and overflow pipe are plugged to prevent leakage, and an air hose is attached to the drain cock hole or one of the hose connection plugs. The radiator is then submerged and tested under a pressure of 5 to 8 pounds of air. No air should escape from any part of the radiator. If there is a leak, note the spot from which the air is coming. Remove the radiator, let out the air and solder the leak with wire solder and the torch.

## Touching Up a Repaired Radiator

862 A repaired radiator should be put in good condition, particularly in so far as the repair work is concerned.

863 If tubes are repaired, no excess solder should be left sticking to the tubes or fins. The fins should be lined up with weaver's pliers and straightened out with the comb (See Fig. 424). The face of the fins should be given a coat of black paint.

## Removing Dents from Top and Bottom Tanks

864 It is possible to remove small dents from the radiator top and bottom tanks without disassembling the radiator. If the filler has been driven into the tank it can be pulled out by screwing the cap into the filler and placing a small iron bar under the top shoulder of filler flange and driving filler up into position with a hammer (See Fig. 425). If there is a small dent in the tank, solder the dent puller into the center of the dent as shown in Fig. 415, and draw it out.

Larger dents may be drawn out by removing that part of the assembly and reshaping it on the bench. The repairman may judge the advisability of reforming the part; if he considers the dent bad enough he should replace the damaged part.

## Installing Radiator in Car

865   (a) Position radiator shell on radiator and run down the four radiator shell screws.

(b) Position radiator over radiator studs (See Fig. 103) inserting radiator connections into hose connections.

(c) Place radiator thimbles over studs and run down the two stud nuts (See "A" and "B" Fig. 104) sufficiently for to permit locking the nuts by inserting cotter pins through radiator studs.

(d) Screw radiator rod into upper tank and run down and tighten radiator rod nut (See Fig. 105).

(e) Tighten radiator hose clips.

(f) Connect carburetor priming rod as described in Par. 129.

(g) Install hood; close radiator drain cock and fill radiator with clean water.

866

# Time Study
## Repairing the Radiator

(One man doing the job)

| | | Hrs. | Min. |
|---|---|---|---|
| 1 | Install new filler neck | | 25 |
| 2 | Install new overflow pipe | | 15 |
| 3 | Replace bottom tank | 1 | 15 |
| 4 | Install new bottom header | 2 | 00 |
| 5 | Change rear wall | | 45 |
| 6 | Change front wall | | 30 |
| 7 | Replace upper tank top | 2 | 00 |
| 8 | Replace top header | 3 | 00 |
| 9 | Change core | 4 | 00 |
| 10 | Replace radiator support | 5 | 00 |
| 11 | Install new top tank support | | 15 |
| 12 | Repair broken tube | | 30 |
| | | 19 | 55 |

# CHAPTER XXVII

# Carburetor Overhaul

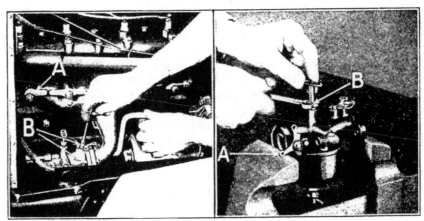

Fig. 426    Fig. 427

## Removing Carburetor from Car

867   Lift off hood.

868   Disconnect carburetor pull rod at throttle and adjusting rod at needle valve by withdrawing cotter pins (See "A" and "B" Fig. 28).

869   Disconnect the two priming wires at carburetor butterfly (See Fig. 18).

870   Shut off gasoline at sediment bulb underneath gasoline tank.

871   Disconnect feed pipe at carburetor by running off pack nut (See Fig. 29).

872   Loosen manifold stud nut which holds carburetor hot air pipe to manifold (See "A" Fig. 426) and withdraw hot air pipe from carburetor.

873   Run off the two carburetor flange bolt nuts "B" and withdraw bolts.

874   Lift out carburetor and place in vise, holding it at throttle and intake flange.  In order to hold carburetor in this manner, it is necessary to pull intake lever back (See "A" Fig. 427).  This prevents shearing the pin in the intake plate.

## Overhauling the Carburetor

875   Remove spray needle by running out spray needle clamp nut "B" (Fig. 427).

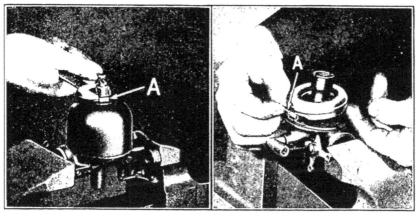

Fig. 428          Fig. 429

**876** Remove drain valve plug assembly and mixer chamber gasket, by running out mixer chamber nut (See "A" Fig. 428). Float chamber can now be lifted off mixer chamber flange.

**877** Remove float by withdrawing float lever pin (See "A" Fig. 429).

**878** Withdraw gasoline inlet needle from inlet seat (See "A") Fig. 430.

**879** Run out spray nozzle and gasket from mixer chamber (See Fig. 431).

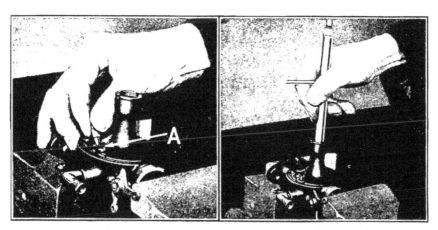

Fig. 430          Fig. 431

**880** Run out inlet seat (See "A" Fig. 432) from mixer chamber. Carburetor is now completely disassembled.

**881** Before reassembling caburetor, examine all parts carefully. It is advisable to use new gaskets when reassembling. See that inlet needle and seat are free from burrs or ridges and that seat is not worn oversize or threads cracked. See that spray needle point is not loose or scored, also that the spray nozzle is not worn oversize or scored. Check metal float for leaks by placing it in boiling water; if

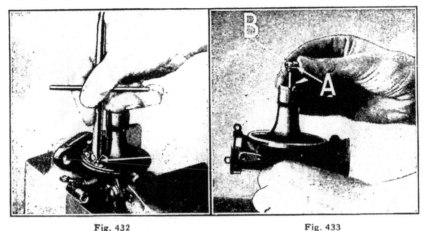

Fig. 432                              Fig. 433

bubbles rise to surface there is a leak. Examine intake lever spring for tension, also make sure that throttle and intake levers have not become loosened.

882   To assemble carburetor position spray nozzle gasket (See "A" Fig. 433) over end of spray nozzle "B" and run down spray nozzle into mixer chamber with a spray nozzle wrench.

883   Insert inlet seat gasket and inlet seat into mixer chamber (See "A" Fig. 432).

884   Place inlet needle into inlet seat. Needle is seated by tapping it very lightly using a small hammer and a seating tool and turning the tool while tapping (See Fig. 434). It is important that the needle be tapped very lightly to avoid scoring needle or enlarging the seat.

885   Place float on mixer chamber and insert float lever pin (See "A" Fig. 429). Float should be moved up and down to see that inlet needle and lever pin are working freely (See Fig. 435). Check adjustment of float with a gauge (See Fig. 436). On the Ford Model N. H. Carburetor, the distance from top of float to machined flange on mixer chamber is $\frac{15}{64}''$ to $\frac{1}{4}''$. (On the Kingston car-

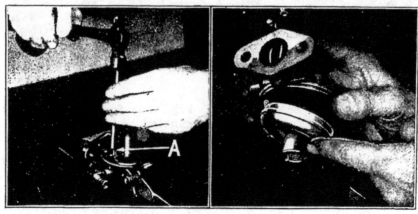

Fig. 434                              Fig. 435

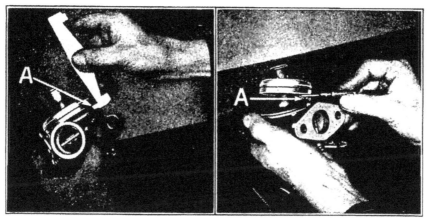

Fig. 436          Fig. 437

buretor this dimension is $\frac{7}{16}''$.) The adjustment is obtained by slightly prying open float spring (See "A" Fig. 437) and raising or lowering the float until the correct setting is obtained.

**886** Position mixer chamber gasket on flange of mixer chamber (See "A" Fig. 438). Install float chamber "B" over mixer chamber. Place mixer chamber nut gasket "C" on float chamber and run down and tighten drain valve assembly "D".

**887** Install spray needle assembly (See "A" Fig. 439) by running the assembly down until it seats in spray nozzle. Do not use any force in screwing the needle down against the nozzle. If force is used it will enlarge the nozzle hole or score the needle, causing imperfect operation. After needle has been seated in spray nozzle turn needle back $\frac{7}{8}$ to 1 turn. This will give the correct opening. Spray needle clamp nut "B" is then run down sufficiently tight to clamp the needle.

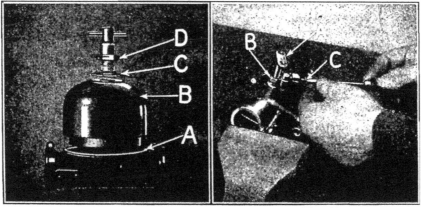

Fig. 438          Fig. 439

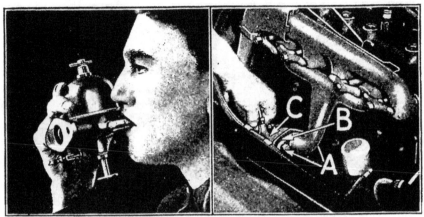

Fig. 440                              Fig. 441

**888**  Run down the adjusting screw "C" in throttle lever until end of screw is ⅛" from throttle lever stop. Test tightness of gasoline inlet needle by turning carburetor upside down, and sucking lightly on the fuel inlet elbow. If the needle is properly seated, the tongue or lips will stick to the elbow in the same manner as small bottle (See Fig. 440).

**889**          Installing Carburetor in Car

(a) Insert the two carburetor flange bolts through inlet pipe (See "A" Fig. 441) placing carburetor flange gasket "B" over ends of bolts.

(b) Position carburetor so that bolts can be entered through carburetor flange as shown at "C". Run down the carburetor flange bolt nuts on the ends of the bolts. It is essential that these nuts be drawn down tightly in order to prevent any interference with the mixture of gas and air which is drawn into the cylinders.

(c) Insert end of carburetor hot air pipe into carburetor, and tighten the nut which holds hot air pipe to manifold (See "A" Fig. 426).

(d) Connect adjusting rod at carburetor needle valve by inserting forked end of rod through needle valve and inserting cotter pin through end of rod (See "B" Fig. 28).

(e) Connect the two priming wires at carburetor butterfly (See Fig. 18).

(f) Connect carburetor pull rod to carburetor throttle by inserting end of rod through carburetor throttle and locking it in position with a cotter pin (See "A" Fig. 28).

(g) Run down feed line pack nut on carburetor inlet elbow, making sure that feed pipe gasket inside of pack nut is in place (See "A" Fig. 442).

(h) Turn on gasoline by opening stop cock in sediment bulb underneath gas tank.

(i) Install hood.

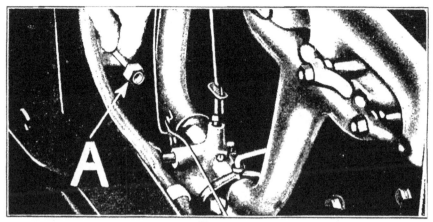

Fig. 442

890               # Time Study
### Carburetor Overhaul
(One man doing the job)

| | | Hrs. | Min. |
|---|---|---|---|
| 1 | Remove carburetor from car | | 15 |
| 2 | Overhaul carburetor | | 30 |
| 3 | Install carburetor in car | | 15 |
| | | 1 | 00 |

# CHAPTER XXVIII

# Installing New Bendix Shaft or Spring

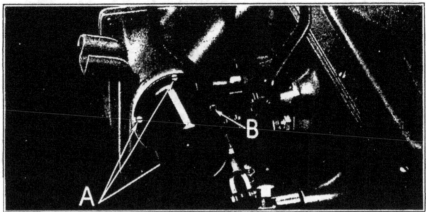

Fig. 443

## Removing Bendix From Car

**891**  Lift off hood.

**892**  Disconnect switch to starting motor cable at starting motor.

**893**  Remove mat and floor boards.

**894**  Remove bendix cover by running out three of the four bendix cover screws (See "A" Fig. 443) and loosening the fourth screw "B". Cover can then be lifted off.

## Installing New Shaft or Spring

**895**  If the bendix spring is broken, it is removed by prying up extension on bendix head spring screw lockwasher (See "A" Fig. 444) and running out screw "B". The bendix shaft spring screw "C" is then removed in the same manner.

**896**  If spring is O. K. but the gear or shaft is broken, run out bendix head spring screw (See "B" Fig. 444), then remove bendix head by slipping it off over end of starting motor shaft. If the head fits tightly it can be withdrawn with a puller (See "A" Fig. 445).

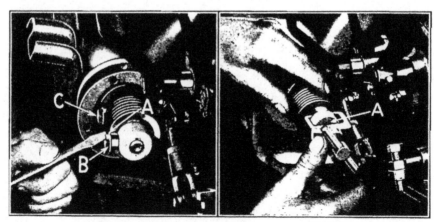

Fig. 444                    Fig. 445

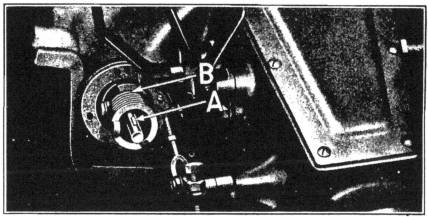

Fig. 446

897   Lift bendix key from starting motor shaft (See "A" Fig. 446).  If key fits tightly in shaft, it can be removed by tapping it with a small hammer and drift.  Bendix shaft, gear, and spring "B" can now be slipped off end of starting motor shaft.  The spring is then removed from bendix shaft by running out bendix shaft spring screw (See "C" Fig. 444).

898   To assemble the bendix, place spring (See "A" Fig. 447) over end of bendix shaft.  Position lockwasher "B" on spring and insert bendix shaft spring screw "C" through lock washer and spring and run down the screw into bendix shaft.  The lock-washer is designed with a small extension on each side of washer.  One of these extensions is bent down against the bendix spring as shown at "B" while the other extension is bent up against the bendix head spring screw.  This eliminates any possibility of the screw working loose.

## Installing Bendix in Car

899   Place a little oil on end of bendix and insert bendix over end of starting motor shaft, making sure that the bendix shaft turns freely in mounting bracket bushing.  If it does not turn freely, remove bendix and dress down end of shaft with an oil stone.

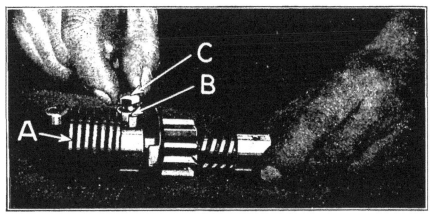

Fig. 447

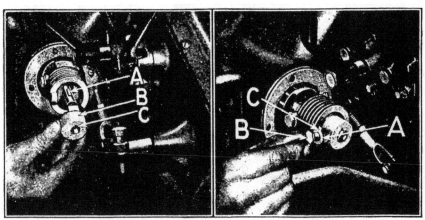

Fig. 448                                 Fig. 449

900   Position bendix on starting motor shaft, install bendix key in keyway on starting motor shaft (See "A" Fig. 448). Replace bendix head "B" by slipping it over starting motor shaft and lining up keyway "C" in head with key in shaft. The head is then pressed onto shaft until screw hole in head lines up with the hole in shaft. Lockwasher and screw are then installed by inserting lockwasher (See "A" Fig. 449) over end of bendix head spring screw "B" and running down screw into bendix head. The screw is locked in position by bending extension "C" on lockwasher tightly against head of screw.

901   After examining bendix cover gasket, position bendix cover over end of bendix, so that one of the four openings in the flange of the cover can be inserted under the head of the bendix cover screw and lockwasher which were not withdrawn when cover was removed. (See "B" Fig. 443). Run in remaining three bendix cover screws and lockwashers, drawing all screws down tightly.

902   Replace floor boards and mat.
Connect switch to starting motor cable.
Install hood.

903

# Time Study

## Changing Bendix or Spring

### (One man doing the job)

|  |  | Hrs. | Min. |
|---|---|---|---|
| 1 | Install car covers, lift out mat and floor boards, remove bendix cover | | 10 |
| 2 | Replace bendix or spring, install screws, replace cover, floor boards and mat, remove car covers | | 20 |
|  |  | | 30 |

# CHAPTER XXIX
# Generator Overhaul

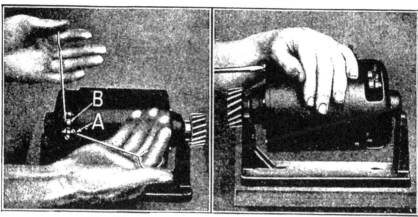

Fig. 450                                    Fig. 451

**904**  Remove generator from car as described in Par. 448.  Remove cover band by loosening cover band bolt (See "A" Fig. 511).

**905**  Place generator on a bench plate and raise the three generator brushes by inserting a brush lifter under each brush terminal and brush spring (See "A" and "B" Fig. 450).  The brushes should be raised about halfway out of brush holders allowing the brush spring to rest against side of brush.

**906**  Loosen the six generator head to yoke screws and run out screws with fingers (See Fig. 451).

**907**  Armature assembly, which comprises the generator head, armature together with large and small bearings can now be withdrawn from yoke (See Fig. 452).

Fig. 452

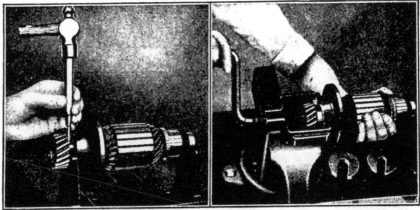

Fig. 453                      Fig. 454

**908** Drive out pinion to shaft pin (See Fig. 453). To prevent damaging the ball bearing when driving out pin, it is necessary to place a lead block or bench plate underneath pinion.

**909** Withdraw pinion from generator shaft by means of a puller (See Fig. 454).

**910** Lift out Woodruff key from generator shaft.

**911** By dropping pinion end of shaft on bench, the generator head (See "A" Fig. 455) can be removed from armature shaft.

**912** Remove large and small bearings (See "A" and "B" Fig. 456) from ends of armature shaft, with a bearing puller.

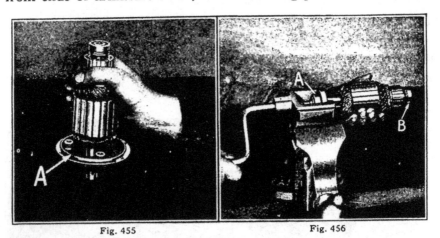

Fig. 455                      Fig. 456

**913** Remove brush end bracket and brush holder assembly—

   (a) Run out the three brush holder screws (See "A" Fig. 457), which hold terminal and field leads to brush holders.

   (b) Run out the four brush end bracket to yoke screws "B". The bracket can then be removed from generator yoke by tapping bracket with a copper hammer as shown in Fig. 458.

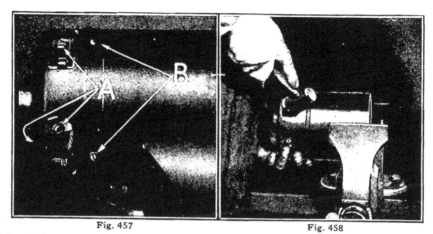

Fig. 457          Fig. 458

**914** Lift generator terminal bolt assembly out of slot in front end of yoke (See "A" Fig. 459).

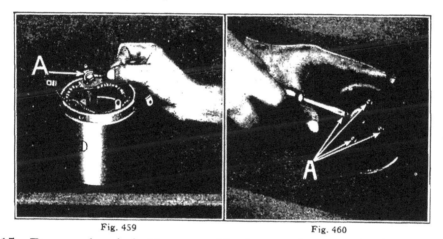

Fig. 459          Fig. 460

**915** Remove brush holder assembly by running out the four brush ring screws in end of brush end bracket (See "A" Fig. 460).

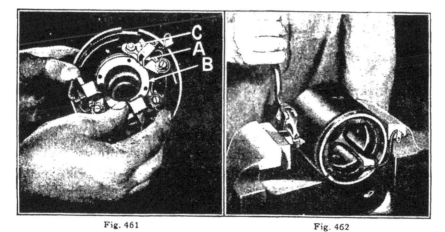

Fig. 461          Fig. 462

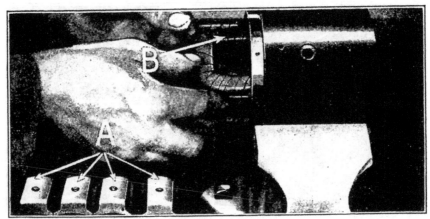

Fig. 463

**916**   Remove third brush holder (See "A" Fig. 461) and retainer ring "B" by running off small brush holder stud nut "C".

**917**   The field coils are next checked for "grounds" and "opens" as described in Par. 925.  If coils test O. K., examine pole pieces to see that they are free from burrs.  The polar diameter is then checked. as explained in Par. 923.  If the test shows an open or ground in the field coils it will be necessary to remove the coils.

**918**   To remove the field coil assembly run out the four pole screws. As the pole screws are tightened with a powerful driver it is necessary to use a pole screw driver, vise and wrench in order to loosen them (See Fig. 462).  After loosening the screws they can be run out with a standard screw driver.

**919**   The four pole pieces (See "A" Fig. 463) and the field winding assembly "B" can now be withdrawn from generator.

## Assembling Generator

**920**   Before re-assembling generator wash all parts thoroughly in gasoline and dry them with a cloth free from lint.  See that the commutator as well as the slots between the segments in commutator are thoroughly cleaned and free from any deposit of carbon and dirt.

**921**   Examine pole pieces to see that they are free from burrs.  Inspect insulation on field coils.  Examine field coil leads to make sure wires are not broken and that all soldered connections are tight.  If insulation is broken, it can be repaired by taping.  When coils and leads are O. K. position the four pole pieces in field windings as shown in Fig. 464.

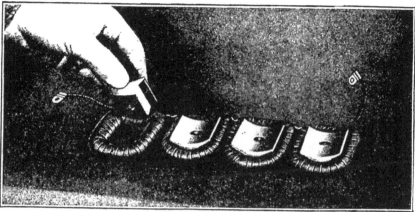

Fig. 464

**922**  Insert field coils and pole pieces into generator yoke with field coil terminals crossed (See "A" Fig. 465) and placed midway between first and second pole screw holes "B" which are located at the right of the terminal slot "C" in yoke.

**923**  Insert the four pole screws into pole screw holes in yoke.  Run down the screws tightly with a standard screw driver, making sure that they enter the pole pieces.  The pole pieces should be forced tightly in place against side of yoke; a pole piece spreader (See "A" Fig. 466) can be used for this purpose.  The polar diameter, i. e., the distance between opposite pole pieces, should measure $\frac{2.838}{2.848}$

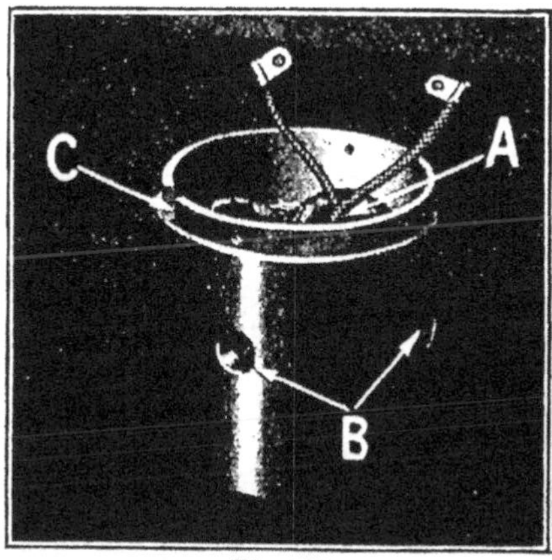

Fig. 465 　　　　　　　　　Fig. 466

The most convenient method of checking this dimension is with a "go" and "no go" plug gauge (See Fig. 467).

**924**  Tighten pole screws with a pole screw driver (See Fig. 462). To prevent any possibility of the pole screws working loose, they should be staked with a center punch as shown at "A" Fig. 468.

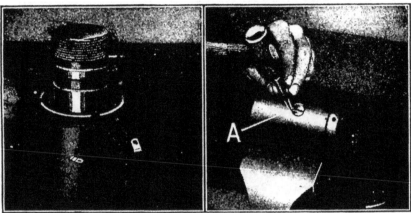

Fig. 467          Fig. 468

925  After assembling field coils in yoke, the coils should be tested for "grounds" and "opens". A "ground" occurs when some part of the insulation is broken or torn, allowing the bare wire to come in contact with the pole piece or yoke. An "open" occurs when a wire is broken and the electrical circuit interrupted. To test for an "open" insert test points through field coil terminals (See "A" and "B" Fig. 469), if circuit is complete, test lamp "D" will light. If lamp fails to light, there is an open in the field coils. To test for grounds, insert one of the test points through either of the two field coil terminals and place the other test point on the yoke as shown at "C." If lamp lights there is a ground between field coils and yoke. If lamp fails to light field coils are O. K. If field coils have a "ground" or "open", which cannot be detected by visual inspection, it is usually less expensive to install new coils rather than attempt to repair them. (Note: Before checking generator or starting motor for grounds, the lamp on the test stand should be checked to make sure it has not burned out. To check the lamp, place the ends of the two test points together; if the lamp lights, it is O. K.)

926  Insert retainer ring (See "A" Fig. 470) into retainer ring groove in brush ring. Position third brush holder "B" into slot in brush

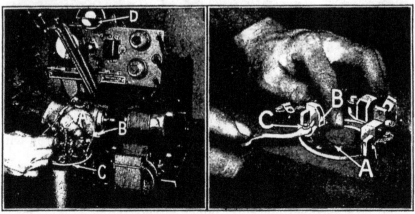

Fig. 469          Fig. 470

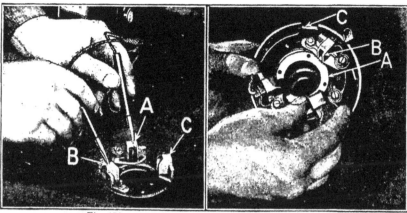

Fig. 471          Fig. 472

ring. Insert brush holder stud through brush ring and third brush holder, running down lockwasher and nut "C" on end of stud.

927  Before installing brush ring assembly into brush end bracket, the ring assembly should be checked for grounds. To check for grounds, place test points on grounded brush holder (See "A" Fig. 471) and third brush holder "B" also on grounded brush holder "A" and positive brush holder "C". If test lamp lights, there is a ground in the brush ring; if lamp fails to light, ring is O. K.

928  Install brush ring assembly (See "A" Fig. 472) into brush end bracket with third brush holder "B" in first position to right of terminal slot "C". Insert the four brush ring screws and lockwashers through end of brush end bracket into brush holder assembly (See Fig. 460).

929  Examine terminal bolt insulator for breaks. If insulator is O. K. insert terminal bolt assembly into terminal slot in yoke, making sure that the flat side of the insulator is up (See "A" Fig. 473), also that the head of the terminal bolt does not come in contact with field coil connection "B".

930  Cross the two field leads (See "A" Fig. 474), so they will be in position to be connected, one to the third brush holder and the other to the grounded brush holder when brush end bracket is installed.

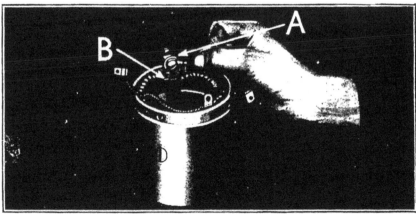

Fig. 473

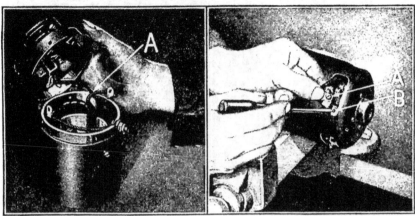

Fig. 474                                    Fig. 475

**931**   Install brush end bracket on yoke and run-down the four bracket to yoke screws (See "B" Fig. 457).

**932**   Line up screw holes in terminal leads and brush terminals. Position lock washer over end of brush holder screw. Insert the screw through lead and brush terminals (See "A" Fig. 475). Run down screw into screw hole "B" in brush holder.

**933**   Before installing armature, test for shorts and grounds.

**934**   To test for grounds, place test points in center of armature laminations and commutator segment (See "A" and "B" Fig. 476). If test lamp "C" lights, there is a ground in the armature and a new armature should be installed. If test lamp fails to light armature is not grounded.

**935**   To test for short circuits; position armature in growler and turn on growler switch. Place a piece of flat steel such as a scale or hack-saw blade across top of armature (See "A" Fig. 477), and slowly revolve armature with fingers. If the steel vibrates, it indicates that the armature is short circuited. If steel does not vibrate, armature is O. K.

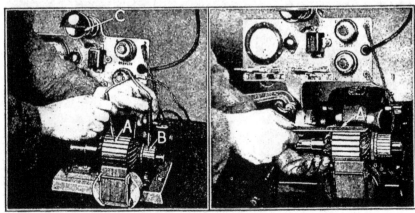

Fig. 476                                    Fig. 477

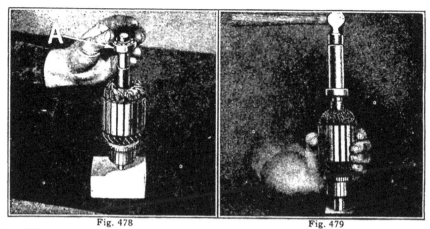

Fig. 478            Fig. 479

**936** Wash large and small ball bearings with gasoline. Inspect bearings for wear, cracked or pitted balls, and cracked ball races. If balls or ball races are cracked or pitted, install new bearings.

**937** Position large ball bearing (See "A" Fig. 478) over pinion end of armature shaft. Press bearing down tightly on shaft until bearing seats squarely on shoulder of shaft. A driver, lead block and hammer are used for performing this operation (See Fig. 479).

**938** Position large bearing disc (See "A" Fig. 480) over end of shaft and force it down on shaft with the driver in the same manner as ball bearing was installed until disc seats squarely on inner race of large ball bearing.

**939** Position generator head (See Fig. 480) over large bearing disc and bearing on armature shaft, making sure that generator head seats firmly on bearing. Insert Woodruff key into keyway on pinion end of armature shaft. Key should fit tightly in keyway.

**940** Examine teeth of pinion for burrs and wear. If O. K., press pinion onto shaft on an arbor press, resting the small bearing end of shaft on a lead block (See Fig. 481). Press pinion down on shaft until pin hole in pinion lines up with the pin hole in shaft. Insert pinion to shaft pin through pinion and generator shaft. The ends of the pin are then riveted (See Fig. 453).

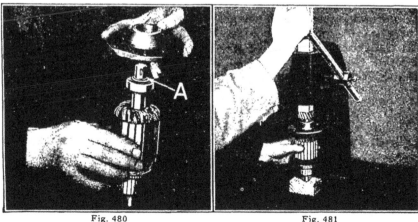

Fig. 480            Fig. 481

Fig. 482          Fig. 483

**941**  Inspect small bearing felt retainer and felt; if badly worn or distorted, install new parts.

**942**  Position small bearing felt retainer (See "A" Fig. 482), felt "B" and small bearing "C" over commutator end of armature shaft, and force parts down on shaft until felt retainer seats on shoulder of shaft "D". Before installing small bearing it should be thoroughly oiled.

**943**  Insert armature assembly into yoke, making sure that the field leads are raised as high as possible so that they will not come in contact with armature; also that the beveled side of the generator head (See "A" Fig. 483) fits onto yoke a trifle below right center of generator terminal "B" when facing pinion end of generator.

**944**  Run in the six screws and lockwashers "C" which hold generator head to yoke (See Fig. 483).

**945**  Press the two main brushes down into brush holders until they seat squarely on commutator positioning the brush springs over the brushes. Allow the third brush to remain raised half way up in holder until the brushes have been checked for correct setting.

**946**  There are two methods used for setting the generator brushes: One method is used when the generator is removed from car and the setting is obtained on the test stand. The other method is used with the generator installed in car. This latter method is perhaps the most efficient as plenty of power is available for rotating the armature and as a result a more accurate adjustment is obtained.

## Setting Generator Brushes on Test Stand

**947**  Position generator so that side of generator yoke comes in contact with frame of test stand; this forms a ground. Connect test stand terminal lead to generator terminal. With the third brush raised approximately half way out of brush holder and the brush spring placed against side of brush, loosen the four brush ring screws in end of brush end bracket, (about one half turn); close the battery switch on stand to the left.

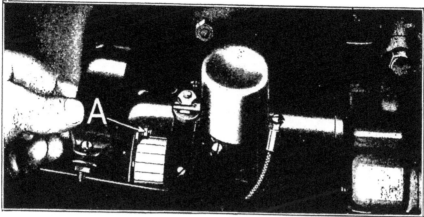

Fig. 484

**948** The brush ring should now be shifted first one way and then the other. This causes the armature to revolve clockwise and counterclockwise, as you look at the gear. While shifting the brush ring, find the point at which the armature will not rotate either way, but has a tendency to move clockwise. Lock the brush ring in this position by tightening the four brush ring screws. Lower third brush and position brush spring over brush.

**949** Replace generator in test stand and start motor; loosen the third brush nut and shift the third brush holder (in the direction of rotation to increase the charging rate, or reverse to decrease) until the ammeter registers a charge of 10 to 12 amperes.

**950** The generator is now installed in car as described in Par. 450.

## Setting Generator Brushes with Generator Installed In Car

**951** To set the generator brushes with generator in the car:—

(a) Loosen the dust cover bolt and lift off dust cover.

(b) Loosen the third brush nut (See "A" Fig. 484) and shift the third brush to the left as far as possible i. e. toward the engine.

(c) Loosen the four brush ring screws (See "A" Fig. 485) approximately half a turn which will allow the brush holder assembly (See "A" Fig. 486) to be moved freely in either direction; care should be taken not to run out the screws more than is actually necessary to allow the brush holder assembly to move freely. (If the screws are run out too far, the clamp ring will fall off inside the generator, and to replace it would necessitate removal of the generator).

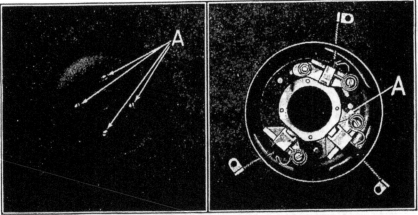

Fig. 485              Fig. 486

(d) Start the engine, opening the throttle until the engine is running at a speed equivalent to approximately 20 miles per hour; then rotate the brush holder assembly until the ammeter indicates the maximum output; tighten the four screws which hold the brush holder assembly in position, and next shift the third brush until the ammeter registers a charge of 10 to 12 amperes, then tighten the third brush nut.  Once the adjustment has been set it should not be changed unless a new armature or brush holder assembly is installed.  It is of course understood that the third brush can be shifted to meet varying conditions, for instance a car that is driven only on short trips, necessitating frequent starting with consequent drain on the battery, would require a higher charging rate than the car which is driven only on long runs.  For average conditions, however, a charging rate of 10 to 12 amperes is the most suitable.

## 952      Time Study

### Generator Overhaul

(one man doing the job)

|   |   | Hrs. | Min. |
|---|---|---|---|
| 1 | Install car covers and remove generator............ |  | 10 |
| 2 | Overhaul generator............................... | 1 | 00 |
| 3 | Install generator, test and remove car covers....... |  | 15 |
|   |   | 1 | 25 |

# CHAPTER XXX

# Starting Motor Overhaul

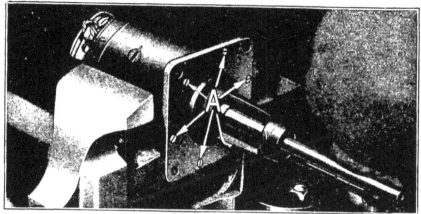

Fig. 487

## Removing Starting Motor from Car

**953**  To remove the starting motor from the car it is first necessary to disconnect the starting motor to switch cable (See "C" Fig. 35). Lift out mat and floor boards and remove bendix cover and bendix as described in Pars. 894, 896 and 897; the four motor mounting screws are then run out and the starting motor withdrawn.

## Disassembling Starting Motor

**954**  Remove cover band by loosening cover band bolt (See Fig. 511).

**955**  Raise the four brushes approximately half way out of brush holders in the same manner as the generator brushes were raised (See Fig. 450).

**956**  Run out the six mounting bracket to yoke screws (See "A" Fig. 487).

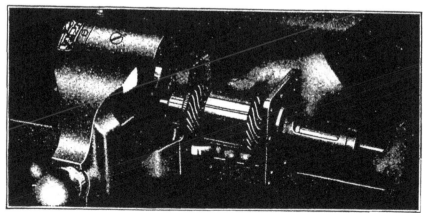

Fig. 488

Fig. 489　　　　　　　　　Fig. 490

957　Mounting bracket and armature can now be withdrawn from yoke (See Fig. 488). If armature sticks in yoke it can be loosened by tapping edge of yoke against bench.

958　Run out the four brush end bracket to yoke screws (See "A" Fig. 489) together with the two screws "B" which hold the two field leads to brush holder.

959　Remove brush end bracket from yoke by lightly tapping the bracket with a copper hammer (See Fig. 458).

960　Run out the four pole screws in the same manner as generator pole screws were removed (See Fig. 462).

961　Loosen terminal nut (See "A" Fig. 490) and lift out pole pieces and field coil assembly "B".

962　If the shaft bushing in brush end bracket shows evidence of wear it can be removed with a bearing puller as shown in Fig. 491 and "A" Fig. 492.

Fig. 491　　　　　　　　　Fig. 492

## Assembling the Starting Motor

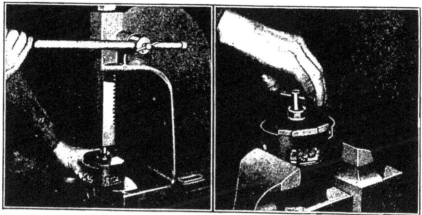

Fig. 493          Fig. 494

**963**  Before assembling starting motor, wash all parts thoroughly in gasoline and dry them with a cloth free from lint.  Clean the commutator with fine sandpaper (Grade 00).

**964**  Install a new shaft bushing into brush and bracket.  When pressing in a new shaft bushing it is absolutely essential that the bushing be pressed in squarely.  A guide plate can be used satisfactorily for this purpose (See Fig. 493).

**965**  After the new bushing has been installed it is necessary to line ream it (See Fig. 494).

**966**  Inspect pole pieces, field coils, and field coil leads as outlined in Par. 921 in assembling generator.

**967**  Insert pole pieces into field coil assembly and position field coil assembly and pole pieces into yoke (See Fig. 464).  Run in the four pole screws as described in Par. 923.

**968**  The pole pieces should be forced tightly in place against side of yoke with a pole piece spreader as shown in Fig. 466.  The polar diameter, which is $\frac{2.838}{2.848}$, is then checked with the plug gauge as shown in Fig. 467, and the pole screws tightened as described in Par. 924.

**969**  To make sure that none of the metal parts on the windings are coming in contact with pole pieces or yoke, the field coil assembly should be tested for grounds.  This is done by placing one test point on motor terminal (See "A" Fig. 495), and the other on yoke "B". If test lamp "C" lights there is a ground in the coils.  If lamp does not light, field coils are O. K.

**970**  Check motor brush ring for grounds with the test points, in the same manner as generator brush ring was checked (See Par. 927). It is unnecessary to remove the starting motor brush ring from brush end bracket when making this test.

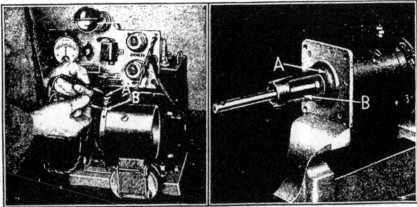

Fig. 495  Fig. 496

**971** Install brush end bracket on end of yoke by running in the four screws which hold it in place, also the two screws which hold field leads to brush holders (See Fig. 489). (The starting motor field leads are not crossed when installing brush end bracket as they are on the generator, but are connected direct to the insulated brush holders.

**972** Armature is now placed in growler and tested for shorts and grounds in the same manner as generator armature as described in Pars. 934 and 935.

**973** If the commutator is rough it can be dressed down as described in Par. 1085, by using an attachment with the stand.

**974** Insert armature into yoke placing mounting bracket "A" over end of shaft and positioning it against yoke. The bracket is installed with the opening "B" in bracket placed to the right when facing front end of starting motor as shown in Fig. 496. Run in the six mounting bracket to yoke screws and lockwashers (See Fig. 487). Lower brushes into brush holders and position brush springs over brushes.

**975** Replace dust cover by inserting it over end of starting motor and running down dust cover screw.

## Installing Starting Motor in Car

**976** Place starting motor gasket on motor mounting bracket and position starting motor on transmission cover running down the 4 motor mounting screws and lockwashers which hold starting motor to transmission cover.

**977** Install bendix and bendix cover; connect switch to starting motor cable and replace hood, floor boards and mat as described in Pars. 899 to 902.

**978**
## Starting Motor Overhaul
(one man doing the job)

| | | Hrs. | Min. |
|---|---|---|---|
| 1 | Install car covers, remove bendix and starting motor | | 20 |
| 2 | Overhaul starting motor. . . . . . . . . . . . . . . . . . . . . . | 1 | 00 |
| 3 | Install starting motor, bendix and remove car covers | | 20 |
| | | 1 | 40 |

# CHAPTER XXXI

# Tracing Car Troubles

**979** The ability to locate and correct car troubles quickly is a valuable asset to the repairman.

**980** While difficulty is sometimes experienced in locating the source of the trouble promptly, if systematic methods are used, the procedure can be reduced to a comparatively simple formula.

**981** In this section of the book, methods for tracing car troubles are described, which will simplify this work and assist the mechanic in locating the trouble quickly.

## Engine Fails to Start
### Cars Equipped with Starters

**982** Failure of the engine to start when turned over with the starter or hand crank is due to trouble either in the electrical or fuel system, or in extremely rare cases, a broken part. (Broken parts can usually be detected by the noises which they make or lack of resistance when turning the engine over with the starting crank.)
If the car is not equipped with a starter, see Par. 991.

**983** If the car is equipped with a starter and the engine fails to turn over when the starting switch is depressed, check the battery as described in Par. 1119 and "e" Par. 1115. (If the engine turns over but car will not start, see Par. 989. If the battery checks O. K. short across the starting switch terminals. This is done by placing the ends of a pair of pliers on both terminals. If a good live spark occurs, the trouble lies in the starting switch and a new switch should be installed. (If no spark occurs, see Par. 988.) If but little or no sound now comes from the starting motor when the starting switch is depressed, it indicates that the bendix is binding due to a bent armature shaft or the bendix gear is not meshing properly with the flywheel ring gear. The bendix can usually be freed by proceeding as follows:

**984** Turn off the ignition switch; place hand brake lever in forward position and rock the car backward and forward. If this does not free the gear, loosen the four starting motor mounting screws three or four turns and again rock the car backward and forward until bendix gear clears ring gear.

**985** While this procedure will usually free the gear, in order to avoid a repetition of the trouble, the bendix should be removed as described in Pars. 891 to 897, and examined, also the teeth on the flywheel ring gear should be inspected for badly worn or broken teeth. With the bendix removed, the teeth on the flywheel ring gear can be inspected through the opening in the transmission cover where the bendix was withdrawn. To facilitate this operation have some one slowly turn the engine over with the starting crank while making the inspection.

**986** If the bendix and ring gear are O. K. the trouble is due to a sprung armature shaft and the starting motor should be removed as described

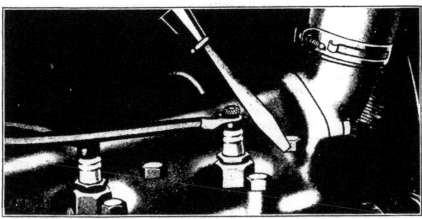

Fig. 497

in Par. 953 and the armature shaft checked for alignment and straightened on a press in the same manner as the crankshaft (See Figs. 162 and 163).

**987**　If a whirring noise is heard when the starting switch is depressed, it indicates either a broken bendix part or stripped teeth on the flywheel ring gear and it will be necessary to remove and inspect the bendix as well as the flywheel ring gear teeth, as outlined in Par. 985.

**988**　If no spark occurs when the starting switch terminals are shorted as described in Par. 983, the trouble is probably due to loose or dirty connections. Examine connections at starting motor terminal, point 5 (Fig. 498), starting switch terminals, points 25 and 26, positive and negative posts on battery, points 27 and 28 and battery ground connection on frame, point 29. If connections are clean and tight, the trouble lies in the starting motor, and it will be necessary to remove the starting motor and check for shorts and grounds or shaft bushing binding on armature shaft as described in Chapter XXXVII.

**989**　If the engine turns over freely but does not start when the starting switch is depressed, place a screw driver with a wooden handle on the cylinder head, holding it about $\frac{1}{8}''$ away from the top of the plug, as shown in Fig. 497 while some one turns the engine over rapidly with either the starter or hand crank. If a good live spark occurs at all of the plugs, the trouble lies in the fuel system and can be remedied as explained in Pars. 1014 to 1018. If a spark does not occur the trouble lies in the electrical system. On cars equipped with a starter, this test should be tried with the ignition key turned on both battery and magneto. If the car will run on battery but not on magneto, inspect the magneto contact post as described in Par. 991. If magneto post is O. K., the trouble is due either to excessive end play in the crankshaft, weak magnets or a ground or short in the magneto coil assembly. See Pars. 992 to 999.

**990**　If the trouble indicates itself as lying in the ignition system, remove and inspect commutator case and spring as described in Par. 1003. If the commutator is O. K., examine magneto and battery wire terminals on terminal block, points 12 and 13 (Fig. 498); ignition switch wire terminal at point 8, commutator terminals on coil box, point 10, also the two soldered connections on terminal to bus bar

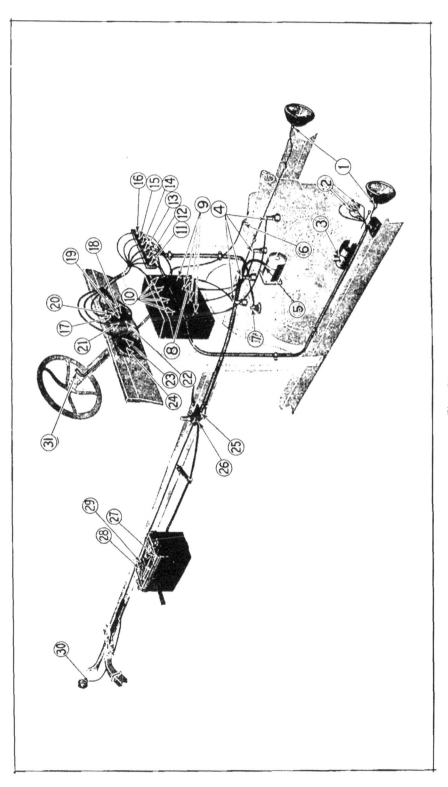

Fig. 498

wire in coil box, and the battery wire, ignition wire and magneto wire terminals, points 18, 19 and 20 on back of switch to see that they are clean and tight. If the trouble is not due to loose or dirty connections at these points, place ends of a pair of pliers across coil terminal, point 19 and battery terminal, point 18 on back of switch; then depress starting switch. If engine starts, the trouble lies in the ignition switch and a new switch should be installed.

## Cars Not Equipped with Starter

991   If the car is not equipped with a starter and fails to start when turned over rapidly with the hand crank and with the switch key turned to point marked "MAG," check the spark plugs as described in Par. 989 to determine whether the trouble lies in the ignition or fuel system. If the trouble indicates itself as lying in the ignition system, inspect the magneto contact post. While someone cranks the car, short the magneto contact post, point 7 (Fig. 498) by placing the ends of a pair of pliers, or a screw driver on the contact post and transmission cover and moving the end of the pliers or screw driver back and forth on the cover to make a good contact. If a good live spark occurs the magneto is O. K. (See Par. 999). If no spark or a very weak spark occurs, remove magneto post and examine contact spring to see that it is not weak, or broken, or that there is no dirt or foreign matter between the contact and contact post spring. After cleaning the contact point and contact post, replace magneto terminal and again short the terminal to cover. If no spark, or a very weak spark occurs the trouble is due either to excessive end play in the crankshaft, weak magnets or a ground or short in the magneto coil assembly.

992   End play in the crankshaft can be checked by inserting a large screw driver or a flat piece of stock between crankcase front wall and crankshaft pulley and noting the movement of the crankshaft when it is forced back and forth. If there is more than .015″ end play in the shaft the trouble is probably due to a worn bearing and an oversize rear main bearing cap T-3031-405AR should be fitted.

993   If there is no appreciable end play in the crankshaft, the strength of the magneto should next be checked. An easy way to prove a weak magneto on a car not equipped with a battery is to run one wire from a six volt storage battery or three or four dry cells to the left hand terminal connection on the terminal block when facing front of dash (See point 11 Fig. 498), and the other wire to some metal part of the engine. Turn the switch key to the right instead of the left and try starting the engine. On cars equipped with starters simply turn switch key to point marked "Bat".

994   If the engine starts, the magneto is either weak or dead. With the engine running take a volt meter reading (See Fig. 499). This can be done by disconnecting magneto terminal wire at magneto contact assembly. One wire on the volt meter is then connected to magneto contact, while the other wire on volt meter is pressed against a clean part of the cylinder or transmission cover. Throttle the engine down

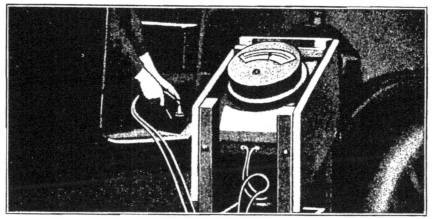

Fig. 499

to about 400 R. P. M. (revolutions per minute). This can be done by removing the valve cover and counting the pulsations of one valve. There are two revolutions of the crankshaft to each pulsation. The magneto should generate at least 7 volts at 400 R. P. M.

**995**   If magneto fails to generate 7 volts, one or more of the magneto coils are shorted or the magnets are weak. To remedy these troubles it will be necessary to remove engine from frame and remove magneto coil assembly, as described in Pars. 163 to 206.

## Locating a Grounded or Shorted Coil

**996**   To locate a grounded or shorted coil, use electric light current, (110 or 220 AC or DC), first passing it through an electric soldering iron or other electrical resistance, which draws between three and five amperes. Fasten one wire of this testing outfit to a bare spot on the coil support, (points "D" Fig. 500). With the other wire touch

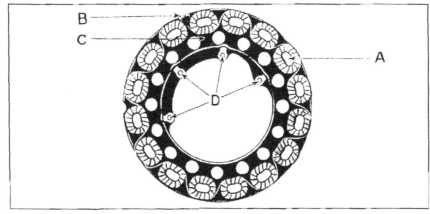

Fig. 500

Fig. 501

contact "B". While the current is passing through the coil assembly, lay a piece of steel, about four inches long, across the cores of adjoining coils, as shown in Fig. 501, until all cores have been touched. If a coil is found where all the coils beyond it give no magnetic pull, that coil (the last live one) is grounded. Examine it to see if the wire leading from it to the first dead coil is grounded on the casting. If not, the last live coil is grounded on its core (See "A" Fig. 500) and by lifting it off of the casting, the dead coils will become alive, unless there is another grounded coil.

997   If all of the coils are dead and there is a spark produced when contact "B" is touched with the test wire, contact "B" is grounded. If there is no spark at contact "B" there is an "open", which can be located by taking the test wire off contact "B", and placing it upon a bared spot on each coil until a spark can be produced. The "open" will be just ahead of this point. If a spark cannot be produced at any coil, the last coil is not grounded at point "C" as it should be.

998   If the coils are not shorted or grounded the trouble is due to weak magnets and new magnets should be installed as described in Par. 281.

999   If a spark occurs after shorting magneto contact post, as described in Par. 991, remove the commutator and inspect commutator case and spring as described in Par. 1003. If commutator is O. K., examine all connections on coil box, terminal block, and back of switch as outlined in Par. 990, and see that they are clean and tight. If the trouble is not due to a loose connection at these points, place the ends of a pair of pliers on the magneto and coil terminals on back of switch, points 19 and 20 (Fig. 498), while some one cranks the car. If the car starts, the trouble lies in the ignition switch and a new switch should be installed.

# CHAPTER XXXII

# Misfiring

## Misfiring Caused by Trouble in Ignition System or Valves

Fig. 502

**1000** Misfiring (missing) may result from trouble in either the fuel system, ignition system or in the valves. If the miss is irregular and cannot be located by shorting the plugs as described in Par. 1001, the trouble is probably in the fuel system (See Pars. 1014 to 1020).

**1001** If the trouble indicates itself as lying in the ignition system or valves, start the engine and place a screw driver on the cylinder near one of the spark plugs, then lean it against terminal of spark plug (See Fig. 502). This shorts the current past the spark plug. A screw driver with a wooden handle should be used when making this test to prevent receiving a shock. Check each plug in this manner until one is found which makes no change in the sound of the exhaust from the engine. When this plug is found, the trouble lies in the ignition or valves of that cylinder. (As the miss is more likely to be due to ignition than valve trouble it is advisable to check the ignition first.)

**1002** Next, stop the engine and disconnect the spark plug wire from the plug in the missing cylinder, then start the engine and hold this wire approximately $\frac{1}{8}''$ away from any part of the cylinder head. If a spark occurs the trouble lies in the plug and can be overcome by cleaning, or if necessary, replacing the plug. Before replacing the plug, check the spark plug points for gap, the gap between the points should measure approximately $\frac{1}{32}''$. Also examine the porcelain to make sure that it has not been cracked.

**1003** If no spark occurs when the above test is made, again hold the spark plug wire approximately $\frac{1}{8}''$ away from the engine, at the same time shorting the commutator terminal of the missing cylinder at the coil box by placing a screw driver on the terminal and resting it against the radiator stay rod (See Fig. 503). (The commutator ter-

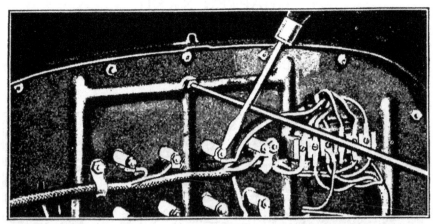

Fig. 503

minals on the coil box are the four upper terminals and for conven- ience are numbered 1, 2, 3 and 4 to correspond with the cylinders.) If a spark occurs between spark plug wire and cylinder the trouble lies in the commutator or commutator loom and can be corrected by inspecting the loom for breaks in the wire and insulation and noting whether commutator loom terminals are properly soldered and that the points where they are connected to commutator case and coil box are clean and all connections are tight. (If no spark occurs, see Par. 1004.) If the trouble is not in the loom or connections, remove commutator as described in Par. 454. Clean the commutator thoroughly by washing it with kerosene. Inspect interior surface of commutator where the roller travels; this surface should be clean and smooth. If the surface is uneven and as a result, the roller fails to make a good contact with any one of the four contact points, its corresponding cylinder will not fire. This usually occurs when driv- ing at high speed. Examine roller for wear. Inspect brush spring to see that spring is not weak or broken. If commutator case or roller is badly worn or the spring is weak or broken, new parts should be installed.

1004   If no spark occurs between spark plug wire and cylinder head when commutator terminal is shorted to radiator stay rod, as de- scribed in Par. 1003, the trouble lies either in the coil unit of the cylin- der which is missing or in the coil box and can be remedied by check- ing the coil unit as described in Pars. 1005 to 1011 and checking the coil box. When checking the coil box, examine the contact points inside of coil box to make sure they are not bent or broken. See that the two soldered wire connections in coil box are tight and that there is no foreign substance in the coil box which prevents the coil units seating squarely in box. If the soldered wire connections in coil box are loose, it will be necessary to remove the coil box and solder them.

# Testing and Adjusting the Coil Units

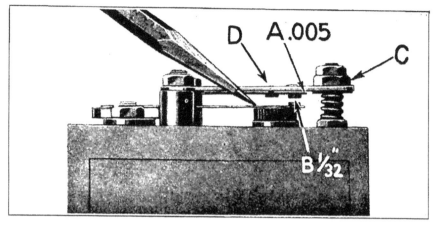

Fig. 504

**1005** Inspect the tungsten points on both vibrator and bridge. If points are badly pitted or burned a new vibrator and bridge should be installed. If points are only slightly pitted they can be removed and dressed down with an oil stone.

**1006** When installing a new vibrator and bridge, it is very important that a uniform clearance of approximately .005″ be maintained between cushion spring and vibrator bridge (See A Fig. 504). This clearance should extend the full length of the cushion spring.

**1007** With the vibrator and bridge held open, adjust the gap between the tungsten points to ⅟₃₂″ as shown at B. The adjustment is obtained by loosening the lock nut and tightening or loosening adjusting nut "C". The tungsten points should meet squarely when they come together. See that the four lock nuts on top of the coil units are drawn down tightly.

**1008** Place coil unit in a coil tester and revolve crank until the volt meter on the machine registers six volts then adjust vibrator tension until the ammeter registers 1.3 amperes. A uniform reading of 1.3 amperes should be obtained on all four coil units. To increase the amperage lightly tap outer edge of vibrator bridge with a small hammer as shown in Fig. 505. To lower the amperage slightly pry up the outer edge of the bridge. Either a special hammer or a screw driver can be used for this purpose (See Fig. 506).

**1009** When a coil unit is correctly adjusted it will show one good spark at each of the 16 points around the ring with the ammeter on the stand registering 1.3 amperes and the volt meter registering six volts. If more than one spark occurs at any of the sixteen points, it indicates that the cushion spring is not working freely. This can be corrected by lightly tapping the vibrator on the cushion spring rivet (See "D" Fig. 504).

Fig. 505                    Fig. 506

**1010**  If only a very weak spark, or no spark at all shows on test ring on stand after dressing down or installing new points and adjusting coil unit as outlined above, the trouble lies in the interior of the coil and it is less expensive to install a new coil unit than to attempt to repair the old one.

**1011**  Before replacing the coil units, see that the contact points on the back and bottom of the units are clean.  The contact points can be cleaned by lightly scraping, or rubbing them with fine sand-paper.

## Inspecting The Valves

**1012**  If the trouble does not lie in the ignition, remove the valve cover and see that the valve spring seat pins are in the valves.  If pins are in place, check the clearance between valves and push rods. If clearance is O. K. (not less than $\frac{1}{64}$ inch or more than $\frac{1}{32}$ inch), start the engine and test for weak valve springs.  This can be done by inserting a screw driver between the coils and forcing the spring down.  If this causes the engine to pick up speed, the spring is weak and should be replaced.  (To check the strength of the valve springs accurately the tension of the springs should be checked as described in Par. 258.)

**1013**  See that the valves are not sticking in guides.  This is done by running the engine slowly and watching the travel of the valves and push rods and checking the gap.  If a valve is sticking the push rod will travel down faster than the valve, leaving a large gap between valve and push rod.  If the valve is sticking due to a heavy deposit of carbon on the stem or guide, it can be loosened by flowing a mixture of oil and kerosene on the stem.  If, however, it is sticking due to a bent or warped stem, it will be necessary to install a new valve.

## Misfiring, or Engine Fails to Start, Caused by Trouble in the Fuel System

**1014**  After making sure there is gasoline in the tank and the vent hole in the filler cap is not plugged, examine spray needle for correct

setting and see that adjusting nut is tight. The correct setting is
$\frac{7}{8}$ to 1 turn of the needle. See that the choke valve is fully open;
if valve is not opened, inspect for a weak or broken choke spring.

1015 If spray needle adjustment and choke spring are O. K., open
the drain valve plug in carburetor bowl; if gasoline fails to flow,
tap the carburetor lightly. This will sometimes loosen dirt which
may have lodged in the jets. If this fails to remedy the trouble
disconnect the feed pipe at the carburetor. If gasoline flows freely
out of feed pipe the trouble lies in the carburetor and it will be
necessary to remove the carburetor and overhaul it as outlined in
Chapter XXVII. The principal points to check are the spray needle,
the spray nozzle, inlet needle and seat, and the correct setting of the
float.

1016 If gasoline fails to flow out of the feed pipe when disconnected
at carburetor, or only flows in a thin or broken stream, close the
shut off cock in sediment bulb underneath gasoline tank and disconnect feed pipe from bulb, then open the shut off cock. If fuel
now flows freely out of the gasoline tank, the trouble lies in the
feed pipe and the pipe should be cleaned with compressed air or by
running a wire through it.

1017 If, however, fuel fails to flow freely from the tank, close the
shut off cock and screw off the screen cap at the side of the sediment
bulb to which the feed pipe was attached. If the screen is clogged
it can be cleaned with compressed air. If screen is broken a new
part should be installed, as a broken screen allows dirt to pass
through the feed pipe and lodge in the carburetor.

1018 Before replacing the screen cap, see that the sediment bulb is
clean and free from any obstruction; the bulb can be cleaned by
opening the drain cock and allowing the gasoline to flow for a few
seconds, at the same time running a wire up and down through the
bulb. After cleaning the sediment bulb, replace the screen cap and
connect feed pipe to sediment bulb and carburetor.

1019 If the carburetor and fuel line are O. K., see that the intake
manifold is clamped tightly to cylinder and that there is no leak at
the manifold gaskets. A leak around the gaskets can be located by
flowing a little oil around the gaskets. If there is a leak, the oil will
be drawn into the cylinder.

1020 Water leaks between the water jacket and cylinders are indicated by drops of water forming at the muffler outlet immediately
after starting the engine and can be felt by holding the hand near
the end of the muffler. Water leaks which cause a miss in the
engine usually result from a worn or damaged cylinder head gasket
or a cracked cylinder head.

# CHAPTER XXXIII

# Back Firing

**1021** Backfiring should not be confused with an explosion in the exhaust muffler. Backfiring is setting fire to a charge of gas and air before the piston arrives near enough to the top center for the momentum of the flywheel to carry it over, or firing the mixture in the inlet manifold and carburetor.

**1022** There are three causes for backfiring, given below, listed in the order in which they are most likely to occur:

(a) Backfire caused by a slow burning mixture.

(b) Backfire caused by a pre-ignition due to a faulty ignition system.

(c) Backfire caused by incandescent carbon in the cylinders.

**1023** A slow burning mixture may be caused by poor compression in the cylinders, faulty valve action, or a faulty carburetion system. A slow burning mixture may be either too rich or too lean. A rich mixture will show a dark smoke at the exhaust. It causes a carbon deposit in the cylinders, eventually resulting in continual backfiring due to incandescent carbon.

**1024** Backfire due to faulty ignition is usually caused by a ground in the wiring between the coil units and the commutator or the commutator being worn or dirty.

**1025** Pre-ignition may be due to incandescent carbon, faulty cooling system or the spark being advanced or retarded too far. The order of testing given above should be varied according to the conditions under which the tests are made and the previous knowledge of the car available to the party making the test. Often the trouble can be located quickly by changing the carburetor adjustment, tapping the carburetor to loosen a sticking float, finding the ground in the ignition system, or cleaning the commutator.

**1026** If changing the carburetor adjustment does not overcome the trouble, check the carburetor and fuel line as described in Pars. 1014 to 1020.

**1027** The first thing to do in locating the cause of the backfire is to determine whether or not it is being caused by pre-ignition due to incandescent carbon. Turn off the ignition switch and if the engine continues to fire, the trouble is pre-ignition due to incandescent carbon. See if the cooling system is overheated. If it is, allow the engine to cool. When the system is cool, start the engine and note whether the backfire occurs before the water boils. If it occurs before the system boils, the trouble is due to hot carbon. If it boils before the engine backfires the fault lies in the cooling system. If the backfire occurs immediately on starting the engine, after the system has been allowed to cool, it is due to ignition or valve trouble.

**1028**  While the engine is running, short the spark plugs as previously described until a cylinder is located where shorting eliminates the backfire.  Test the ignition wires of this cylinder for a ground, or the valves for failure to seat.

**1029**  See that there is no gasket leak.  See that the cylinder head bolts are drawn down tightly.  See that the spark plug is tight by pouring a little oil around it and watching to see if gas blows by.  In extreme cases, the sound of escaping gas may be heard.

**1030**  Remove the valve door and examine the valve action.  When examining the valves, see that the stem of the inlet valve is not too loose in its guide.  Too much clearance at this point allows the cylinders to suck in an excessive amount of air.

**1031**  If the compression is even in all cylinders, but the backfiring occurs steadily in one cylinder, the trouble lies in the ignition system (look for a short in the commutator wire) or less frequently, a leak around the inlet valve stem.

**1032**  If it is necessary to short one and two, or three and four cylinders, to overcome the backfire, the trouble is probably due to a poor gasket between the inlet manifold and the cylinder or an air leak in that branch of the inlet manifold.

**1033**  If the backfire is irregular and cannot be located by shorting one or two cylinders, the trouble probably lies in the carburetor system.  Having tried the carburetor adjustment, examine the inlet manifold and gasket for an air leak, by pouring a little oil on any doubtful spots.  If there is a leak the oil will be drawn into the cylinders.

**1034**  The typical indication of backfiring to ignition trouble is the coil buzzing continually.  However, backfiring may be caused by the commutator not being set properly, dirty commutator, secondary wires shorting one into the other, or a wet coil box.  With the exception of a wet coil box, these troubles may be located by visual inspection.  This inspection should be made immediately after trying the carburetor adjustment, as backfire due to a faulty commutator, may indicate on a test the same as a carburetor trouble.

**1035**  If the coil vibrates continually, examine the wire between that coil and the commutator as the trouble must necessarily lie in this part of the system.  In the majority of cases it is due to faulty wiring at the commutator or a shorted commutator.

# CHAPTER XXXIV

# Engine Knocks

1036 While it would be impractical to describe in detail every knock that might possibly occur in an automobile engine, there are certain knocks which comprise the bulk of this trouble and with which the mechanic should be familiar.

1037 Carbon knock—A carbon knock is a clear sounding knock which develops after the engine becomes warmed. It is heard most plainly when ascending a steep grade in high gear. Carbon knocks can be remedied by cleaning the carbon as described in Chapter IV.

1038 Loose piston knock—A loose piston knock sounds more like a rattle or slap than a knock; it is heard most plainly when the engine is cold, or when the engine is suddenly accelerated. Piston knocks indicate worn pistons and these parts should be checked for wear as described in Chapter VI.

1039 Connecting rod bearing knocks—A connecting rod bearing knock is a rapid hollow pounding which soon becomes worse if not attended to. It is heard most plainly when the engine is speeded up to about 25 miles per hour, and the throttle is suddenly closed. Rod knocks indicate worn bearings and the bearings should be taken up as described in Chapter V.

1040 Main bearing knock—A main bearing knock is a deep heavy toned knock, which is frequently accompanied by a jarring in the floor boards. It is particularly noticeable when the engine is under a load; for example when ascending a steep grade in high gear or pulling through heavy sand. Main bearing knocks indicate worn bearings and the bearings should be tightened as described in Chapter VII.

1041 Piston pin knock—A piston pin knock is a metallic tapping which is heard most plainly when driving about 25 miles per hour. It indicates either a worn piston pin or piston pin bushing, and these parts should be inspected for wear as described in Chapter VI.

1042 With the exception of a carbon knock the particular cylinder in which any of these knocks occur can be located by short circuiting each spark plug with a screw driver as described in Par. 1001.

1043 If, when No. 1 spark plug is shorted, the knock is no longer heard, the knock is either in the front main bearing or in the piston and connecting rod assembly of No. 1 cylinder, the sound of the knock determining whether it is in the bearing or in the assembly. This also applies to No. 4 cylinder, the knock being either in the piston and connecting rod assembly of No. 4 cylinder or in No. 3 main bearing.

1044 If shorting No. 2 spark plug eliminates the knock, the trouble lies in the piston and connecting rod assembly of No. 2 cylinder. If, however, the knock can still be heard but not as plainly, the trouble is probably due to a worn center main bearing. The same applies to No. 3 cylinder.

1045 Sounds are deceiving and hard to describe, so when the trouble is located as being in a particular cylinder, it is a good plan to take out the piston and connecting rod assembly and inspect it carefully.

1046 Noisy valves—A light tapping noise, which is present at all speeds usually indicates too great a clearance between the valves and push rods. Check the clearance between the valves and push rods as described in Par. 372, also make sure that none of the valves are sticking in the guides.

1047 A light tapping noise may also indicate a loose camshaft bearing. If the adjustment between the valves and push rods has been checked and found O. K., start the engine and insert a thin piece of metal, such as a hack saw blade between valve and push rod, repeating the operation until each valve and push rod has been checked. If the knock disappears, the nearest camshaft bearing is loose and the fit of the bearing should be checked. This can be done by removing the cylinder front cover and inserting a brass bar between each side of camshaft gear and cylinder block and forcing the camshaft back and forth in the bearing at the same time noting whether there is any movement of the shaft. If there is play in the bearing it will be necessary to remove the camshaft and install new bearings as described in Chapter IX.

## Conditions Which Sometimes Cause Knocks

1048 Flywheel loose on crankshaft, caused by flywheel cap screws not being drawn down tightly or the threads being stripped.

1049 Loose pulley pin or fan drive pulley loose on crankshaft; caused by excessive wear.

1050 Time gear loose on camshaft; caused by camshaft lock nut not being drawn down tightly.

1051 Excessive end thrust in camshaft front bearing indicates a badly worn bearing.

1052 Ignition timed incorrectly (See Par. 126).

1053 Pistons striking cylinder head or gasket; caused by crowding cylinder head towards valve side of cylinder block when assembling.

1054 Excessive end play in crankshaft; caused by a worn rear main bearing.

1055 Magnets striking magneto coil spools; caused by too small a gap between magnet clamps and magneto coil spools or excessive end play in crankshaft.

1056 Generator bearings tight or broken.

1057 Loose fan bushing; caused by a badly worn fan bushing.

1058 Crankcase loose in front bearing; caused by worn bearing cap, or loose cap screws.

# CHAPTER XXXV

# Clutch Troubles

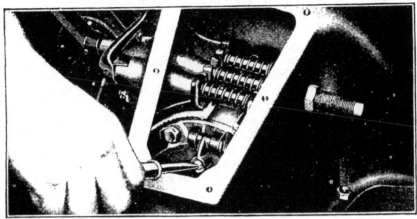

Fig. 507

## Slipping Clutch

**1059**  If the engine races, but the car does not pick up speed when changing from low to high speed or when the engine is suddenly accelerated, the trouble is probably due to wear on the transmission clutch disc and the clutch should be adjusted.

**1060**  To adjust the clutch, jack up one of the rear wheels and remove the mat, floor boards, and transmission cover door.  Place hand brake lever in forward position and turn the engine over  with the starting crank until one of the three clutch fingers is directly below the opening in the transmission cover.  Withdraw cotter pin from clutch finger screw and give the screw (See Fig. 507) one-half turn (clockwise), then replace the cotter pin and adjust the two other clutch finger screws in the same manner.  The transmission cover door is then replaced and the clutch tested for correct adjustment. If the clutch still slips, give each of the three screws another half turn, making sure that all three screws receive exactly the same number of half turns.  (If the car has been in service for a long period and the clutch still slips after the clutch finger screws have been run down to the end of their adjustment, the trouble is due either to worn clutch plates or a weak or broken clutch spring.)

**1061**  After tightening the clutch finger screws, check the adjustment of the low speed connection.  This is done by withdrawing cotter key and removing the clevis pin, then pull the clutch pedal back and check the play in the pin hole in the clevis and clutch lever shaft.  If there is less than $\frac{1}{16}''$ play, loosen the clevis lock nut and run the clevis in on the low speed connection until there is $\frac{1}{16}''$ play in pin holes in

246

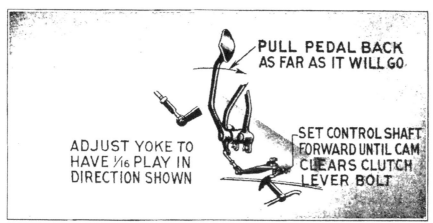

Fig. 508

clevis and clutch lever shaft, (See Fig. 508).   The pin is then inserted
through clevis and clutch lever shaft and locked with a cotter key
and the lock nut run down tightly against the clevis.   The clutch
lever screw is next run down until it holds the clutch in neutral
when the hand brake lever is pulled back to a vertical position.

## Car Creeps Forward With Hand Brake Applied

1062   If, when the engine is warm, and with the hand brake on, the
car has a tendency to creep forward when the engine is started, the
clutch lever screw probably requires adjusting.

1063   To adjust the clutch lever screw, remove mat and floor boards
and loosen the clutch lever screw lock nut (See "A" Fig. 509) and
turn the screw "B" one turn in a clockwise direction or until the
low speed pedal moves down $1\frac{3}{4}''$ when the hand brake lever is
pulled back as far as it will go.

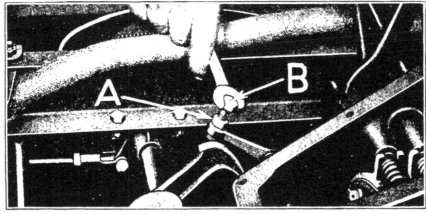

Fig. 509

**1064**  If the car still creeps forward when the engine is warm, the trouble is due either to the clutch or the low speed band being adjusted too tightly.  The clutch can be loosened by reversing the procedure for tightening the clutch as described in Par. 1060. The low speed band is adjusted as outlined in Par. 524.

**1065**  During cold weather, when the oil becomes congealed, it will sometimes cause the clutch plates to stick and this will have a tendency to make the car creep forward.  This condition disappears, however, as soon as the engine becomes warm.

## Clutch Pedal Sticks in Low Speed

**1066**  If the clutch speed pedal sticks when pressed down to engage the low speed, see if the pedal is striking against the floor boards.  If the pedal is not striking the floor boards, the trouble is caused by too loose an adjustment of the low speed band and can be remedied by adjusting the band as described in Par. 524.

# CHAPTER XXXVI

# Tracing Trouble in the Generator

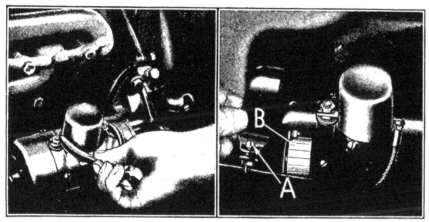

Fig. 510          Fig. 511

**1067** Trouble in the generator is indicated by the ammeter failing to register a charge. Occasionally it is indicated by a pronounced magnetic or singing noise in the generator.

**1068** If a magnetic or singing noise is heard in the generator and the ammeter fails to register a charge, place the ends of a pair of pliers across the cutout terminals (See Fig. 510) while the engine is running at a speed equivalent to 20 miles per hour. If the ammeter now registers a charge, the trouble lies in the cutout and a new cutout should be installed. If ammeter fails to register a charge the trouble is probably due to an open in the charging circuit and can be remedied as described in Chapter **XXXIX**.

**1069** If no humming noise is heard in the generator but the ammeter does not register a charge, short the cutout terminals with a pair of pliers as described above. If ammeter then shows a charge, remove the pliers and see if ammeter still registers a charge; if it does the trouble is due to a dirty or oily commutator, and can be remedied by cleaning the commutator. If ammeter stops registering when pliers are removed, the trouble lies in the cutout and a new cutout should be installed.

**1070** To clean the commutator, loosen the dust cover bolt and lift off dust cover (See "A" Fig. 511). With engine running, hold a piece of fine sandpaper (grade 00) against commutator "B" until commutator is clean and bright.

**1071** Occasionally generators fail to charge due to dirt or carbon deposits from the brushes lodging in the slots between the commutator bars. This condition can be noted by visual inspection, and the foreign matter removed with a small stiff wire.

Fig. 512

1072   If the above tests fail to locate the trouble remove generator from car. The trouble may be due to any of the following causes.

(a) Short circuit, or grounds in the armature.

(b) Grounded brush holder, or grounded or open field coil.

(c) Worn brushes.

(d) Excessive arcing at brushes.

1073   In addition to electrical trouble the generator is subject to mechanical trouble as follows:

(a) Commutator rough.

(b) Bearings broken or worn.

(c) Brush ring shifting or third brush shifting to incorrect position.

1074   After removing generator from the car inspect generator for worn brushes; weak or broken brush springs or broken brush or field connections. If brush springs and connections are O. K. place generator in a test stand; connect wire on test stand to generator terminal and close switch on stand to left; (this will make the generator run as a motor) and note the following conditions: (when making this test it may be necessary to give armature a turn with the hand in order to make it revolve See Fig. 512).

1075   If generator runs but ammeter hand flutters, it indicates armature trouble, and the armature should be removed and checked for shorts and grounds as described in Pars. 934 and 935.

1076   If the ammeter hand moves clear across the dial, open the switch on the stand at once, then check for a ground in generator terminal or brush holder as described in Pars. 927 and 929.

1077   If the generator runs and the ammeter registers over five amperes it indicates either a ground in the fields (check for grounds with the test points as described in Par. 925) or a tight bearing. If a bearing is tight it should be removed and thoroughly cleaned, or if necessary replaced.

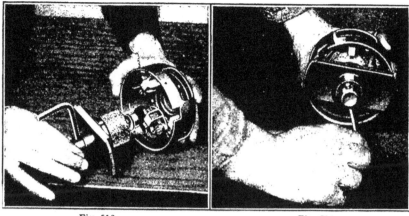

Fig. 513                    Fig. 514

**1078**  If ammeter registers two amperes or less, check for broken or loose field connections as described in Par. 921.

**1079**  While making these tests, worn and loose bearings can be readily detected by the noise which they make.

**1080**  A generator which is O. K. should run steadily and draw approximately three to five amperes and when the speed of the generator is slackened by holding the coupling with the fingers, the ammeter should register more and more until a reading of 18 to 20 amperes is attained just before armature stops revolving.

**1081**  Brush and spring troubles can be noted by visual inspection. If brushes are worn undersize, chipped, or springs are broken or weak, they should be replaced with new parts.  When new brushes are installed it is necessary to sand them in order to insure brushes seating squarely on commutator.  This is essential if correct brush setting is to be obtained.  The brushes should be sanded until they have a 75% or better bearing on the commutator.  A sanding tool can be used for this purpose (See Fig. 513).

**1082**  To sand the brushes, raise the brushes in the brush holders as described in Par. 905 and remove brush end bracket as described in Par. 913.  The sander (See Fig. 513) is then inserted into brush end bracket and the brushes lowered into the brush holders until they rest on sander.  The brush springs are then positioned over brushes; this provides the correct brush tension when sanding. The three brushes are sanded at the same time by revolving the handle on the sander (See Fig. 514).  It is very important that good brush seats be obtained before installing generator in car.

**1083**  When brushes stick in brush holders it is usually caused by the interior surface of the brush holder being rough or having a burr in it.  This can be remedied by lightly filing the holder with a fine file as shown in Fig. 515.  If the trouble is due to an oversize brush, it should be dressed down until it fits evenly in holder.

**1084**  If the positive or grounded brush springs are weak or broken it is less expensive to install a brush holder assembly rather than attempt to install new springs.

**1085**  Excessive arcing at brushes is due to three causes:

(a)  Incorrect brush setting, See Pars. 946 to 951.

(b)  Rough or dirty commutator:  If commutator is rough, place

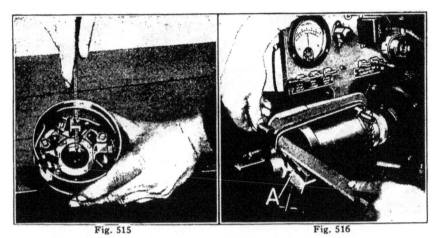

Fig. 515        Fig. 516

generator on test stand. Install commutator filing fixture (See "A" Fig. 516) and revolve armature. Hold a fine file lightly on commutator and dress commutator down until a smooth even surface is attained.

(c) Brushes not seating squarely on commutator: If brushes do not seat squarely on commutator, it will be necessary to sand them as described in Par. 1082.

1086    To test for opens or grounds in field coils without disassembling the generator, place generator on stand and raise third brush as described in Par. 905. Connect test stand terminal (See "A" Fig. 517) to brush terminal on third brush "B". If field coils are O. K. ammeter on stand will show a reading of 2 to $2\frac{1}{2}$ amperes with switch "C" on stand closed. If ammeter fails to show a charge it indicates an open in the field coils and new coils should be installed, providing a visual inspection fails to disclose the trouble. If a high reading is shown on ammeter either the brush holder or field coils are grounded. If brush holder is grounded a new brush ring should be installed. If field coils are grounded, they should be removed and inspected for broken wires, loose connections and broken insulation.

1087    After locating the trouble, the generator is assembled and installed in the car as outlined in Par. 450.

Fig. 517

# CHAPTER XXXVII

# Tracing Trouble in the Starting Motor

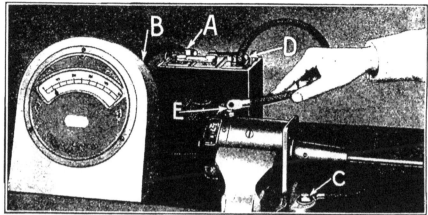

Fig. 518

**1088** If, when the starting switch is depressed, the engine fails to turn over and the tests described in Par. 988 indicate the trouble lies in the starting motor, it will be necessary to remove the starting motor from the car. (See Par. 953).

**1089** The starting motor is then placed in a vise, which is connected to a storage battery by means of a cable extending from the negative post on battery (See "A" Fig. 518), to ammeter "B" and to vise "C". The meter should have a range of from 0 to 500 amperes. A cable is then run from the positive terminal "D" on battery to starting motor terminal "E". When connected in this manner a charge of 50 to 75 amperes should register on the meter if starting motor is O. K.

**1090** If a high reading is shown on the ammeter and the armature revolves slowly, it indicates a grounded armature and the armature should be removed and tested for grounds in the same manner as the generator armature (See Par. 934).

**1091** A high meter reading, accompanied by a slow and jerky movement of the armature shaft, when the shaft is revolving, indicates a shorted armature and the armature should be removed, and tested for shorts as described in Par. 935.

**1092** If a high reading is shown on ammeter and the armature fails to rotate, it indicates either grounded field coils or a grounded brush holder and these parts should be removed and tested for grounds in the same manner as the generator field coils and brush ring assembly (See Pars. 925 and 927). It is unnecessary to remove the starting motor brush ring from brush end bracket when checking for a grounded brush holder.

**1093** If the armature fails to rotate and cannot be turned by hand and the meter shows a reading of from 100 to 200 amperes, it indicates that the shaft is bent or else binding in the shaft bushing. The shaft can be checked and straightened on a press in the same manner as the crankshaft (See Figs. 162 and 163).

**1094** If the shaft bushing is binding the old bushing should be removed as described in Par. 962 and a new bushing installed as described in Pars. 964 and 965. This condition can also be caused by the pole screws working loose in yoke, allowing a pole piece to come in contact with the armature.

# CHAPTER XXXVIII

# Tracing Trouble in the Lighting System

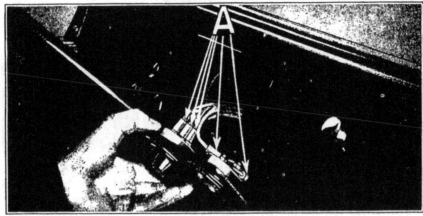

Fig. 519

**1095** Trouble in the lighting system is indicated by the failure of one or more of the lamps to light when the lighting switch lever is turned to points marked either "dim" or "bright".

## All Lamps Fail to Light

**1096** If all lamps fail to light when the lighting switch lever is turned on, turn off switch at once and see if ammeter registers a discharge. (If only one lamp fails to light, see Par. 1099.) If a heavy discharge is registered on the ammeter there is a ground in the wiring, which can generally be detected by the odor of burning insulation. Check headlamp wires at headlamp wire bushings in hood blocks to make sure that the insulation on the wires has not become chafed or worn. Inspect tail lamp wire at the point where it leaves switch to motor cable sleeve at starting switch, and examine the wire clear back to where it enters tail lamp to make sure there is no break in the insulation. If a spot light or dash light has been installed on the car, check the wires on these items for breaks in the insulation.

**1097** If the ammeter fails to show a discharge, and an examination discloses that the trouble is not due to the lamps being burned out, check battery wire connection on terminal block, point 13 (Fig. 498), and on back of ignition switch, point 18, and on ammeter, points 23 and 24, also at starting switch, point 26, for an open or loose connection. See that the rubber insulators on the ends of the wires on back of switch (See A, Fig. 519) are in position so that it is impossible for the metal part of any of the terminals to come in contact with each other. If these connections are clean and tight, the trouble is undoubtedly in the lighting switch, which should be checked as outlined in Par. 1101.

**1098** If all of the lamps burned out simultaneously the trouble is due to an open in the charging circuit between ignition switch, point 18, and ground connection on frame, point 29, and a check for opens in the charging circuit should be made as described in Chapter **XXXIX**.

## Tail Lamp or One Headlamp Fail to Light

**1099** When a headlamp or the tail lamp fails to light it is usually due to a burned out lamp. Remove lamps which fail to light and examine them to see if filament is broken. If filament is O. K. the trouble is probably due to loose connections. If it is the headlamp that fails to light, clean and tighten headlamp wire connections in plugs, point 1, Fig. 498, and headlamp wire connections on terminal block, points 15 and 16. If the filament in the tail lamp is O. K. but tail lamp fails to light when switch is turned on, the trouble is probably due to a loose connection at tail lamp plug, point 30, or on terminal block, point 14. All of these connections should be thoroughly cleaned and tightened. It is also advisable to check head and tail lamp wiring to make sure insulation is not broken.

**1100** If the lamps now fail to light, remove ignition switch and examine all connections on the back of switch to see that they are clean and tight, also that the rubber insulators on the ends of the wires (See "A", Fig. 519) are in position so that it is impossible for the metal part of any of the terminals to come in contact with each other.

**1101** If lamps still fail to light, the trouble lies in the ignition switch or a broken wire in the loom assembly. Check ignition switch by shorting across headlamp wire terminal (bright) and battery wire terminal, points 22 and 18 (Fig. 498) and battery wire terminal and headlamp wire terminal (dim), points 18 and 17, and tail light wire terminal and battery wire terminal, points 21 and 18, with the ends of a pair of pliers. If this test causes the lamps to light, the trouble lies in the ignition switch and a new switch should be installed. If the lamps still fail to light the trouble is undoubtedly due to a broken wire in the loom assembly and a new loom should be installed.

# CHAPTER XXXIX

# Tracing Trouble in Charging Circuit

**1102** The charging circuit (generator to battery) is one of the most important circuits on the car. It is in continuous operation whenever the engine is running at or above normal road speeds. Its proper operation determines to a large extent the life of the generator and battery.

**1103** The functioning of the circuit is indicated by the ammeter located on the instrument board. The ammeter hand should remain on or near the zero mark when the engine is idling, no lights burning, and the ignition switch turned on the magneto side. It should read 10 to 12 amperes charge at 20 to 25 miles per hour when the lights are off and the ignition switch is turned to magneto. It should read 3 to 4 amperes discharge when the engine is not running and the lights are burning on bright.

## Short Circuits

**1104** In tracing a short in the generator to battery circuit, it should be borne in mind that the current flows from each end, for example, from the generator when running at a charging speed, and from the battery to cutout when the generator is not charging. A short in this circuit is usually indicated by the odor of burning insulation, and if this warning is not heeded, the wire is likely to melt, resulting in an open circuit, and the possibility of fire. If the short circuit is between the battery and the ammeter, no indication of trouble will be shown on the ammeter. If it lies beyond the ammeter, it will be registered.

**1105** An ammeter is a delicate instrument, and if a heavy discharge from the battery is passed through it the ammeter hand is likely to become bent causing it to register inaccurately. To determine whether or not the ammeter hand is bent or whether its failure to register accurately is due to a short in the ammeter or wires, proceed as follows:

**1106** Disconnect "terminal block to starting switch" wire at the terminal block, point 13, Fig. 498. If the ammeter now registers zero, the hand is not bent but there is a short in the ammeter wire from the ammeter to cutout, points 3, 11 and 23, or ammeter to ignition switch wire, points 18 and 24, or in the light and ignition switch, or in the head or tail lamp wires. To find the short, examine these wires carefully for a break in the insulation; also note whether rubber insulators are in place on the terminals on back of ammeter and ignition switch (See "A" Fig. 519).

## Open Circuits

**1107** An "open" in the charging circuit is a condition to be guarded against, as running the car for any length of time with the charging

256

Fig. 520

circuit open will result in a burned out generator. While the engine is running at a fair rate of speed an open is indicated by the ammeter showing no charge and a decided hum in the generator. When this condition occurs the trouble should be located and corrected immediately. If it is necessary to run the engine while the charging circuit is open, the generator should be grounded. This can be done by running a piece of wire from the generator terminal to one of the brush end bracket screws, (See Fig. 520).

1108 Never turn the lights on when the charging circuit is open, and the engine is running, as it will burn out the lamps.

1109 To locate an open in the charging circuit, turn on the lights (the engine should not be running when making this test). If the lights burn, the battery wire on ignition switch is O. K., and the trouble lies between the ignition switch and the cutout, points 18 and 3 (Fig. 498). If the lights do not burn, ground the two ammeter terminals, points 24 and 23. If a spark occurs the open does not lie in the ammeter. If no spark occurs the trouble lies between the ammeter and ground connection on frame, points 24 and 29. Next ground the battery wire on terminal block, point 13. If no spark occurs, the trouble lies between the battery wire on terminal block and ground connections on frame, points 13 and 29. The starting switch terminal on battery side, point 26, should then be tested in the same manner. If, when the positive battery post, point 27, is grounded, no spark occurs the indications are that the battery is dead or there is an open at either the negative post on battery or ground connection on frame, points 28 and 29. A visual inspection at negative post connection on battery and ground connection on frame, points 28 and 29, will detect at which of these points the open is located, as no spark, of course, will occur, when points 28 and 29 are grounded. (A test lamp, made with a six volt headlamp bulb, can be used in making these tests in place of grounding for a spark).

# CHAPTER XL

# Horn Fails to Sound

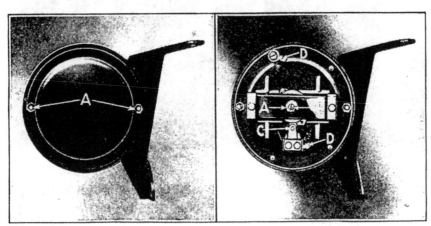

Fig. 521                 Fig. 522

**1110** Failure of the horn to sound when the horn switch button is depressed is due to:

    (a)  Loose or dirty connection either at the horn, terminal block or switch, points 6, 13 and 31 (Fig. 498).

    (b)  Worn horn button.

    (c)  Broken contact spring.

    (d)  Horn wires broken or insulation worn.

    (e)  Incorrect adjustment.

    (f)  Breaker points sticking or burned.

    (g)  Lead wires broken at soldered connection.

**1111** If the trouble is not due to loose or dirty connections at points 6 or 13, run out the horn switch bolt and nut and lift out horn button and switch. Examine the point of the button for wear. If the point is badly worn, the spring will fail to make contact when the horn button is depressed.

**1112** If the horn button is O. K., inspect the switch for loose connections or broken contact spring. Examine the wires for breaks where they enter the switch assembly. If wires and switch are O. K. replace the switch and run off the two horn cover nuts (See "A", Fig. 521) and lift off horn cover. See that plunger lock nut (See "A", Fig. 522) is drawn down tightly. If the nut is loose, tighten it and then try the horn.

**113** If the horn still fails to sound, check the play between plunger and diaphragm. If the distance is less than $\frac{1}{16}$" or more than $\frac{3}{32}$" loosen the plunger lock nut and turn adjusting screw "B" until the correct adjustment is obtained. (On the magneto type horn the adjusting nut is located at the front of the diaphragm and can be adjusted by inserting a small wrench into the funnel end of the horn and loosening or tightening the nut.)

**1114** After checking the adjustment, depress the horn button; if no sound comes from the horn, examine for burned or sticking breaker points at point "C". See if the lead wires from the coil are broken at their soldered connections (See point "D"). If the wires are broken, they can be repaired by soldering. Examine the breaker points; if slightly burned they can be dressed down with a fine file.

# CHAPTER XLI

# Battery Care

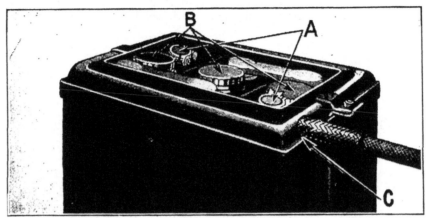

Fig. 523

**1115** While the battery requires comparatively little attention it is absolutely essential that it receive some care. The care it requires may be summed up as follows:

(a) See that the cable connections on the positive and negative posts (See "A" Fig. 523) are clean and tight and are covered with a coating of vaseline.

(b) Keep the filling plugs tight (See "B"), and battery dry and clean. Failure to screw the plugs down tightly will permit the electrolyte to spray out.

(c) Keep the nuts on the ends of the battery clamp bolts drawn down tightly.

(d) Add water frequently, enough to keep the plates covered at all times. Distilled water or clean rain water that has not come in contact with metal should be used for this purpose.

(e) Take hydrometer readings every two weeks at any time except just after adding water and be guided by their indications as follows: Readings between 1.250 and 1.300 indicate a fully charged battery. Readings less than 1.225 but more than 1.150 indicate a battery less than half charged; at such time the lights and starter should be used sparingly until the readings become more than 1.250. Readings less than 1.150 indicate complete discharge, in which case the battery should be given a bench charge. This discharged condition may be due to trouble other than in the battery in which case all connections should be examined; a loose or dirty connection is often the cause of trouble.

**1116** If the connections between battery and cable terminals are not kept clean they will corrode, causing a poor connection or else opening the circuit altogether. The corrosion will also consume the battery cable insulation (See "C") causing a short circuit when the exposed part of the cable comes in contact with the metal battery container and resulting in the battery becoming discharged. If the corrosion is not removed from the positive post of the battery, it will continue to build up until a sufficient amount has accumulated on the post to reach the metal battery cover and form a ground.

1117 If the battery wire terminal becomes corroded and is causing trouble, remove it and clean the parts thoroughly with weak ammonia. Remove all foreign matter and give all connections a coating of vaseline and securely tighten.

1118 There may be a leak or ground in the wiring, which is causing the battery to run down. Test for this by turning on the lights, then remove the bulbs from their sockets. Disconnect one of the cables at the battery. Then rub the cable terminal against the battery terminal post from which it was removed. If sparks are noticed, there is a ground in the wiring, which must be looked for and removed. (See Chapter **XXXIX**.)

1119 If starter will not crank engine, turn on lights and attempt to start in the usual manner. If lights go out or become quite dim, the battery is in poor condition and should be given a bench charge and the cause of the trouble located and removed. If lights continue to burn brightly, the trouble is elsewhere than in the battery.

1120 Detailed instructions for servicing batteries is described in the Ford battery manual, a copy of which will be furnished to dealers upon application to nearest Ford Branch.

# Chapter XLII
# Servicing the Improved Car

Fig. 524

1121   The numerous improvements made in the improved 1925 car have to some extent altered former methods of removing and installing certain parts.

1122   So that no difficulty will be experienced when replacing a new part, we will, wherever an improvement has altered former replacement methods, describe in detail how the new part is removed and installed.

## Replacing the New Type Fenders

1123   In addition to being of a wider and heavier construction, the new crown type fenders extend lower and are hung closer to the wheels, thus affording maximum protection against road splash.

1124   In place of mounting the fenders on fender irons, the new type fenders are bolted direct to the body and frame. This method of assembly affords exceptional rigidity and eliminates fender vibration.

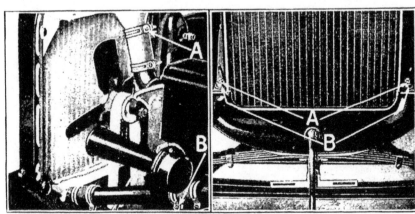

Fig. 525                              Fig. 526

Fig. 527                    Fig. 528

## Removing the Front Fender—

1125   To remove the new type front fender, it is first necessary to remove the radiator; the radiator is removed as follows:

1126   Open pet cock underneath radiator and while water is draining, lift off hood and disconnect priming rod (see "A" Fig. 524) by unhooking it from carburetor butterfly "B."

1127   Loosen cylinder head outlet hose clip screw (see "A" Fig. 525) also cylinder water inlet hose clip screw "B".

1128   Withdraw cotter pins and run off radiator stud nuts (see "A" Fig. 526) and lift off upper thimbles "B".

1129   Pry up the three loom clips on radiator bottom tank (see "A" Fig. 527) and lift out lighting wire loom from underneath clips.

1130   Loosen radiator stay rod lock nut (see "A" Fig. 528) and lift rod out of radiator stay rod bracket "B".

1131   Lift radiator off of studs—radiator inlet connection together with outlet pipe can then be withdrawn from hose connections (see "A" and "B" Fig. 529) and radiator lifted from car.

1132   Remove starting crank ratchet pin (see "A" Fig. 530) by withdrawing cotter key "D" and driving the pin out of the ratchet with a hammer and drift.   Ratchet "C" can then be withdrawn from end of starting crank.

Fig. 529                    Fig. 530

Fig. 531

**1133**   Withdraw starting crank together with radiator apron spacer (see "A" Fig. 531). Radiator lower thimbles "B", stud springs "C", and radiator apron can now be lifted off over ends of radiator studs.

**1134**   Run off the nuts on the ends of the two engine pan bolts (see "C" Fig. 524) also the nuts on the ends of the two hood block bolts

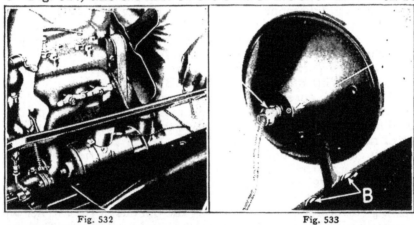

Fig. 532                Fig. 533

"D" Fig. 524. Hood block can then be lifted from frame as shown in Fig. 532.

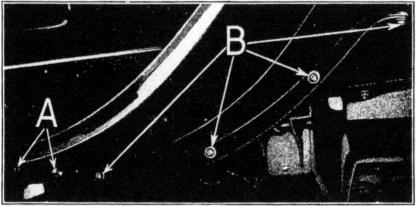

Fig. 534

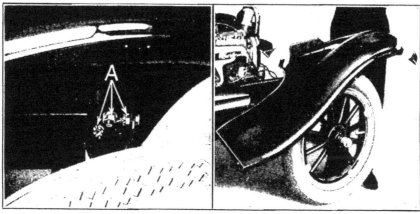

Fig. 535          Fig. 536

**1135** Disconnect headlamp plug (see "A" Fig. 533) at headlamp by pressing in on plug and turning it counter clockwise.

**1136** Run off the nuts on the ends of the two headlamp bracket bolts (see "B" Fig. 533). Headlamp can then be withdrawn from fender apron.

**1137** Run off the nuts on the ends of the two front fender to running board bolts (see "A" Fig. 534) and withdraw the bolts.

**1138** Run off the nuts on the ends of the four front fender to dust shield bolts "B" and withdraw the bolts.

**1139** Run off nuts on the ends of the three front fender to bracket bolts (see "A" Fig. 535) and withdraw bolts. Fenders can now be lifted off as shown in Fig. 536.

### Installing Front Fender—

**1140** To install the new type front fender, position it against frame and fender bracket, lining up the bolt holes in fender with holes in frame. The three front fender to bracket bolts are then inserted through bracket and fender. Castle nuts are run down on the ends of two of the bolts, but are not locked with cotter keys until all bolts and nuts are entered. The third bolt is locked in position with a lockwasher and hexagon nut. (See Fig. 535.) Do not draw nuts down tightly until all fender bolts have been entered.

**1141** Place flat washers over the ends of the four front fender to dust shield bolts and insert the bolts through fender and dust shield (see "B" Fig. 534). The bolts are locked in position by means of a flat washer and a lockwasher which are placed over the ends of each bolt and nuts run down but not tightened until all bolts are entered.

**1142** Insert the two fender to running board bolts through running board and fender (see "A" Fig. 534). Place lockwashers and nuts over the ends of the bolts and run down nuts but do not tighten until all bolts are entered.

**1143** Insert headlamp wire into notch in hood block and position hood block on frame lining up bolt holes in hood block with holes in frame. The two engine pan bolts (see "C" Fig. 524) are then inserted through hood block, frame and engine pan; lockwashers being placed over the ends of each bolt and nuts run down but not tightened until all fender bolts are entered.

1144 Place a flat washer over the end of one of the two hood block bolts (see "D" Fig. 524) and insert the bolts through the hood block. Place a lockwasher and nut over the ends of each of the two bolts and draw the nuts down tightly.

1145 Draw all fender bolts and nuts down tightly, locking the two fender to bracket bolt nuts with cotter keys (see Fig. 535).

### Installing the Radiator—

1146 Position radiator apron (see "E" Fig. 530) over ends of radiator studs "B". Place radiator apron spacer over end of starting crank (see "A" Fig. 531). Insert starting crank through radiator apron and starting crank sleeve. (It is very important that the radiator apron spacer is installed, as the spacer holds the crank firmly in the sleeve and prevents any possibility of a rattle.) Position starting crank ratchet over end of crank (see "C" Fig. 530). Line up hole in ratchet with hole in crank and insert starting crank ratchet pin (see "A" Fig. 530) through ratchet and crank. The pin is locked in position by means of a cotter key which is inserted through end of pin as shown at "D".

1147 Position springs (see "C" Fig. 531) and lower thimbles "B" over ends of radiator studs.

1148 Insert cylinder head outlet hose over end of radiator inlet connection (see "A" Fig. 529). Insert radiator outlet pipe into outlet hose connection "B" making sure that the lower hose connection is underneath lighting wire loom. Position radiator over ends of studs, seating radiator firmly on lower thimbles. Place upper thimbles (see "B" Fig. 526) over ends of studs. Run down radiator stud nuts "A" sufficiently far to permit locking them with cotter keys. Insert radiator stay rod into bracket on dash and run down and tighten lockwasher and nut (see Fig. 528). Tighten hose clip screws on top and side hose connections.

1149 Position headlamp on fender, lining up bolt holes in headlamp with bolt holes in fender. Insert the two headlamp bolts through headlamp and fender, running down lockwashers and nuts on ends of bolts.

1150 Connect headlamp plug to headlamp by pressing in on plug and turning it clockwise.

1151 Insert lighting wire loom under the three clips on radiator bottom tank, bending the clips down until loom is held firmly in position. (See Fig. 527.)

1152 Connect carburetor priming rod to carburetor butterfly by inserting priming rod through radiator apron and hooking it into carburetor butterfly. (See "B" Fig. 524.)

1153 Replace hood; close drain cock underneath radiator and fill radiator with clean water.

1154 The headlamps should now be checked for alignment and focus.

### Focusing and Aligning the Headlamps—

1155 On the improved car, the headlamps are set higher and further apart; this has been accomplished by mounting the headlamps on the fenders. The new method of assembly necessitates dealers making a few changes in the dimensions of their shop layouts used for focusing and aligning headlamps. Fig. 537 shows the new layout.

1156 Headlamps are aligned and focused with the empty car standing on a level surface in front of a white wall or screen 25 feet from the

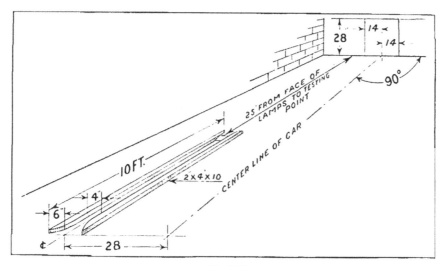

Fig. 537

front of the headlamps. This wall must be in semi-darkness or sufficiently shielded from direct light so that the light spots upon it from the headlamps can be clearly seen. The wall or screen must be marked off with black lines as shown in Figs. 124 and 125.

**1157** To focus the headlamps:

(a) Turn on bright lights.

(b) Focus, by means of focusing screw (see "C" Fig. 533) at back of lamps, first one lamp and then the other, adjusting the bulb filament at the focal center of the reflector to obtain an elongated elliptical spot of light on the wall, with its long axis horizontal (see Figs. 124 and 125).

With lamps thus focused for the "bright" filament, the "dim" will be in correct position.

**1158** The headlamps are aligned after they are assembled to the car by bending the headlamp brackets as follows: (A new type bending iron is used, details of which are shown in Fig. 538).

(a) The tops of the bright spots on the 25-foot wall are to be set at a line 28 inches above level of surface on which car stands. (See Fig.

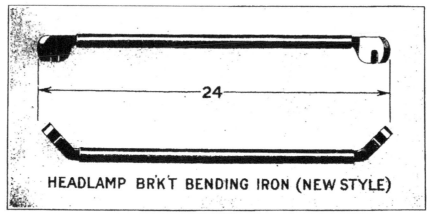

HEADLAMP BRK'T BENDING IRON (NEW STYLE)

Fig. 538

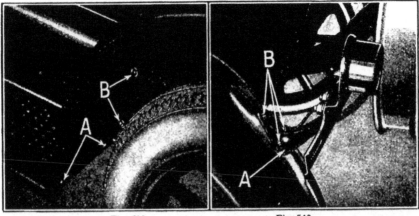

Fig. 539             Fig. 540

537.) With top lines thus set for empty car, the headlamps will also have the proper tilt under full loads as required by the various states.

(b) The beam of light from each headlamp is to extend straight forward, that is, the centers of the elliptical spots of light must be 28 inches apart.

**1159** Proper alignment is readily checked by means of a horizontal line on the wall in front of the car 28 inches above the level surface of car, and two vertical lines 28 inches apart, each one 14 inches from center line of car. Proper alignment of car relative to marks on the wall may be readily provided by use of wheel guide blocks for one side of the car, as shown in Fig. 537. If it is impractical to tie up the floor space required by these blocks, marks painted on the floor can be used to show where one set of wheels should track and where the car should be stopped.

## Replacing Rear Fenders

**1160** To remove the new design rear fender, run off nuts on the ends of the two rear fender to running board bolts (see "A" Fig. 539).

Run off nuts and withdraw the two fender to dust shield bolts "B". Run out the four fender to body bolts (see "A" Fig. 541). (The nuts

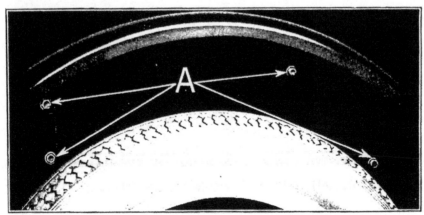

Fig. 541

on the ends of these bolts are fastened in the body and remain there when the bolts are withdrawn.)

Fender can now be lifted from body.

1161  The new tail lamp and license bracket assembly is installed on the left rear fender (see "A" Fig. 540). When changing a left rear fender, it is therefore necessary to remove the bracket. This is done by disconnecting the tail lamp wire at tail lamp and running off the nuts from the ends of the three bracket to fender bolts "B". Bracket can then be lifted off of fender. To install the new tail lamp and license bracket, the procedure is reversed.

### *Installing Rear Fender—*

1162  To install the new type fender, place lockwashers over the ends of the four fender to body bolts. Position fender against body and line up the bolt holes. Insert the four fender to body bolts (see "A" Fig. 541) through fender and run them down into the fender bolt nuts which are held stationary in body. Do not tighten until all bolts have been entered.

1163  Insert the two fender to running board bolts through fender and running board (see "A" Fig. 539). Place lockwashers over the ends of the bolts and run down the nuts. Do not tighten the nuts until all fender bolts and nuts are entered.

1164  Place flat washers over the ends of the two fender to dust shield bolts and insert bolts through fender and dust shield (see "B" Fig. 539). Place a flat washer, also a lockwasher over the ends of each of the two bolts. Start nuts on ends of bolts and draw them down tightly.

1165  Draw down all fender bolts and nuts tightly.

## Replacing the New Design Running Boards

1166  The new design running boards are $1\frac{1}{2}''$ wider than the old style board and in addition they are set closer to the ground, thus affording maximum convenience when entering or leaving the car.

1167  The new running boards can be easily removed by running out eight bolts and nuts as follows:

1168  *Removing.* Run off the nuts on the ends of the two front fender to running board bolts (see "A" Fig. 534) and withdraw bolts.

1169  Run off the nuts on the ends of the two rear fender to running board bolts (see "A" Fig. 539) and withdraw bolts.

1170  Run off the nuts on the ends of the four running board bolts (see "A" Fig. 542) and withdraw bolts. Running boards can now be lifted from brackets.

1171  *Installing.* Place the two running board blocks on running board brackets. Position running board on top of blocks, lining up bolt holes in running board with holes in blocks and brackets.

1172  Insert the four running board bolts (see "A" Fig. 542) through running board blocks and brackets, placing lockwashers over the ends of the bolts and running down the nuts. (Do not draw nuts down tightly until all bolts have been entered.)

1173  Insert the two rear fender to running board bolts (see "A" Fig. 539) through fender and running board. Place lockwashers over the ends of the bolts and run down the nuts but do not tighten until all bolts have been entered.

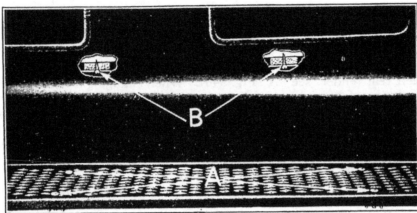

Fig. 542

**1174** Insert the two front fender to running board bolts through running board and fender. Place lockwashers over the ends of the bolts and run down and tighten nuts (see "A" Fig. 534).

**1175** Draw down nuts tightly on the ends of the four running board bolts, also the two rear fender to running board bolts.

## Replacing the New Dust Shield

**1176** *Removing.* To remove the new design dust shield, it is first necessary to remove the running board as described in Pars. 1168 to 1170.

**1177** After removing the running board, run out the two wood screws which hold dust shield to body (see "B" Fig. 542).

**1178** Withdraw cotter pin from end of rear hood clip; hood clip washer, and spring can then be lifted off and hood clip (see "A" Fig. 543) withdrawn.

**1179** Run off nut on end of hood block bolt (see "B" Fig. 543) and withdraw bolt.

**1180** Run off the nuts on the ends of the four front fender to dust shield bolts (see "B" Fig. 534) and withdraw the bolts.

**1181** Run off the nuts on the ends of the two rear fender to dust shield bolts (see "B" Fig. 539) and withdraw the bolts.

Fig. 543

Fig. 544

1182 By sliding the dust shield back until it clears the front fender, the shield can be withdrawn as shown in Fig. 544.

1183 *Installing.* To install the new dust shield, insert end of shield between rear fender and frame (see Fig. 544).

1184 Position hood block support in channel of hood block, lining up bolt and hood clip holes in support with bolt and clip holes in hood block.

1185 Draw dust shield forward until shield rests on hood block bracket, lining up the hood block bolt hole in the shield with the bolt hole in bracket.

1186 Insert hood block bolt (see "B" Fig. 543) through hood block, support and bracket. Place a lockwasher over end of bolt and run down nut but do not tighten until all dust shield bolts have been entered.

1187 Insert hood clip (see "A" Fig. 543) through hood block and support. Position hood clip spring and washer over end of clip, locking them in position by inserting a cotter key through end of clip.

1188 Place a flat washer over the ends of the two rear fender to dust shield bolts and insert the bolts through fender and dust shield. A flat washer and a lockwasher are then placed over the ends of the bolts and the nuts run down but not tightened until all dust shield bolts are entered.

1189 Place flat washers over the ends of the four front fender to dust shield bolts and insert the bolts through fender and dust shield (see "B" Fig. 534). Place a flat washer and lockwasher over the end of each of the bolts and run down nuts tightly.

1190 Tighten nuts on the ends of the hood block bolt and the two rear fender to dust shield bolts.

1191 Run down the two dust shield to body screws through dust shield into body (see "B" Fig. 542).

1192 The running boards are now installed as described in Pars. 1171 to 1175.

# The New Type Coil Box

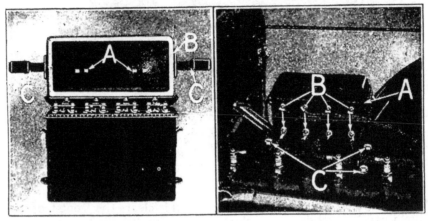

Fig. 545                                    Fig. 546

**1193**   In place of being bolted to the back of the dash, the new design coil box is mounted on the left hand side of the cylinder head.

**1194**   The new location provides easy access to the coil units and affords quieter operation as the action of the vibrators cannot be heard by the occupants of the car.

**1195**   The hold down springs which are riveted to the inside of the cover (see "A" Fig. 545) hold the coils tightly against the box contacts, insuring perfect contact at all times.   By means of a special composition gasket (see "B" Fig. 545) and two heavy type spring latches "C" which are hinged to the coil box cover, a dust and waterproof joint is formed between cover and box.   A trough (see "A" Fig. 546) which has been made an integral part of the cover prevents any water reaching the terminals on the back of the coil box.

**1196**   To remove the new type coil box: run off the nuts on the ends of the eight coil box terminal posts (see "B" Fig. 546) and lift off commutator loom and spark plug wires.

**1197**   Run off ignition wire terminal nut on bottom of coil box and lift off ignition wire.

**1198**   Run out the three cylinder head bolts which hold coil box to cylinder head (see "C" Fig. 546), coil box can then be removed.

**1199**   To install the new type coil box, the procedure is reversed.

# New Design Fan Bracket

**1200** To obtain maximum cooling efficiency, the fan on the improved car has been placed at a higher elevation. This improvement has been accomplished by means of a new type fan bracket which is designed as an integral part of the cylinder head outlet connection. (See "A" Fig. 547.)

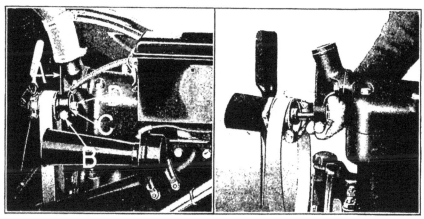

Fig. 547          Fig. 548

## *Adjusting Fan Belt*

**1201** To adjust the new fan belt, loosen lock nut on end of adjusting screw (see "B" Fig. 547) then turn the adjusting screw "B" to the right, this will tighten the belt. To loosen the belt, turn the adjusting screw to the left. (The method of obtaining the correct tension of the fan belt is described in Par. 127.) When correct tension is obtained, tighten lock nut on end of adjusting screw "B" making sure that the cotter key in the end of the screw is in good condition.

## *Replacing Fan Belt*

**1202** To remove the new fan belt, loosen lock nut on end of adjusting screw (see "B" Fig. 547) and turn the screw to the left until the fan shaft in the eccentric reaches the lowest point of the bracket (see "C" Fig. 547). Fan belt can then be slipped from fan and drive pulleys and lifted off over fan.

**1203** *Installing.* The new fan belt is installed by slipping it over the fan and positioning it on fan and drive pulleys. The belt is then adjusted as described in Par. 1201.

## *Replacing Fan*

**1204** To remove the fan, loosen the fan belt as described in Par. 1202 and run off fan shaft nut (see "D" Fig. 547). The fan shaft can then be withdrawn from the eccentric as shown in Fig. 548.

**1205** To install the fan, simply reverse the procedure.

# New Design Transmission Brake Band

Fig. 549

**1206** The new transmission brake band has been increased from $1\frac{1}{8}''$ to $1\frac{3}{4}''$ wide, an improvement which affords an exceptionally smooth and positive braking effect as well as contributing to the ease of braking. In addition, the increased width of the band (see Fig. 549) makes adjustments infrequent and materially increases the life of the lining.

**1207** To facilitate replacement, all transmission bands are equipped with detachable ears. This improvement permits new linings being installed without removing the transmission cover, thereby effecting a saving in time and labor, as well as lowering replacement cost to the customer.

**1208** Installation instructions contained in Chapter XIII apply to the present design bands.

## Transmission Brake Drum

**1209** To provide ample braking surface for the improved brake band, the new design transmission brake drum has been increased from $1\frac{1}{8}''$ to $1\frac{3}{4}''$ wide (see "A" Fig. 550).

**1210** Hardened steel shoes are fitted over each of the six lugs inside of the new drum as shown at "A" Fig. 551. The steel shoes prolong the life of the drum by absorbing any clutch disc wear which would otherwise be directed on the lugs.

**1211** The shoes can be easily replaced by withdrawing them from the brake drum lugs with a pair of pliers; new shoes being installed by placing them over the lugs and tapping them down into position with a small hammer.

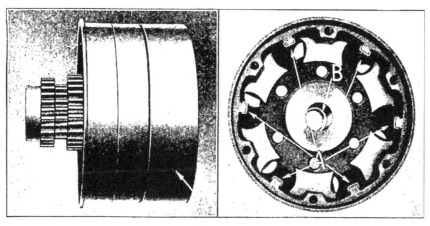

Fig. 550            Fig. 551

**1212** When rebushing the brake drum, only one driven gear sleeve bushing is now used in the brake drum sleeve (see "B" Fig. 551) instead of the two bushings formerly used. This bushing (3320C-T712) is pressed in from the driven gear end of the sleeve.

## The Transmission Cover

**1213** The new transmission cover is designed with an extension at the top of the cover behind which are placed steel shims as shown at "A" Fig. 552. This extension acts as an added support to the crankcase while the shims which are inserted between extension and cylinder block insure accurate alignment of the universal ball cap.

**1214** When overhauling an engine or transmission, or in fact performing any repair operation which requires the removal of the crankcase, it is extremely important when reassembling to see that the universal ball cap bearing lines up accurately on the drive plate shaft.

Fig. 552

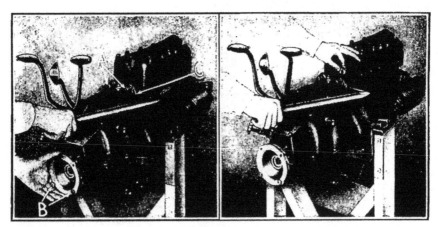

Fig. 553              Fig. 554

**1215** To insure these parts being in exact alignment the crankcase and transmission cover should be installed as described in Pars. 326 to 330 inclusive. The two transmission cover to cylinder bolts are then inserted into extensions on transmission cover and run down about half way into cylinder block (see "A" Fig. 553).

**1216** The fit of the ball cap on the drive plate shaft is then checked by loosening the two ball cap screws (see "B" Fig. 553) and moving the ball cap back and forth on the shaft. If the cap moves freely on the shaft, the alignment of the crankcase and cylinder block is OK and the two transmission covers to cylinder block bolts can be tightened. If ball cap does not move freely on drive plate shaft, insert a flat bar between cylinder block and transmission cover (see "C" Fig. 553) and slightly pry the transmission cover back until ball cap moves freely on shaft. This will leave a small gap between extensions on transmission cover and cylinder block. With the flat bar still in position, insert sufficient shims between cylinder block and transmission cover (see Fig. 554) to completely fill the gap between these parts. When sufficient shims have been installed, withdraw the flat bar and run down the two transmission cover to cylinder block bolts tightly (see "A" Fig. 553).

**1217** A second check should now be made to insure that the ball cap moves freely on drive plate shaft. If ball cap binds on shaft, remove or install additional shims between cylinder block and transmission cover until correct alignment is obtained, after which the two ball cap screws are tightened.

**1218** When performing repair operations requiring the removal of the transmission cover only, care must be exercised when installing the cover to replace the exact number of shims which were removed from between transmission cover and cylinder block.

# Replacing the Hub Brake Shoe

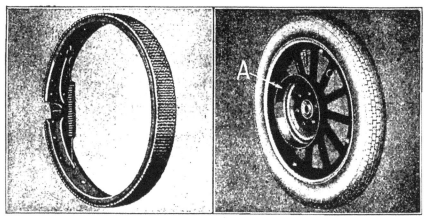

Fig. 555                    Fig. 556

**1219**  The new hub brake shoe has been increased from $7\frac{15}{16}''$ in diameter to $10\frac{15}{16}''$ in diameter, the width of the shoe being increased from $1''$ to $1\frac{1}{2}''$ (see **Fig. 555**).

**1220**  The hub brake shoes are now made of pressed steel in place of cast iron, and are covered with a heavy asbestos lining which renders braking smooth and positive and eliminates all metal to metal contact between brake shoe and drum.

**1221**  To provide ample braking surface for the new shoe, the hub brake drum has been increased from $8''$ in diameter to $11''$ in diameter, the width of the drum being increased from $1\frac{13}{16}''$ to $1\frac{27}{32}''$ (see "A" Fig. 556).

**1222**  The shoe is assembled to the axle housing plate by means of four steel clips which are riveted to the plate (see "A" Fig. 557). A heavy coil spring shown at "B" holds the shoe firmly against the hub brake cam.

Fig. 557                    Fig. 558

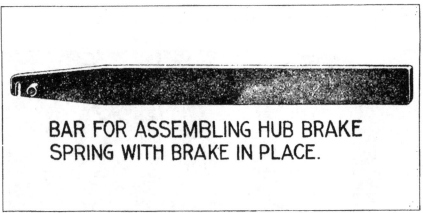

BAR FOR ASSEMBLING HUB BRAKE
SPRING WITH BRAKE IN PLACE.

Fig. 559

**1223**   After removing the rear wheel the new brake shoe is removed as follows:

*Removing—*

**1224**   Disconnect brake shoe spring by withdrawing it from lugs on brake shoe.   As the new spring is larger and has a much stronger tension than the old type spring, a special tool has been designed (see Fig. 559) to facilitate its removal and installation.   Fig. 560 shows how the new tool is used to remove the spring.   After removing the spring, the brake shoe can be lifted off of axle brake housing plate, as shown in Fig. 558.

*Installing—*

**1225**   To install the new brake shoe, position it on axle brake housing plate, inserting the flange on the edge of the shoe behind the four steel clips on housing plate (see "A" Fig. 557).   Line up brake shoe so that hub brake cam (see "A" Fig. 558) can be entered between ends of brake shoe.

**1226**   Install brake shoe spring by placing it over lug on upper side of brake shoe and hooking it over the lower lug with the special tool as shown in Fig. 560.

**1227**   The rear wheel is then replaced.

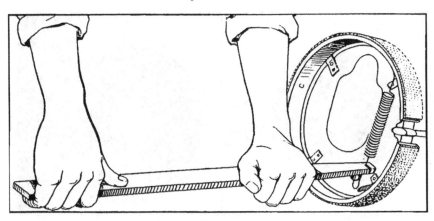

Fig. 560

# Removing and Installing the Gasoline Tank

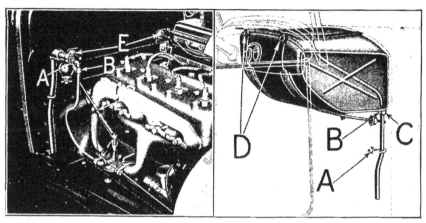

Fig. 561                    Fig. 562

**1228** The new design gasoline tank is placed underneath the cowl between the instrument board and dash. The new location places the tank at a higher elevation, bringing it almost directly over the carburetor, thus insuring a steady flow of fuel to the carburetor even when ascending the steepest hills.

**1229** The sediment bulb is conveniently located underneath the hood. This has been accomplished by means of a flanged pipe connection extending from the gasoline tank through the dash. The new location affords easy access to the sediment bulb and simplifies the operation of removing water and foreign matter which the sediment bulb collects.

**1230** The tank is filled from the outside of the car, the filler cap being located in the center of the cowl underneath a rain proof cover. A large trough or wall built around the filler and connected to an overflow pipe, carries any spillage direct to the ground.

**1231** *Removing—*

To remove the new tank:

Close shutoff cock on sediment bulb. See "A" Fig. 561.

Run off feed pipe pack nut "B" at sediment bulb outlet elbow and withdraw feed pipe from elbow.

Drain gasoline from fuel tank. A quick method of draining the fuel is as follows: (a) Place a 10 gallon or larger gasoline container near car. (b) Insert a large funnel into the end of a 5 or 6-foot length of hose. (c) Place end of hose in the container. (d) Remove filler cap on tank. (e) Loosen the sediment bulb, then while holding the funnel underneath end of sediment bulb connection, run out the sediment bulb. The gasoline will then flow freely into the funnel and through the hose into the container. (f) (Caution: When draining gasoline, keep fires away.)

**1232** After draining gasoline from tank, loosen nut on end of overflow pipe clamp (see "A" Fig. 562).

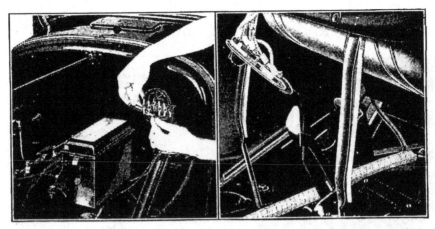

Fig. 563            Fig. 564

1233   Run out overflow pipe set screw "B". Pipe can then be withdrawn from gasoline tank connection "C".

1234   Remove cotter key (see "C" Fig. 561) and withdraw carburetor adjusting rod "D" through dash.

1235   Run off the two gasoline tank strap nuts (see "E" Fig. 561 and lift off washers.

1236   Hold the nuts stationary on the ends of the two ignition switch screws and run out the screws.

1237   Withdraw ignition switch from instrument board (see Fig. 564).

1238   To prevent any possibility of a spark occurring should the gasoline tank touch the terminals of the wires on the back of the switch when withdrawing the tank, it is a good plan to disconnect the battery wire and insert a small piece of rubber tubing over the end of the battery wire terminal (see Fig. 563).

1239   Lift out mat and floor boards.

1240   Run out the six transmission cover door screws (see "B" Fig. 299). Back up the two adjusting nuts (see "C" Fig. 307) to the end of the reverse and brake pedal shafts.

1241   After loosening the reverse and brake pedals, the transmission cover door should be temporarily replaced; this will prevent any parts dropping into the transmission; one screw is sufficient to hold the door in position.

1242   Withdraw gasoline tank straps through dash into body, bending the straps straight down as shown in Fig. 564. The straps are hooked into brackets which are located at the top of the cowl (see "D" Fig. 562). By unhooking the straps from these brackets, the straps can then be withdrawn.

1243   Force the brake and reverse pedals forward as far as they will go so there will be plenty of clearance to withdraw the tank.

1244   Move tank back and forth until sediment bulb connection on tank clears opening in dash. To facilitate this operation have someone stand at front of dash and guide the sediment bulb connection through the opening while the tank is being withdrawn. When connection clears opening in dash the tank can then be lifted out as shown in Fig. 565.

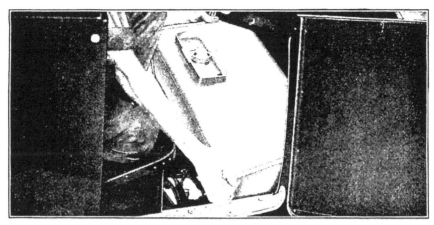

Fig. 565

*Installing—*

**1245**  Position tank in car, inserting sediment bulb connection through opening in dash.  (Have someone stand in front of dash to guide connection through opening.)

**1246**  Hook the two tank straps into brackets at top of cowl (see "D" Fig. 562).  Bend the straps so they will fit closely against tank and insert the threaded ends of straps through holes in dash.  Place a spacer washer and lock washer over ends of straps.  Start nuts on ends of straps and run them down tightly (see "E" Fig. 561).

**1247**  Insert overflow pipe into sediment bulb connection (see "C" Fig. 562) lining up screw hole in pipe with set screw "B" in connection.  The set screw is then run down until it enters pipe.

**1248**  Position overflow pipe clamp over pipe (see "A" Fig. 562) running down nut tightly on end of clamp.

**1249**  Screw sediment bulb into sediment bulb connection.

**1250**  Insert feed pipe into sediment bulb elbow and run down feed pipe pack nut (see "B" Fig. 561).

**1251**  Open shutoff cock on sediment bulb (see "A" Fig. 561).

**1252**  Insert carburetor adjusting rod "D" through instrument board and dash.  Place priming rod lift over end of adjusting rod and insert rod into carburetor adjusting rod sleeve.  Lock priming rod lift in position by inserting cotter pin "C" through adjusting rod.

**1253**  Position ignition switch on instrument board.  Insert the two ignition switch screws through switch and instrument board.  Start lockwashers and nuts on ends of screws.  Hold the nuts stationary and draw down the screws tightly.

**1254**  Remove transmission cover door and adjust brake and reverse pedals.  Replace transmission cover door by running down the six screws which hold door to transmission cover.

**1255**  Replace floor boards and mat.

**1256**  Withdraw rubber tubing which was inserted over end of battery wire to prevent a spark (see Par. 1238) and insert terminal of wire under head of battery wire screw on terminal block.

**1257**  Install hood and fill gasoline tank with fuel.

# More Room for the Driver

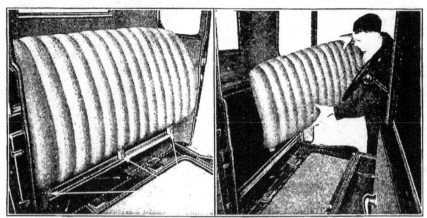

Fig. 566       Fig. 567

**1258** While the standard seating arrangement in the improved Coupe and Tudor is designed to furnish maximum riding comfort for the average size driver, provision has also been made for the accommodation of owners of larger than average size. This has been accomplished by designing the seats so they can be easily adjusted to provide additional space between driver's seat and steering wheel as well as increased leg room.

### Adjusting the Coupe Seat—

**1259** In addition to the increased space obtained by inserting the two dowels in seat riser into the two forward holes in bottom of seat cushion (see Fig. 576), the seat and seat back in the new Coupe can be moved back to provide additional space between steering wheel and seat back, as well as increased leg room, by proceeding as follows:

**1260** Lift out seat cushion.

**1261** Run off the nuts on the ends of the three seat back strainer bolts (see "A" Fig. 566), and withdraw the bolts.

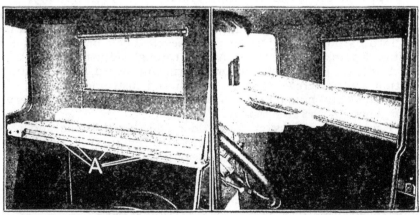

Fig. 568       Fig. 569

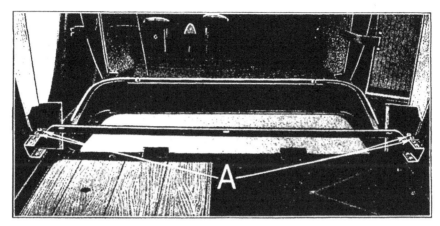

Fig. 570

**1262** Raise the seat back approximately 2″, this will release the clip which holds seat back to spacer board. Seat back can then be lifted out of car as shown in Fig. 567.

**1263** Run off the nuts on the ends of the five spacer board to body bolts (see "A" Fig. 568) and withdraw the bolts.

**1264** By tipping up the back of the spacer board, it can be lifted out as shown in Fig. 569.

**1265** The seat can now be moved back 2″ by running off the nuts on the ends of the four seat bar to bracket bolts (see "A" Fig. 570) and withdrawing the bolts. Then slide the seat bar back approximately 2″ on brackets or until rear bolt hole in seat bar lines up with rear hole in bracket. The four bolts are then inserted through seat bar and brackets (see "A" Fig. 571) and lock washers and nuts run down tightly on ends of bolts.

**1266** This change necessitates two additional bolts, lock washers and nuts being used to hold each end of the body supports to the brackets as shown at "B."

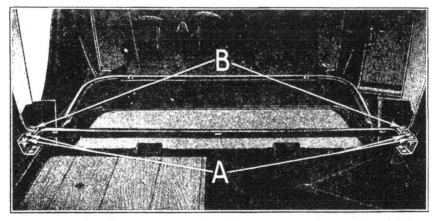

Fig. 571

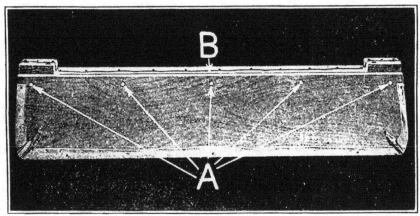

Fig. 572

1267   The width of the spacer board should next be cut down 2″ to correspond to the distance which the seat was moved back. This will preserve the comfortable angle at which the seat back is set and in addition provide greater space between steering wheel and seat back.

1268   To cut down the spacer board proceed as follows:

1269   Place spacer board on a flat surface with the bottom side up and run out the five wood screws (see "A" Fig. 572) which hold spacer block to board. Spacer block "B" can then be removed.

1270   Withdraw tacks from edge of fabric on spacer board where spacer block was withdrawn and fold the fabric back as shown at "A" Fig. 573. Mark off a section 2″ in width extending the full length of the spacer board as shown at "B," and saw it off. If an owner is unusually stout and requires a larger amount of space between steering wheel and seat back, an additional 2″ can be cut from the spacer board.

1271   In instances where the owner does not desire the seat moved back, but simply desires more clearance between steering wheel and seat back, the maximum width of the strip sawed from the spacer board should not exceed 3″.

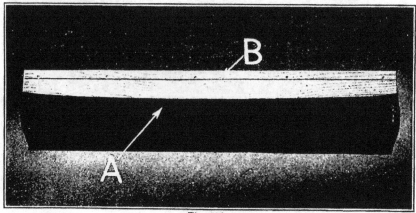

Fig. 573

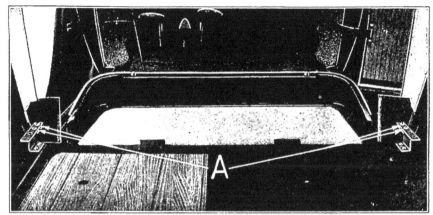

Fig. 574

**1272** To eliminate any possibility of cutting off too wide or too narrow a strip, it is a good plan to keep several spacer boards on hand from which strips varying in width from 1″ to 3″ have been cut. By trying out these different width spacer boards in an owner's car, the owner himself can determine which is the most suitable for his needs.

**1273** After cutting down the width of the spacer board, drill five new holes in spacer board for the five wood screws which hold block to board. Smooth out the fabric on the board (see "A" Fig. 573) and tack it securely to spacer board. Any excess fabric can be cut off with a pair of scissors or a sharp knife.

**1274** Assemble spacer board block to spacer board by running in the five wood screws (see "A" Fig. 572) which hold block to board.

**1275** Install spacer board in body, running down the five bolts and nuts (see "A" Fig. 568) which hold spacer board to body.

**1276** Position seat back in car, hooking the clip on the back of the seat back into the spacer board block. Line up the three bolt holes in seat back strainers with bolt holes in seat bar and run down the three seat back strainer bolts and nuts. (See "A" Fig. 566).

**1277** Replace seat cushion, making sure to insert the two dowels on seat riser (see "A" Fig. 576) into the two forward holes "B" on bottom of seat cushion board.

## Different Adjustment Methods Used on Coupes Equipped with Former Type Seat Bar Brackets

**1278** In the first run of the improved Coupes, the seat bar brackets were of a slightly different type than the present design. This necessitates a little different method being used in moving back the seat.

**1279** A simple method of moving back the seat in Coupes equipped with the former style bracket is to first remove the seat bar as described in Par. 1265. Then bolt a small steel plate to each of the two brackets as shown in Fig. 574. This plate serves as an extension to the bracket and permits moving back the seat 2″ in the same manner as is done with the present design bracket. Details

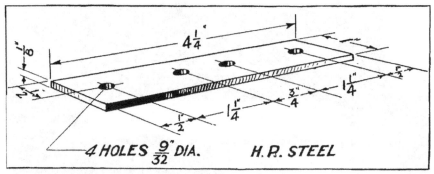

Fig. 575

of the plate which can be easily made locally, are shown in Fig. 575.
When replacing the seat cushion insert the two dowels on seat riser
(see "A" Fig. 576) into the two forward holes "B" on bottom of seat
cushion board.

## Moving Back the Seats in the Improved Tudor

1280   The driver's seat in the improved Tudor can be set back $1\frac{1}{2}''$
by simply moving back the seat and inserting the seat legs into the
two forward holes at bottom of seat assembly. This is done as
follows:

1281   Lift out seat cushion.

1282   Run off the two seat leg nuts and washers (see "A" Fig. 577).
Seat legs can then be withdrawn from bottom of seat assembly by
tipping the seat backwards.

1283   Insert seat legs into the two forward holes in bottom of seat
assembly shown at "B." If the finishing material extends over the
bottom of the holes it can easily be cut out with a knife.

1284   Place a flat washer and a lockwasher over the end of each seat
leg and run down the two seat leg nuts.   (See "A" Fig. 577).

1285   Replace seat cushion.

1286   The rear seat can be moved back by sliding back the cushion
into the seat back and positioning dowels on seat riser into the two
forward holes in cushion frame, in the same manner as shown in
Fig. 576.

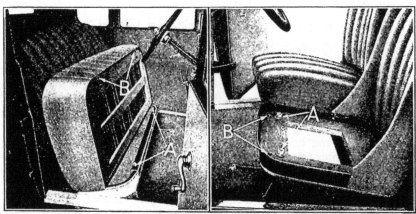

Fig. 576                          Fig. 577

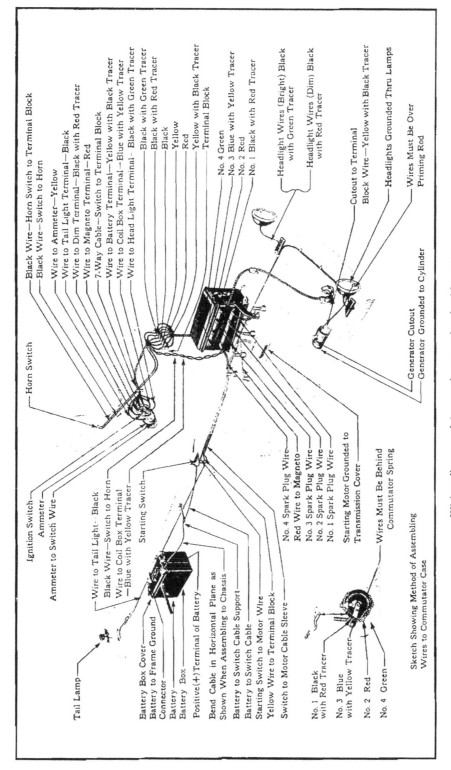

Wiring diagram of improved car equipped with starter

Tail Lamp

Ignition Switch
Ammeter
Ammeter to Switch Wire

Horn Switch

Black Wire—Horn Switch to Terminal Block
Black Wire—Switch to Horn
Wire to Ammeter—Yellow
Wire to Tail Light Terminal—Black
Wire to Dim Terminal—Black with Red Tracer
Wire to Magneto Terminal—Red
7-Way Cable—Switch to Terminal Block
Wire to Battery Terminal—Yellow with Black Tracer
Wire to Coil Box Terminal—Blue with Yellow Tracer
Wire to Head Light Terminal—Black with Green Tracer
Black with Green Tracer
Black with Red Tracer
Black
Yellow
Red
Yellow with Black Tracer
Terminal Block

No. 4 Green
No. 3 Blue with Yellow Tracer
No. 2 Red
No. 1 Black with Red Tracer

Headlight Wires (Bright) Black
with Green Tracer
Headlight Wires (Dim) Black
with Red Tracer

Cutout to Terminal
Block Wire—Yellow with Black Tracer
Headlights Grounded Thru Lamps
Wires Must Be Over
Priming Rod

Generator Cutout
Generator Grounded to Cylinder

Wire to Tail Light—Black
Black Wire—Switch to Horn
Wire to Coil Box Terminal
—Blue with Yellow Tracer

Starting Switch

Battery Box Cover
Battery to Frame Ground
Connector
Battery
Battery Box
Positive (+) Terminal of Battery
Bend Cable in Horizontal Plane as
Shown When Assembling to Chassis
Battery to Switch Cable Support
Battery to Switch Cable
Starting Switch to Motor Wire
Yellow Wire to Terminal Block
Switch to Motor Cable Sleeve

No. 4 Spark Plug Wire
Red Wire to Magneto
No. 3 Spark Plug Wire
No. 2 Spark Plug Wire
No. 1 Spark Plug Wire

Starting Motor Grounded to
Transmission Cover

Wires Must Be Behind
Commutator Spring

No. 1 Black
with Red Tracer
No. 3 Blue
with Yellow Tracer
No. 2 Red
No. 4 Green

Sketch Showing Method of Assembling
Wires to Commutator Case

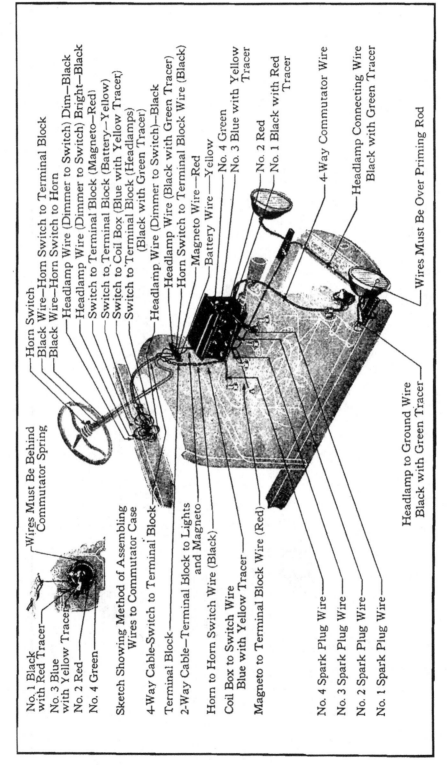

No. 1 Black
with Red Tracer
No. 3 Blue
with Yellow Tracer
No. 2 Red
No. 4 Green

Sketch Showing Method of Assembling
Wires to Commutator Case

4-Way Cable–Switch to Terminal Block

Terminal Block

2-Way Cable–Terminal Block to Lights
and Magneto

Horn to Horn Switch Wire (Black)

Coil Box to Switch Wire
Blue with Yellow Tracer

Magneto to Terminal Block Wire (Red)

No. 4 Spark Plug Wire
No. 3 Spark Plug Wire
No. 2 Spark Plug Wire
No. 1 Spark Plug Wire

Wires Must Be Behind
Commutator Spring

Horn Switch
Black Wire–Horn Switch to Terminal Block
Black Wire–Horn Switch to Horn
Headlamp Wire (Dimmer to Switch) Dim–Black
Headlamp Wire (Dimmer to Switch) Bright–Black
Switch to Terminal Block (Magneto–Red)
Switch to Terminal Block (Battery–Yellow)
Switch to Coil Box (Blue with Yellow Tracer)
Switch to Terminal Block (Headlamps)
(Black with Green Tracer)
Headlamp Wire (Dimmer to Switch)–Black
Headlamp Wire (Black with Green Tracer)
Horn Switch to Terminal Block Wire (Black)
Magneto Wire–Red
Battery Wire–Yellow
No. 4 Green
No. 3 Blue with Yellow
Tracer
No. 2 Red
No. 1 Black with Red
Tracer

4-Way Commutator Wire

Headlamp Connecting Wire
Black with Green Tracer

Wires Must Be Over Priming Rod

Headlamp to Ground Wire
Black with Green Tracer

Wiring diagram of improved car not equipped with starter

# INDEX

NOTE: Numbers refer to paragraphs

## A

Note: Numbers refer to paragraphs.

Note: Numbers refer to paragraphs.

Note: Numbers refer to paragraphs.

Note: Numbers refer to paragraphs.

Note: Numbers refer to paragraphs.

Note: Numbers refer to paragraphs.

Note: Numbers refer to paragraphs.

Note: Numbers refer to paragraphs.